The Theological
and
Philosophical Works
of
Hermes Trismegistus

The Theological
and
Philosophical Works
of
Hermes Trismegistus

John David Chambers, M.A., F.S.A.

Athens ‡ Manchester

The Theological and Philosophical Works of Hermes Trismegistus

Old Book Publishing Ltd

Book Cover Design: Old Book Publishing Ltd

Copyright © 2011 Old Book Publishing Ltd
All rights reserved.

Title of original: The Theological and Philosophical Works of Hermes Trismegistus, Christian Neoplatonist
Originally published in 1882

Cover image: Mosaic floor in the Cathedral of Siena: Hermes is shown on the right. At the bottom the inscription says: *"Hermes Mercurius Trismegistus, contemporary of Moses"*.

ISBN–10: 1-78107-051-2
ISBN–13: 978-1-78107-051-2

EDITOR'S NOTE

Old Book Publishing Ltd takes care in preserving the wording and images of the original books. For this reason we have invested in technology that enables us to enhance the quality of such reproduction. This investment helps overcome problems encountered when reproducing old books, such as stains, coloured paper, discolouration of ink, yellowed pages, see-through and onion skin type paper.

This reproduction book, produced from digital images of the original, may contain occasional defects such as missing pages or blemishes due to the original source content or were introduced by the scanning process.

These are scanned pages and the quality of print represents accurately the print quality of the original book, though we may have been able to enhance it.

As this book has been scanned and/or reformatted from the original we cannot guarantee that it is error-free or contains the full content of the original.

However, we believe that this work is culturally important, and despite its imperfections, have elected to bring it back into print as part of our commitment to the preservation of printed works.

Old Book Publishing

THE
THEOLOGICAL AND PHILOSOPHICAL WORKS

OF

HERMES TRISMEGISTUS,
CHRISTIAN NEOPLATONIST.

*TRANSLATED FROM THE ORIGINAL GREEK, WITH
PREFACE, NOTES, AND INDICES.*

BY

JOHN DAVID CHAMBERS, M.A., F.S.A.,
OF ORIEL COLLEGE, OXFORD, RECORDER OF NEW SARUM.

"With thrice-great Hërmes."—MILTON's "*Il Penseroso.*"

EDINBURGH:
T. & T. CLARK, 38, GEORGE STREET.

MDCCCLXXXII.

PRINTED BY THE COMMERCIAL PRINTING COMPANY
FOR
T. & T. CLARK, EDINBURGH.

LONDON, ...		HAMILTON, ADAMS, AND CO.
DUBLIN, ...		GEORGE HERBERT.
NEW YORK, . . .		SCRIBNER AND WELFORD.

CONTENTS.

PART I.

POEMANDRES.

CHAP.		PAGE
I.	Poemandres,	1
II.	To Asclepius. Catholic Discourse,	16
III.	Sacred Discourse,	24
IV.	To his own Son Tat. Discourse: The Crater or Monas,	30
V.	To his own Son Tat. That the Invisible God is most Manifest,	36
VI.	That in The God alone is The Good, and by no means anywhere else,	42
VII.	That the greatest evil among men is ignorance of The God,	45
VIII.	That none of the Entities perish; but mankind erroneously call the changes destructions and deaths,	47
IX.	Concerning Understanding and Sense, and that in The God only is The Beautiful and The Good, but elsewhere not at all,	50
X.	The Key. To his Son Tat,	55
XI.	Mind to Hermes,	68
XII.	Respecting Common Mind. To Tat,	77
XIII.	To his Son Tat. On a Mountain. Secret Discourse about Regeneration and Profession of Silence,	87
	Secret Hymnody,	93
XIV.	To Asclepius. To be rightly wise,	96

PART II.

EXCERPTS FROM HERMES BY STOBÆUS.

I.	Of Truth. From the things to Tat,	100
II.	Of Death. From Asclepius,	104
III.	Of God. From the things to Tat,	105

CONTENTS.

	PAGE
IV. From Stobæus, Physica, 134,	106
V. Hermes to the Son,	107
VI. Concerning the Economy of the Universe. Of Hermes from those to Ammon,	108
VII. Of Hermes from those to Ammon,	109
VIII. Of Hermes from the things to Tat,	109
IX. Of Hermes from the things to Tat,	111
X. Of Hermes from that to Tat,	111
XI. Of Hermes from the things to Ammon,	116
XII. Of Hermes from the things to Tat,	117
XIII. Of Hermes from those to Ammon,	122
XIV. Of Hermes from those to Ammon to Tat,	123
XV. Of Hermes,	125
XVI. Of Hermes,	126
XVII. Of the Same,	127
XVIII. Of the Same,	128
XIX. Of the Same,	129
[As to the Sacred Book.]	
XX. Of Hermes,	131
XXI. Of Hermes from that to Tat,	132
[As to the Decans.]	

PART III.

NOTICES OF HERMES IN THE FATHERS.

I. Justin Martyr,	138
II. Tertullian,	139
III. Cyprian,	140
IV. Eusebius Pamphilus,	140
V. Clemens Alexandrinus,	141
VI. Firmianus Lactantius,	141
VII. Arnobius,	148
VIII. Augustine of Hippo,	149
IX. Cyrillus Alexandrinus,	149
X. Suidas,	154
INDEX,	156

Addendum to Note 2 on page 9.

It is possible also that Hermes may here refer to the traditional "Seven Wise Men" mentioned by Philo Judæus in his Treatise, "Every man virtuous also free," ch. xi., whom he speaks of as then "being very ancient."

PREFACE.

THE Mercurius or Hermes Trismegistus of legend was a personage, an Egyptian sage or succession of sages, who, since the time of Plato, has been identified with the Thoth (the name of the month September) of that people. This Thoth is the reputed author of the "Ritual of the Dead," or, as styled in Egyptian phraseology, the "Manifestation of Light" to the Soul, who through it declared the will of the Gods and the mysterious nature of Divine things to Man.[1] Dr Pietschmann, in his work on Hermes, which exhaustively treats of this subject,[2] gives a list of authorities for these facts, ranging from Plato down to Syncellus, *circa* A.D. 790. He states, however (p. 33), that by the time that the so-called Hermeneutical writings were collected together, the identity of Hermes with Thoth was forgotten, and Thoth became his son Tat, and Asclepius his disciple, both of whom he instructs in the writings now translated. Subsequently Pietschmann informs us, quoting Letronne,[3] that the epithet "Trismegistus" appears first in the second century of the Christian era, and that, before that period, Hermes was designated by the repetition of the "$\mu\acute{\epsilon}\gamma\alpha\varsigma, \mu\acute{\epsilon}\gamma\alpha\varsigma, \mu\acute{\epsilon}\gamma\alpha\varsigma$" only, as on the Rosetta Stone.

He was considered to be the impersonation of the religion, art, learning, and sacerdotal discipline of the Egyptian priesthood. He was, by several of the Fathers, and, in

---

[1] Rawlinson's Egypt, i. 136, and the authorities there quoted.

[2] Leipsic, Engelmann, 1875, pp. 31-33.

[3] *Ibid.* p. 35, "Inscription Grecque de Rosette," Letronne, Paris, 1841.

modern times, by three of his earliest editors, supposed to have existed before the times of Moses, and to have obtained the appellation of " Thrice greatest," from his threefold learning and rank of Philosopher, Priest, and King,[1] and that of "Hermes," or Mercurius, as messenger and authoritative interpreter of divine things. In the Hieroglyphics he, like Horus, is represented by a bird with a hawk's head, and to him was sacred the Ibis and the Moon.[2]

This Hermes—and there was but one among the ancient Egyptians[3]—was worshipped as a god by them. Tertullian[4] says, " In ancient times most authors were supposed to be, I will not say god-like, but actually gods; as, for instance, the Egyptian Hermes, to whom Plato paid very great deference."

Clement of Alexandria[5] writes, " Hermes of Thebes and Esculapius of Memphis *ex vate Deus;*" and he subsequently gives a detailed account of his works, forty-two in number—four of astrology, others of astronomy, geology, and hieroglyphics, and thirty-six of philosophy, hymns to God, religious ceremonies, and sacerdotal discipline.[6] Lactantius[7] expresses himself thus (quoting Cicero, "De Naturâ Deorum," Lib. iii.): "Although a man, he was of great antiquity, and built Hermopolis, and is there worshipped as well as at Pheneus. He was most fully imbued with every kind of learning, so that the knowledge of many subjects and arts acquired for him the name of

---

[1] See the edition of the works of Hermes by François de Foix, Comte de Candalle, assisted by the younger Scaliger.

[2] Champollion the younger ("Panthéon Egyptien"). Several hieroglyphical representations of him, under various Egyptian names, are given by Pietschmann, p. 1.

[3] See Pietschmann, *ibid.* pp. 35, 36.

[4] "De Animâ," ch. 2.

[5] Stromata, I., ch. 21, p. 389, Oxford Edition, Lib. vi., ch. 4, p. 757.

[6] The "Ritual of the Dead," vulgarly attributed to Hermes, as at present discovered, consists of three Books redivided into 23 portions and about 165 chapters. See Rawlinson's Egypt, i. 138.

[7] Lib. i., ch. 6.

Trismegistus." Further, S. Augustine[1] relates, "He, the fifth Mercury (as Lactantius had thought also), and his friend Esculapius (or Asclepius, grandson of the first) were men, and became gods, Mercurius and Æsculapius, after the Greek fashion." Cyril of Alexandria ("Contr. Julian.," i. 30*a*, *circa* 412), speaks of Hermes in general thus:— "This Hermes then, him of Egypt, although being initiator (τελεστής), and having presided at the fanes of idols, is always found mindful of the things of Moses, &c.; and made mention of him in his own writings, which, being composed for the Athenians, are called 'Hermaica,' fifteen books." And subsequently, "I speak of Hermes, him having sojourned, third, in Egypt" (Lib. v., 176*b*).[2]

The majority of the Fathers, in their uncritical mode, even Lactantius himself, confounded the original Hermes with our author, in the same way that they ascribed to the Sybilline verses a far too high antiquity; and the later Fathers, moreover, especially Lactantius, made no distinction between the genuine works of our Hermes and others which falsely bear his name; some of them, as, for instance, "Asclepius," having been written at least a century later; and those, as, for instance, "The Sacred Book" and the Dialogue between Isis and Horus (Stobæus, "Physica,' 928, 1070, edit. Meineke, i. 281, 342), to which it is impossible to assign a date, are all indiscriminately ascribed to the same Hermes, although it is absolutely certain that the author of "Poemandres" never can have written them.

What is strange is, that several of the learned editors of the works of our Hermes consider him to have lived before Moses. Vergicius, in his preface to the edition printed at Paris by Turnebus in 1554, states this. Flussas (1574), after discussion, leaves the question as to his age undetermined; but Patricius (Patrizzi), in his "Nova de Universis Philosophia," printed at Ferrara in 1591, and at Venice

---

[1] "City of God," viii. 23, 26.

[2] See the extracts from Cyril of Alexandria, *post*, Part III., and the note from Pietschmann there.

1593, says that Hermes lived some time before Moses, and quotes Eusebius in his "Chronicle" as stating that Cath or Tat his son flourished in the first year of Armeus, king of Egypt, which was twenty years before the death of Moses. On the other hand, John Albert Fabricius, the learned author of the "Bibliotheca Græca" (published 1705-1728), has relegated all the "Hermaica," in his "Historia Literaria," to the later times of Jamblichus and Porphyry. Even Pietschmann, whose dissertation has been already mentioned, makes no distinction between the legendary Hermes and the author of "Poemandres."

Notwithstanding these opinions, it is certain that the Hermes who was the author of the works here translated must, as Causabon and later writers (such as L. Ménard, who thinks he was probably contemporaneous with St. John) have shown, have been a Greek living at Alexandria, subsequently to Philo Judæus and Josephus, in the end of the first and beginning of the second century; who, it would seem, assumed the name of Hermes in order to give greater weight to his teaching. The Fathers above quoted, Lactantius himself, and the editors of Hermes above named, may have been misled as to his great antiquity by the hieroglyphical representations of him; but the facts, then unknown, but now demonstrated, that the use of these characters lasted in Egypt down to the tenth year of Diocletian (he died A.D. 313) at the least, and that, as Henry Brugsch and later investigators have shown, the ordinary writing on papyrus in the National Library at Paris, some of which is entirely in Greek characters, is not earlier than the times of Nero, refute their suppositions. It is, moreover, quite impossible that an author who shows an intimate acquaintance with the phraseology of Plato, with the Hebrew Scriptures as extant in the Septuagint version (sometimes using the very expressions therein contained), who reproduces the language of the Sermon on the Mount and of the Gospel, Epistles, and Revelation of St. John, and sometimes of St. Paul, can have flourished at so early a period.

PREFACE.

These same facts serve also to indicate his actual epoch. Although, as De Rougé[1] has shown, very early Egyptian monuments now at Berlin and elsewhere express or insinuate the idea of the Eternal Father-Creator, and of his Son begotten before the worlds, yet the dogma of the Holy Trinity is, as we shall find, expressed in far more categorical terms, and almost in the very words of St. John, by our Hermes in his "Poemandres;" so also the doctrine of Baptism and the Regeneration or new birth, as set forth by St. John in the third chapter of his Gospel, as due to The Man, the only Son of God.

Asclepius was said to be the grandson of Hermes, and the work which bears that name refers unmistakably to times near to those of Constantine, when the ancient religion of Egypt was tottering to its fall. Moreover, that author refers therein repeatedly to Ammonius Saccas, who is called the founder of the Neoplatonic School, and who died *circa* A.D. 241. On the other hand, the clear reference, by Justin Martyr, to the teaching of Hermes as to the Unity of the Godhead,[2] and the identity, almost verbal, of a passage in that Father with a passage in the "Poemandres," and the mention of him by Tertullian, demonstrate that he wrote before or contemporaneously with the earlier of these Fathers. Many of the works of our Hermes are probably still entombed in the libraries on the Continent; but those which have come to light, and are now translated, are most remarkable and of very considerable importance, since they are the only treatises we possess of the kind belonging to that epoch. The emphatic praise bestowed upon them by the Fathers, from Justin Martyr[3] downwards, ought to commend them to our notice. The eulogium of Lactantius,[4] "Trismegistus who, I know not how, investigated almost all truth;" and as he and Cyril

---

[1] Etude sur le Rituel Funéraire des Egyptiens," "Revue Archéologique," 1860, p. 357; and see Rawlinson's Egypt, i. 320.
[2] See Part III., *post*.   [3] See Part III., *post*.
[4] "Divin. Instit.," iv. 9.

of Alexandria[1] and Suidas[2] remark, his enunciation of the doctrine of the Incarnation of the Son of God for the regeneration of man,[3] and of the Holy Trinity in Unity,[4] of the immortality of the soul of man, is plain; whilst his undoubted adherence to much of the philosophy of Plato (the Attic Moses), especially in the "Timæus," entitles him to be considered the real founder of Neoplatonism in the best and most Christian sense.

The former editors of Hermes were of like opinion. Thus Vergicius, in his preface to the edition of Turnebus (Paris, 1554), "His teaching appears to be most excellent and evangelical." "Behold in his theology how wonderfully and evangelically he hath plainly instructed us as to the Most Holy Trinity." So also Flussas, with Scaliger the younger (Bordeaux, 1574), "He deserves the name of an evangelical philosopher, for he first expounded the chief effects of divine grace upon man, and first declared how his salvation depended upon the Son of God—the one Man given for the regeneration of mankind." So Patricius also, in his "Nova de Universis Philosophia" (Ferrara, 1591; Venice, 1593), which comprised the principal works of Hermes, speaks thus,—"In these books and fragments of Hermes will appear a philosophy pious towards God and, in most respects, consonant to the dogmas of faith. It will appear also that all the Greek philosophies, Pythagorean and Platonic in divine things and the dogmas of morals, those of Aristotle and of the Stoics in physics and medicine, were all taken from these his books and from those which have perished." But although this may be so, the reader must be forewarned that he will not find in these writings a complete Christianity. There is no express notice of the Nativity, of the Crucifixion, Resurrection, or Ascension, or coming of Christ to Judgment, to be found therein, although there is also nothing inconsistent with

---

[1] "Contra. Jul.," 33c.   [2] Lexicon, *voce* "Hermes."

[3] "Poemandres," ch. xiii. 4.

[4] *Ibid., passim;* and see Suidæ Lexicon, *voce* "Hermes," for a passage to this effect not now extant elsewhere.

these facts. On the other hand, as has been already seen, they teach emphatically the Unity of the Godhead, the dogma of the Holy Trinity—God the Father, the Word, the Son begotten of Him before the worlds, of the Holy Spirit proceeding from the Father through the Son, instrumental in creation, and the Sanctifier; and there are clear allusions to the effusion of this Holy Spirit on the World, with its Seven Gifts in the shape of Fire. Thus Hermes was not a mere Platonist propounding the means of attaining moral and intellectual perfection without reference to the facts and doctrines of Holy Scripture, but, in theory at least, in great part a Christian.

The "Hermaica" have been unaccountably neglected in England. That these works were not unknown here in the time of Milton is proved by his words from "Il Penseroso," "With thrice-great Hermes;" but they received little further attention in this country. On the Continent, however, as soon as the originals of his principal treatises was discovered, the value of them was perceived, and immediately after the invention of printing they were committed to the press.

The "Poemandres," the principal work, was translated into Latin and published by Marsilius Ficinus at Treviso in 1471, divided into fourteen chapters, which were afterwards increased to twenty by Patricius. This edition of Ficinus was several times republished; at Ferrara and Venice in 1472; at Mayence in 1503; and especially at Cracow, but in a Latin translation only, by the Carmelite Rosselli, in six volumes folio, in 1584, with a commentary so voluminous, discursive, and argumentative that it is nearly useless. Nevertheless, this was reprinted, with what professed to be the original Greek, at Cologne, in 1638, in one volume folio. The original Greek of the "Poemandres," and of the "Definitions of Asclepius to Ammon the King" (which, we shall see presently, is not a work of our author, but subsequent to his epoch), were first printed and published by Adr. Turnebus, edited, with a preface, by Angelus Vergicius, at Paris, in quarto, in 1554. D. Franciscus Flussas republished the "Poemandres" in Greek and Latin, in quarto, at Bordeaux in 1574. Francis Patricius (Cardinal Patrizzi) reprinted the works attributed to Hermes which are extant in Greek (some of which, as already stated, we shall find are not his) among his "Nova de Universis Philosophia" at Ferrara, in folio, in 1591; and again under a new title, "Nova de Universis Philosophia libris quinquaginta comprehensa, auctore Francisco Patritio," at Venice, in folio, in 1593, Robertus Meiettus being the printer. Gustave Parthey has done a great service to early Christian literature by publishing at Berlin, in 1854, an entirely new edition of the "Poemandres" in the original Greek, from a MS. of the end of the 13th century, No. 1220 in the National Library at Paris; others, Nos. 1297, 2007, 2518, of the 16th century, in the same library having, with 1220, been collated by D. Hamm with the edition of Turnebus and that numbered 2518, which had been written by the hand of Angelus Vergicius at Venice. Parthey also consulted another MS. of the 14th century, Plut. lxxi., No. 33, in quarto, in the Laurentian library at Florence, collated, at the request of Parthey, by Francis de Furia with the Turnebus edition. This publication of G. Parthey is most carefully edited, and accompanied by a close and admirable Latin translation of his own. In the preface he promised an edition of the other remains of Hermes to be found extracted in Stobæus and several of the Fathers, which promise, it is to be lamented, he has not yet performed.

There exist several old French translations of the "Hermaica:" one by G. de Preau, published at Paris in 1557; "Two books of Hermes Trismegistus, one 'Of the Power and Wisdom of God,' the other 'Of the Will of God;'" another of the "Poemander," by Foye de Candalle, with a comment, at Bordeaux, 1574; another, by G. Joly and Hub, in folio, at Paris, in 1579, again printed in 1626. A complete translation into modern French of all the works attributed to Hermes was published at Paris, by Dr Louis Ménard, in 1866, in quarto, and again in 1868 in small octavo. This translation is by no means literal, often an abbreviation, and sometimes incorrect. It is prefaced by a critical dissertation on the authorship and contents of the Hermetic books respectively, which contains much curious information. This work was crowned by the Academy of Inscriptions and Belles Lettres, but is discursive and not sufficiently discriminative. Nevertheless the conclusions of the writer have often been adopted as correct in the present volume.

In 1781 Dietrich Tiedemann, Professor of Philosophy at the University of Marbourg, the author of several works on the philosophies of the Greeks and Egyptians, published at Berlin and Stettin a translation into German of the Poemandres, or Treatise by the Hermes Trismegistus of "God's Might and Wisdom."

In 1875, as already stated, Engelmann at Leipsic published a dissertation on Hermes Trismegistus by Dr Richard Pietschmann, "after Egyptian, Greek, and Oriental sources," which, however, relates mostly to the legendary Hermes, and not to our author, but which contains a mine of information on the general subject from a vast variety of authorities, and may be considered introductory to the present volume.

At Bologna, 1820, was printed a dissertation on the Hermaica, of which, however, the translator has not been able to obtain a copy. Some others are referred to by Ménard in the preface to his volume.

At 1855-1860 were published at Leipsic the complete works of Stobæus in six volumes, correctly edited by Augustus Meineke as part of the "Bibliotheca Scriptorum Græcorum et Romanorum Teubneriana," which, in his "Physica et Ethica et Florilegium," contain large Excerpts from Hermes. These constitute almost all we have of his genuine works, beyond the "Poemandres," which we possess entire, and the notices we have of them in the Fathers of the Church.

The genuine works of our Hermes now extant and here translated, and presumably belonging to the latter part of the first century and beginning of the second, are—

1. The "Poemandres," of which he is by common consent the author, which consists mostly of dialogues after the manner of Plato. The first alone bears that name, being a colloquy between that personage who represents "Νοῦς," or "Mind"—the Wisdom and Power and Providence of God, Life, and Light—with Hermes himself. The eleventh chapter also contains a dialogue of a similar character. In the remainder Hermes instructs his son Tat and his disciple and grandson Asclepius, and in part mankind generally, in the wonderful Knowledge of God and of the Creation and of Piety, which he had learned from Νοῦς.

2. Several portions of the books of Hermes and his son Tat, for which we are mainly indebted to the excerpts made by Stobæus in his "Physica," "Ethica," and the "Florilegium." Also fragments of the first book of the "Digressions to Tat," which are quoted in the works of Cyril of Alexandria against Julian; and some portions of the books of Hermes to the earlier Ammon, which are extracted from that work by Stobæus in his "Physica," with a few sentences quoted by Lactantius which are not to be found elsewhere. The citations from Hermes contained in the Christian Fathers will be found in Part III.

Other discourses commonly called "Hermaica," but which are not his,—because containing statements and doctrines which are inconsistent with his, and are either of Egyptian and heathenish origin, or savour of the later teaching of Plotinus and Jamblichus, and besides contain evident anachronisms, are therefore not included in this volume, although we find there plagiarisms from the original Hermes and many statements accordant with Christianity. These are :—

1. The "Perfect Discourse" (λόγος τέλειος), which bears the title of Asclepius. The author speaks of Hermes as "my grandfather," and calls Ammon into council—presumably that Ammonius Saccas who was the master of

PREFACE. xvii

Plotinus, and died in Alexandria A.D. 241. Of this, except such of the extracts in Stobæus and Lactantius as are in Greek, there is only one version extant—a Latin translation falsely ascribed to Apuleius (which existed also solely in the time of St Augustine, who cites it in chs. 23 and 26 of Lib. viii. of his "City of God "), and which was published with his works by Aldus in 1521, and Almenhorst at Frankfort in 1621. That this is not from the hand of our Hermes is at once apparent from its contents, which are at variance with his genuine writings. It contains, amongst other things, an eloquent address to the Nile, wherein the author, as a prophet, laments in touching terms the abolition of the ancient national religion of Egypt—that holy land—and the approaching triumph of Christianity; the devastation of the country and of its sacred shrines, and destruction of the population. He speaks of Isis and Osiris, and of the cult of animals, of Jupiter Plutonius, of thirty-six horoscopes, and of the Pantomorphosis. Further, it contains a distinct defence of the worship of statues of the gods formed by the hands of men, and maintains that it is a great privilege granted by God to men—the power of making gods. That Lactantius quotes this work more than once as of Hermes himself, and applies his description of the calamities of Egypt as if they were the afflictions to come upon the earth in the last days,[1] is simply a proof of the uncritical judgment of some of the Fathers as to chronology, and sometimes as to exact authorship, which is well known and acknowledged. It is plainly the production of an Alexandrian of the Egyptian religion, who assumed the name and discipleship of, and quoted from, Hermes for his own purposes, and most probably lived some short time before the epoch of Constantine.

A second discourse, also found among the "Hermaica," is a portion of that called the "Sacred Book," denominated Κόρη κόσμου (Patrit., 276, Stobæus, "Physica," Meineke, i. 281), which Patrizzi corrected after Stobæus from a MS.

[1] Lactant., Divin. Instit., VII., 18.

found at Enclistra, in the island of Cyprus. It is a strange production, being a dialogue between Isis and his son Horus, with Momus, on the creation of the world and of souls, and of metempsychosis. It is in places Platonic, as if citing the Timæus; and it quotes also by name Hermes, and partly the account by him of the Creation in " Poemandres." Being apparently a summary of the Græco-Egyptian philosophy, it must be attributed to a Græco-Egyptian, probably of Alexandria; but it is scarcely Greek at all, and there are few indications of its exact date. In this production Hermes is spoken of in these words:— " Hermes, he understanding all things, who also saw the whole of things together, and having seen, considered them, and having considered them was powerful to explain and show them. For what he understood he committed to characters, and having committed them to characters, concealed the most part, being silent with wisdom, and speaking opportunely, in order that all the duration of the world hereafter should search out these things; and thus having ordered the gods, his brethren, to become his escort, he ascended towards the constellations. But he had for successor Tat, his son and heir of his science, and shortly afterwards Asclepius, son of Imothes, by the counsel of Pan and Hæphæstus, and all those to whom the Almighty Providence reserved an exact knowledge of the things of heaven. Hermes then excused himself to all his surroundings for not delivering the entire theory to his son, on account of his youth." From this it would appear that the writer of this discourse was posterior to Asclepius, —that is, of the middle or end of the third century. A third fragment of importance is usually included among the " Hermaica," and is quoted by Lactantius with a like want of critical sagacity. It is denominated the " Definitions ("Ορoι) of Asclepius to King Ammon." He calls " Hermes my master, who conversed with me often alone or in presence of Tat," and quotes many passages of the " Poemandres." It is written with eloquence. Ammon the king is supposed to be present, and the main portion is occupied with the praise of King Ammon and other kings. The whole is alien from the spirit and diction of Hermes himself, and must have been composed many years subsequently to the "Poemandres."

The theological and philosophical teaching of our Hermes—for he was both a theologian and philosopher,—may be thus summed up:—

First and foremost he insists upon the being of The God; an Unconditioned, self-existent Essence, Founder (κτίσας), Maker (ποιητής), Creator (δημιουργὸς), upholder and governor of the Universe at His own mere Will,—the One, the Only, the Supreme—very Life and Light Itself. He is Almighty (αὐθέντης), never inert, but ever acting in every part of His creation, pervading and energizing all things by His particular Providence, to which Fate and Necessity are wholly subject. Nothing can subsist or move apart from Him, Who has in Himself all things that have been, are, or shall be.

He is the perfection and the sum of The Good, the Beautiful, the Holy, and the True; immaterial, infinite, incorporeal, invisible, the object of none of the senses; ineffable, incomprehensible, inimitable, invariable; without form or figure, colourless; Intelligence and Wisdom itself; everlasting, independent of time, the Eternal from eternity; the Light and Life of mankind; Holiness and Goodness itself, and in no sense the author of anything evil or base. If any evil exist in creation, it is as it were by way of rust or excrescence only, and cannot be attributed to the Deity.

This Being, above all, in all, and about all, is Unity. The universal Harmony of the Κόσμος, which is eloquently set forth, demonstrates that He can be but One. Motion exists throughout all the order of the worlds, and is the condition and quality of the Eternal; but this Motion must be generated and continually energized by some Being superior to and stronger than that which is moved, and than the medium in which the motion takes place. If He ever ceased to energize, He would be no longer God; but this never can be. He is inexpressible, and has no name. A name implies an elder or superior to give the name; but there is none such. We call Him Father and Master and Lord of all existences, not as names, but appellations derived from His benefits and His works.

This, The God before the moist Nature which appeared out of darkness, begat the Perfect Word, coessential ('Oμοούσιος) with Himself, the Second God, visible and sensible, First One and only, and loved Him as His own Son—a sacred, ineffable, and shining Word, exceeding all the ability of men to declare—Son of God—The One Man by the Will of God, through Whom is access in prayer to The Father, The Lord of all things.

Through this Word were the World, the Heaven, the Stars, the Earth, Mankind, and all the living existences in them, brought into being, and harmoniously ordered through the operation of Mind ("Νοῦς"), the Wisdom of God, the God of Fire and Spirit proceeding from God, Which with the Seven administrative Spirits created by it, whose administration constitutes Fate, applied themselves to the conformation of the Universe out of chaos, according to the Idea, the Archetype or Pattern, pre-existent in the Mind of the Deity. This "Κόσμος" so created, Hermes calls second God, as being wholly instinct with The One Divinity. He gives the same appellation to the Sun, for the same reason and because it is the instrument of God's Will in new creating. The mode of the creation is shown in the form of a Vision displayed before Hermes, and in several portions is related in the very words of the Septuagint version of Genesis. The Procession of the Holy Spirit and His instrumentality in Creation is enunciated, apparently according to the creed of the orthodox Greeks. Thus, The God created Man after the image of Himself, as His child, an immortal and divine animal, out of two natures, the immortal and mortal, between the two, that viewing all things he may admire them and their wonderful order and harmony. Man has a divine nature, because he has a Soul, an independent incorporeal immortal energizing intelligent Essence, which, being a portion of the Soul with which God animated the Universe, was created before the body, and was infused into it. It is threefold—Mind or Reason, Desire, and Spirit, which can receive God, and become a consort of Deity, having intellect and speech—immortal properties, that Man may contemplate and worship his Creator. The greatest disease of the Soul is ungodliness and ignorance of God.

Man, being an imperfect, fallible, and composite being, cannot know The God of himself; but those to whom The God of His own free will imparts this faculty can do so. He is ever desirous and willing to be known; and to those who are pure, and who wish for this knowledge, He reveals Himself by imparting to them of His Mind, which is of the very essence of the Divinity, and joined to it as the light is to the Sun. Not that Mind is God; but that The God is the cause of Mind. This Mind in men is God. Such men therefore have their humanity near to Deity, for He is their very Father; when they leave the body, they become this Mind. They must seek the knowledge of Him, which is virtue, temperance, piety, salvation, and ascent to Heaven. The God created all things perfect. Man has become depraved; but has free choice of good and evil.

To attain this state, then, men must hate and mortify the flesh, its vices and excesses, reject the depravity and ignorance of earth, where Truth does not exist; the wickedness, darkness, and corruption of the body; they must recur and look in heart to Him, Who can alone show the way of salvation.

The mode of accomplishing this, which can only be done by the help of God, Who is willing to reveal Himself to all, is by ridding themselves of the twelve principal vices, and acquiring in their place the ten cardinal virtues. When these shall be so acquired, man becomes fitted to ascend to the Ogdoad, the eighth Circle, to the presence of God his Father, to become immortal, part of His Essence and of His Powers and Virtues, and divine (θεωθῆναι). This may happen even in the body, by the gift of God. This is the Regeneration (παλιγγενεσία). The author of it is the enlightening Word of God—the One Man by the will of God. Baptism is to be added, and His good Spirit must lead men thereto: those thus regenerate will strive to bring all mankind to the same blessed state.

Neither any evil, nor has Fate, any power over those who are thus pious and regenerate. They are rewarded with immortality both of soul and body, becoming partakers of Divinity, having attained The Supreme Good. In death the union of soul and body is dissolved, but the Soul survives. There can be no destruction of what is of God and in God. From the perishing body (which is not a destruction, but a dissolution of the union in order to be renovated) a new body arises, and becomes immortal through the immortal Soul. This cannot wholly be attained in the present life; but, after death, the Man, becoming entirely in harmony with God, employs himself beyond the eighth or perfect zone in hymns of happiness and praise.

Those who adhere to the body, and surrender themselves to its passions, are abandoned by God; they attain not unto The Good, or to immortality, but becoming more and more wicked they are given over for vengeance to the evil demon, tormented by wicked demons and fire; retrograding to reptilism, they are given over to be tormented by evil passions and lusts, and, condemned to misery, are whirled about the universe—are converted into devils. No allusion is however made by Hermes to the Egyptian judgment by Osiris, or to that by Christ taught in the New Testament.

Finally, the great end of Man is, when thus purified and regenerated, to worship His Creator in His presence, and to be united to Him, and to contemplate and adore Him in holy Silence. In the "Poemandres" are three several anthems of praise and blessing—"verbal rational sacrifices" addressed to the Deity; one of them denominated "The Hymn of the Regeneration"—to The God "whose only passion is to be The Good." There is a certain likeness in these to the ancient Egyptian hymns to Ra, to Hades, and Osiris, and to the Litany of Ra translated and published in the "Records of the Past;" but a much greater resemblance to several of the Psalms. Thus does Hermes inculcate or imply several of the main doctrines and objects of Christianity; but it is fair to admit that, as before observed, he does not notice the fact of the Nativity upon earth, or the Crucifixion, Death, Resurrection, or Ascension of Christ, or His Coming to Judgment. Perhaps they did not come within the purview of his intention, as neither within that of Paley in his "Natural Theology."

The astronomical teaching of Hermes is merely incidental to the rest, and is simple enough. The whole Universe is in the form of a sphere. Nature is composed of four Elements—Earth, Air, Fire, and Water. He appears also to have inferred the rotundity of the Earth from that of the Sun, Moon, and Planets—the latter perhaps revolving round the Sun, but the whole cosmical system round the Earth in an organized Harmony of one external, of seven inner, circles; the varying motion of the Planets being accounted for by a resisting medium. He was aware of the difference between the revolutions of Venus and Mercury and those of the other planets, but does not account for it. He asserts plainly enough that the Earth itself is stable and immoveable; the Constellations, especially the Zodiac, fixed in a solid Firmament, circulating round the Earth also, diagonally to the Equatorial Circle and the orbits of the planets, with the Polar Star for a central pivot, drawn round it by the constellation of the Bear. The whole system of this Κόσμος, or Universe, and of the Harmony thereof, is mainly the same as that of Plato.

It is remarkable that Hermes anticipates modern philosophy by insisting that there is no void in nature, and that none of the works of The God can become extinct or perish, but, if disappearing, are resolved into some other essence or nature, and renovated in another form; thus, it would appear, affirming the future eternity of existing matter, and deducing from this the immortality of the human body. His reasoning resembles that of S. Paul, 1 Cor. xv. 36 : " Thou foolish one, that which thou thyself sowest is not quickened except it die," &c. It is, of course, impossible in this volume to contrast the theology and philosophy of our Hermes, with that of Philo Judæus, with which it has many points of resemblance, or with that of the Grecian sages generally; but in the notes several extracts have been given from the Dialogues of Plato (as edited by C. F. Hermann, at Leipsic, in 1877) and from other authors illustrative of the text. Many passages of Holy Scripture from the Septuagint and the Revised Version of the New Testament have likewise been noted with the same view.

Finally, it is desirable to state that the language and style of our Hermes is semi-classical, though Alexandrian, and without dialect; but often rugged, involved, mystical, tautological, and obscure, with a number of technical words belonging to the Greek philosophy which renders it difficult to translate. It bears much resemblance to that of Plato, whose writings he had certainly studied. The aim of the translator has not been to produce a flowing version, or an elegant paraphrase, or a pithy abbreviation, but to render the original into English with as much literal exactness as practicable.

HERMES TRISMEGISTUS.

POEMANDRES.[1]

CHAPTER I.

1. THOUGHT in me (a) becoming on a time concerning the Entities (b), and my meditation (c) having been exceedingly sublimed, and my bodily senses also calmed down (d), like as those oppressed in sleep from satiety, luxury, or fatigue of body, I supposed some one of very great magnitude, with indefinite dimension, happening to call out my name, and saying to me, "What wishest thou to hear, and to contemplate; what, having understood (e), to learn and to know?" (f)

2. I say, "Thou, then, who art thou?" "I, indeed," He says, "am Poemandres, The Mind (g) of The Supreme Power.[2] I know what thou wishest; and I am everywhere with thee."

3. I say, "I wish to learn the Entities, and to understand the nature of them, and to know The God; this," I said, "I wish to hear." He says to me again, "Have in thy mind whatsoever things thou wouldest learn, and I will teach thee."

(a) ἐννοίας μοί. (b) τῶν ὄντων. (c) διανοίας. (d) κατασχεθεισῶν.
(e) νοήσας. (f) γνῶναι. (g) Ὁ τῆς Αὐθεντίας Νοῦς.

[1] "Shepherd-man," "Flockman." According to Ménard (Preface, p. 3), "Shepherd of man;" but no former editors have adopted this meaning.

[2] Αὐθέντης, according to the scholiast on Thucydides (Hesychius and the "Thesaurus" of Stephens), was formerly synonymous with αὐτόχειρ, but subsequently came to mean ἐξουσιαστής, or Dominus, and the word is used by Hermes several times in that sense.

4. Speaking this, he was changed in the form (*a*), and immediately all things were disclosed to me in a moment; and I see a spectacle indefinable, all things having become light, more pleasant and joyous, and having beheld I was gladdened (*b*); and, after a little, darkness was brought down in part having become dreadful and horrible, sinuously terminated (*c*), so that I imagined myself having seen the darkness changed into a certain moist nature (*d*), unspeakably disturbed, and giving forth smoke as if from fire, and emitting a certain sound ineffable, mournful. Then a noise from it was inarticulately sent out,—as I supposed (*e*) the voice of Light.

5. From the Light a certain Holy Word descended upon Nature, and a pure Fire [1] sprang forth from the moist nature upwards on high. It was light and sharp and drastic also, and the air being light followed The Spirit (*f*); it ascending up to the fire from land and water, so that it seemed to be suspended from it. Earth and water remained mingled in themselves so as not to be distinguished from the water, and they were moved by The on-borne (*g*) Spiritual Word [2] to hearing.[3]

6. Then the Poemandres to me, "Hast thou understood" (*h*), He says, "this the spectacle and what it means? And I shall know," I said, "that the Light." He said, "I am MIND, thy God, Who is before moist nature,

(*a*) τῇ Ἰδέᾳ.   (*b*) ἡράσθην.   (*c*) σκολιῶς πεπερασμένον.
(*d*) εἰς ὑγράν τινα Φύσιν.   (*e*) ὡς εἰκάσαι.
(*f*) τῷ πνεύματι. See ch. iii., *post*.
(*g*) τὸν ἐπιΦερόμενον πνευματικὸν λόγον.   (*h*) ἐνόησας.

[1] It is to be observed, once for all, that the Greek word "πῦρ," translated "Fire," may mean "Heat," whether visible or invisible. Here it would appear to mean the fire of the Holy Creative Spirit.

[2] Compare Ps. civ. 30: "Thou sendest forth Thy Spirit, they are created; and Thou renewest the face of the earth." Also Genesis i. 2: "And the earth was without form (ἀόρατος, Septuagint) and void (ἀκατασκεύαστος, unarranged, Sept.); and darkness upon the face of the deep (ἐπάνω τῆς ἀβύσσου, Sept.); and the Spirit of God moved upon the face of (ἐπεΦέρετο ἐπάνω, Sept.) the water." This description of the primitive Chaos closely resembles that of Plato in "Timæus," 53, which is too diffuse to be here quoted.

[3] See ch. iv. *post*, and note (1) there.

that which appeared out of darkness; but The luminous Word(*a*) out of Mind, Son of God."¹ "What then?" I say. "Know thus: that in thee seeing and hearing is Word of The Lord, but The Mind, Father God; for they are not distinct from each other, for the union of these is the Life."² "I thank thee," I said. "But understand The Light, and become acquainted with that," He says.

7. And saying this He looked me in the face for a long time, so that I trembled at the form of Him. But He having nodded (*b*), I beheld in my mind The Light, being in numberless powers, and the World having become illimitable, and the fire to be restrained by a very great force, and subdued (*c*), to have assumed a stationary (*d*) condition. But I comprehended (*e*) beholding these things, because of the word of the Poemandres.

8. But when I was in astonishment, He says to me again, "Didst thou see in The Mind the Archetypical (*f*) form,³ that existing (*g*) before the indefinite beginning?"

(*a*) ἐκ νοὸς φωτεινὸς λόγος.   (*b*) ἀνανεύσαντος.   (*c*) κρατούμενον.
(*d*) στάσιν.   (*e*) διενοήθην.   (*f*) ἀρχέτυπον εἶδος.   (*g*) προϋπάρχον.

¹ See Lactantius, "Div. Inst.," iv. c. 6, where he quotes, in the original Greek, from the book, "Ὁ λόγος τέλειος" (attributed also to Hermes, but not his work), at length, similar expressions. See the extracts from Lactantius, *post*, Part III.

² Compare John i. 1, 4: "In the beginning was The Word, and The Word was with (The) God, and the Word was God." ("God was The Word," *Greek*). "The same was in the beginning with (The) God. In Him was life, and the life was The Light of (the) men. The Light shineth in the darkness, and the darkness apprehended it not. There was The true Light, which lighteth every man coming into the world." And see *ibid.* v. 26: "God hath given unto us eternal life, and this life is in His Son" (1 John v. 11).

³ Plato, in the "Timæus" (28), had written to this effect (see the paraphrase by Jowett, vol. iii. 532): "All that is generated must of necessity be generated by some cause. When the Creator (δημιουργός), ever looking to what concerns this, having used for this purpose a certain pattern (παραδείγματι), worked out the idea and power of it; thus of necessity to finish all things as beautiful. To have used a created pattern could not have been beautiful. The eternal, ineffable Father of all had in view an eternal archetype (or pattern). To imagine the archetype created would be a blasphemy, seeing that

This Poemandres to me. "These then," I say, "Elements of the Nature, whence constituted (a) are they?" Again He to me, "From the will of God, which, taking the[1] Word (b), and beholding the beautiful World (c), formed an imitation (d), making the World by means of the elements (e) of Itself[2] and progenies of souls." (f)

9. But the Mind, The God, being masculine-feminine, originating (g) Life and Light,[3] begat (h) by Word another Mind Creator (i), Who being God of the Fire and Spirit,[4]

(a) ὑπέστη. (b) λαβοῦσα. τὸν λόγον. (c) κόσμον.
(d) ἐμιμήσατο. (e) στοιχείων. (f) γεννημάτων ψυχῶν.
(g) ὑπάρχων. (h) ἀπεκύησε. (i) νοῦν δημιουργόν.

the world is the noblest of creatures, and God is the best of causes; and the World, being thus created according to the eternal pattern, is the copy of something."

[1] In this treatise λόγος is used with three significations—Reason, Speech, and Word; but with the definite article "The Word" is intended.

[2] Stobæus, in his "Physica" (309, Meineke, i. 82), remarks that Plato held that there were three great beginnings or principles (ἀρχαί)—The God, The Matter, The Idea—by whom, out of which, to which. The God is Mind (of the World): Matter, that subject to generation and destruction; but Idea, incorporeal Essence in the intelligence and phantasies of The God.

In "Timæus" (31, 32) Plato says: "Of the Four the constitution (σύστασις) of the World took each one Whole. For the constitutor constituted it of the Whole of Fire and Water, and Air and Earth, leaving no part nor power of any without; first and especially, because the perfect living creature should be of perfect parts, and also that out of the remnants no other such thing should become." He argues thence that there can be but one κόσμος, and from the whole concludes, moreover, that the visible world is formed after the pattern of the intelligible or invisible (see *ibid.* 31). Compare Rom. i. 20: "For the invisible things of Him, since the creation of the world, are clearly seen, being perceived through the things that are made, His everlasting Power and Divinity;" and Heb. ix. 23, "It was necessary that the copies of things in the Heavens should be purified with these" (*scil.* by sacrifices).

[3] Compare John i. 4, "In Him was Life, and the Life was the Light of the Men."

[4] This paragraph seems to relate that the God of Fire and Spirit proceeds, according to the creed of the orthodox Greek Church, from the Father through the Son. See *post*, ch. iii. 2; ch. xiii. 21, and note.

created some Seven Administrators (*a*),¹ encompassing in circles the sensible world; and their administration is called Fate (*b*).²

10. Immediately from the downborne elements sprung forth The Word of The God to the pure creation of all Nature,³ and was united to the creative Mind (*c*), for it was of the same essence (*d*),⁴ and the irrational downborne elements of Nature were left to be matter only.

11. But the Creator Mind along with The Word, that encompassing the circles, and making them revolve with force (*e*), turned about its own creations and permitted them to be turned about from an indefinite beginning to an interminable end; for they begin ever where they end.

(*a*) διοικητάς.   (*b*) εἱμάρμενη.   (*c*) τῶ δημιουργῷ νῷ.
(*d*) ὁμοούσιος.   (*e*) δινῶν ῥοίζῳ.

¹ "The Seven Spirits which are before His throne" (Rev. i. 4); "The Seven Spirits of God, and the Seven Stars" (*ibid.* i. 20; iii. 1); "Seven lamps of fire burning before the throne, which are Seven Spirits of God" (*ibid.* iv. 5); "The Seven Spirits of God, sent forth into all the earth" (*ibid.* v. 6); "I saw the Seven Angels which stand before God" (*ibid.* viii. 2); "Seven Angels" (*ibid.* v. 7, 8); "Raphael, one of the Seven Holy Angels which present the prayers of the Saints, and which go in and out before the Glory of The Holy One" (Tobit, xiv. 15). See Rev. viii. 3, 4; Ps. ciii. 20; and the extracts from Hermes by Stobæus (188); Meineke, i. 48 (*post*, Part II.).

² That Hermes held that Fate and Necessity are wholly subject to the Providence of the Creator, see ch. x. 20, and the Excerpt by Stobæus (183) (*post*, Part II.); Meineke, i. 47.

³ By the Word of the Lord were the Heavens made, and all the host of them by the breath of His mouth (ἐστερεώθησαν καὶ τῷ πνεύματι (Spirit) "τοῦ στόματος αὐτοῦ πᾶσα ἡ δύναμις αὐτῶν," Septuagint), Ps. xxxiii. 6. "All things were made by Him" (*i.e.*, The Word), "and without Him (χωρὶς αὐτοῦ, "apart from Him") was not anything made that was made" (John i. 3); and see the remainder of the passage before quoted. "Who is the Image of the invisible God, the first born of all creation. For in Him were all things created in the heavens and upon the earth, things visible and things invisible, whether thrones, or dominions, or principalities, or powers. All things have been created through Him and unto Him" (Col. i. 15, Revised Version). See Heb. i. 3, quoted next page.

⁴ It is remarkable to recognise here the test epithet of the orthodox at the Council of Nicæa.

But the revolution (*a*) of these, as the Mind wills from the downborne elements, brought out irrational animals, for it did not afford them reason.(*b*) But the air brought out winged animals, and the water swimming, and both earth and the water were separated from each other,[1] just as The Mind willed, and the earth sent out from itself the four-footed animals which it had, serpents, wild and tame beasts.

12. But the Father of all things, The Mind, being Life and Light, begat (*c*) (engendered) a Man like to Himself,[2] whom He loved as His own child, for He was very beautiful, having the image of His Father. For, in fact, moreover The God loved His own form,[3] and to this delivered over all His own creations.

13. Having considered the formation (*d*) of the Creator in the Father, He too willed to create (*e*), and was parted (*f*) from the Father, becoming (*g*) in the creative sphere. Having all the dominion (*h*), He considered the creations

(*a*) περιφορά.   (*b*) λόγον.   (*c*) ἀπεκύησεν.
(*d*) κατανοήσας τὴν κτίσιν.   (*e*) ἠβουλήθη δημιουργεῖν.
(*f*) ἀπεχωρίσθη.   (*g*) γενόμενος.   (*h*) ἐξουσίαν.

[1] "And God said, Let the waters under the heaven be gathered together unto one place, and let the dry land appear" (Gen. i. 9). "There were heavens from of old, and an earth compacted out of water, and amidst water, by the Word of God" (2 Peter iii. 5). See *post*, ch. iii. 2.

[2] "Wisdom is the brightness of the everlasting Light, the unspotted mirror of the Power of God, and the image of His Goodness" (Wisdom, vii. 26).

"The image of The invisible God, the first born of all creation" (Col. x. 15).

"The only begotten Son, He hath declared Him." "His Son, Whom He appointed heir of all things, through Whom also He made the worlds, Who being the effulgence of His glory and the very image of His substance, and upholding all things by the Word of His power" (Heb. i. 3, Revised Version).

"Who being in the form of God counted it not a prize to be on an equality with God, but emptied Himself, taking the form of a servant, being made in the likeness of men, and being formed in fashion as a man He humbled Himself" (Philipp. ii. 6, Revised Version).

[3] "The kingdom of the Son of His love" (Col. i. 13, Revised Version).

of the brethren who were enamoured of Him;[1] but each made Him participate of his own order(*a*), and having learnt the essence (*b*) of these, and partaken of their nature, He willed to break through the circumference of the circles, and to depress (*c*) the force of Him resting (*d*) on the fire.[2]

14. And He having all dominion (*e*) over the mortal living things of the world, and over the irrational, looked obliquely (*f*) through the Harmony,[3] breaking through the

(*a*) μετεδίδου ἰδίας τάξεως. (*b*) οὐσίαν. (*c*) καταπονῆσαι.
(*d*) ἐπικειμένου. (*e*) ἐξουσίαν. (*f*) παρέκυψεν.

[1] "The first born among many brethren."

"It behoved Him in all things to be made like unto his brethren" (Heb. ii. 17). Lactantius (Divin. Instit. iv. 6) quotes nearly the whole of this passage, together with another similar one from "Asclepius," applying it to Christ, and again (vii. 1), applying it to Man in general. See *post*, ch. iii. and xiii.

[2] An internal Fire was part of the cosmogony of the Platonists.

[3] Plato, in Timæus (53) (in the main according to the Pythagorean system), writes (after saying that God arranged the thin and light elements above and the thick and heavy below), "When God put forth His hand to order the Universe, Fire and Water and Earth and Air having been produced (πεφυκότα), He fashioned them according to forms and numbers, to put them together as far as was possible, as should be most beautiful and best."

The Harmony of Heaven is described in the Timæus (35 and 36): "Heaven revolves round a centre once in 24 hours; the orbits of the Fixed Stars in a different direction from the Planets. The inner and outer sphere cross one another, and meet again at a point opposite to that of their first contact. The first moves in a circle from left to right, along the side of a parallelogram supposed to be inscribed in it, the second also moving in a circle along the diagonal of the same parallelogram from right to left; the first describing the path of the Equator, the second that of the Ecliptic. To the sphere of the undivided He gave dominion, but the sphere of the other or manifold was distributed into seven unequal orbits, having intervals in ratios of twos and threes, three of either sort. He bade them move in opposite directions to one another; three of them, the Sun, Mercury, and Venus, with equal swiftness, the remaining four with unequal swiftness to the three and to one another, but all in due course. The Moon is represented by 1, the Sun by 2, Venus by 3, Mercury by 4, Jupiter by 9, Saturn by 27, being the compound of the two Pythagorean ratios (as to which see ch. iv. *post*), having the might of the circles, and showed to the downward borne (a) Nature the beautiful form of The God, which [Nature] having beheld, having in itself insatiate beauty and all the energy of the Seven Administrators, and the form (b) of The God, smiled (c) for love, as it were having beheld the image of the very beautiful form of the Man in the water and the shadow (d) on the earth. But He having beheld in the water the form like to Him being in Himself, loved it and willed to dwell with it. But along with the will came energy (e) and begat (f) the irrational form.

15. But Nature having received (g) the beloved, completely embraced (h) it, and they mingled, for they were enamoured; and through this, beyond all living upon earth, the Man is twofold, mortal indeed because of the body, immortal because of the essential (i) Man.[1] For being immortal, and having the dominion (k) of all things, he suffers mortal things subject to the fate. Being, then, above the Harmony, he became an harmonious servant. But being masculine-feminine (l), being from a masculine-feminine father, and sleepless, he is dominated by a sleepless.

16. And after these things my Mind; "For also I myself love the discourse." But Poemandres says: "This is the

(a) κατωφερεῖ.   (b) μορφήν.   (c) ἐμειδίασεν.   (d) σκίασμα.
(e) ἐνέργεια.   (f) ἐκύησε.   (g) λαβοῦσα.   (h) περιπλάκη.
(i) οὐσιώδη.   (k) ἐξουσίαν. (l) ἀρρενοθήλυς.

same intervals though not in the same order, being the same mixture as was originally divided in forming the world (see Jowett's "Summary," vol. iii. 578). The Harmony of Man, of his body, of the parts of it, and of the earth, is detailed in the Timæus, 69, 77. It is founded on a complicated system of triangles, which it is not necessary here to explain. But the Harmony of the soul and body of Man has strict analogy to that of the κόσμος (ibid. 38).

[1] Plato ("Parmenides," 144) says: "The Essence (οὐσία) belongs to all beings, although many, and is absent from none of the entities, neither from the least nor from the greatest. This would be foolish to say, for how can the Essence be absent from any entity? The smallest and greatest, and everywhere being and divisible, were they comminuted as much as possible, yet certainly they are infinite parts of the Essence."

Mystery concealed up to this day. For the Nature mingled with the Man produced a certain most admirable wonder; for he having the nature of the harmony of the seven, of which I spoke to you,[1] of fire and spirit, the Nature did not wait, but immediately brought forth the seven men[2] after the natures of the Seven Administrators, masculine-feminine, and sublime " (*a*).

And after these things, "O Poemandres! I have come now to a great desire, and am longing to hear; do not diverge." And Poemandres said, " But be silent, for I have not yet completed to thee the first discourse." " Behold, I am silent," I said.

17. " There happened then, as I said, the generation of these seven in such mode. For the air was feminine, the water, cupiscent (*b*). It received maturity from fire; from ether the spirit; and Nature brought forth the bodies after the likeness of the Man. But the Man became (*c*) from life and light unto soul (*d*) and mind; from life as to soul, but from light as to mind;[3] and thus remained all the

(*a*) μεταρσίους. (*b*) ὀχευτικόν. (*c*) ἐγένετο. (*d*) ψυχήν.

[1] See *ante*, 9, note 4. Also Deuteronomy xxxii. 8, Sept.

[2] For whom these Seven Men are intended is questionable; but the difficulty may perhaps be solved thus: The original pattern Man being masculine-feminine, represents Adam with Eve who was taken out of Adam; and the Seven whom Nature procreated may signify, in like manner, the succeeding Patriarchs named in Genesis, ch. iv. and v., wherein, after detailing the posterity of Cain, it proceeds: " This is the book of the generation of Adam, in the day in which The God made the Adam, after the likeness of God He made him, male and female He made them, and blessed them, and called his name Adam in the day that he made them" (*from the Septuagint, edit. J. Field, Cantab.* 1565). Then follows that Adam begat sons and daughters after his likeness and his image, &c., and the names of the Patriarchs, beginning with Seth, up to and including Lamech the seventh, the father of Noah. Or the number Seven here mentioned may conventionally signify Cain and his posterity.

[3] " And the Lord God formed man of the dust of the ground ('dust of the ground,' Heb.), and breathed into his nostrils the breath of life, and man became a living soul" (Gen. ii. 7, English Version).—" Καὶ ἔπλασεν ὁ Θεὸς τὸν ἄνθρωπον χοῦν ἀπὸ τῆς γῆς, καὶ ἐνεφύσησεν εἰς τὸ πρόσωπον αὐτοῦ πνοὴν ζωῆς, καὶ ἐγένετο ὁ ἄνθρωπος εἰς ψυχὴν ζῶσαν" (Sept. *ibid.*).

members of the sensible world, until the period of the completion of beginnings and progenies.(*a*)

18. Hear the remaining discourse which thou desirest to hear. The period being completed, the connecting bond (*b*) of all things was loosed by the will of God; for all the living creatures being male-female, were loosed apart (*c*) along with the Man, and became partly some male, but some female in like manner. But The God immediately said in Holy Word : ' Increase in increasing, and multiply in multitude all formations and creations'[1](*d*), and let the understander (*e*) recognise himself as being immortal, and the cause of the death love of body, and all Entities.

19. The providence of Him speaking this, by means of Fate and Harmony effected the minglings and established the generations, and all things were multiplied according to kind. And he that recognised (*f*) himself arrived at the superabounding good ; but he that, from error of affection,

(*a*) Τέλους ἀρχῶν καὶ γενῶν. (*b*) σύνδεσμος.
(*c*) διελύετο.   (*d*) κτίσματα καὶ δημιουργήματα.
(*e*) ὁ ἔννους.   (*f*) ὁ ἀναγνωρίσας ἑαυτὸν.

[1] "And God blessed them, saying, Be fruitful and multiply and fill the waters in the seas, and let fowl multiply in the earth" (English Version).—"Καὶ ηὐλόγησεν αὐτὰ ὁ Θεὸς λέγων Αὐξάνεσθε καὶ πληθύνεσθε καὶ πληρώσατε τὰ ὕδατα ἐν ταῖς θαλάσσαις, καὶ τὰ πετεινὰ πληθυνέσθωσαν ἐπὶ τῆς γῆς" (Sept., Gen. i. 22). The Vulgate and English Version agree in reading as to the blessing of Noah and his sons before the creation of man : "Increase or be fruitful and multiply and replenish the earth, and subdue it" (Gen. ix. 1). The Septuagint adds, and "be Lords over it" (see *post*, ch. iii.). A scholiast (Michael Psellus) on one of the MSS. of another work attributed to Hermes, (but not his), "De Operatione Demonum," published by Boissonade, Nuremberg, 1838, and quoted in the notes by Parthey (p. 10), whilst acknowledging that Hermes must have been acquainted with the books of Scripture, and sometimes copied the very expressions, as in this passage, complains that he has not conserved the simplicity and clearness of Scripture, but has amplified and exaggerated them after the Greek fashion ; but the real difference consists only in this, that what in Genesis is enunciated separately, is here extended to all created beings. Yet surely this is within the purview of the Scriptural expressions.

loved the body, this man remaineth wandering in darkness, sensibly (a) suffering things of death."

20. "Why do the ignorant (b) sin so greatly?" said I, "that they should be deprived of immortality?" "Thou seemest," he saith, "O thou (c)! not to have apprehended the things thou hast heard; did not I tell thee to understand?" "I understand," I said, "and remember, and at the same time I thank thee." "If thou hast understood," he saith, "tell me why are those being in death worthy of death?" "Because," I say, "before the peculiar body cometh[1] the fearful darkness (d), out of which the moist nature out of which the body is constituted (e) in the sensible world, whence death is derived."(f)

21. "Thou hast understood rightly, O Thou! But after what mode does he who hath understood himself (g) proceed to God, which the Word of God said? I say that 'from Light and Life is constituted the Father of the Universals (h), from whom the Man was generated.' "Say well speaking," He saith; "for Light and Life are The God and the Father from Whom the Man was generate.[2] If, then, thou hast learnt thyself to be from light and life,[3] and that thou existest (i) of these, thou shalt pass

(a) αἰσθητῶς. (b) ἀγνοοῦντες. (c) ὦ οὗτος. (d) στυγνόν.
(e) συνέστηκεν. (f) ἀρδεύεται, literally, "is watered."
(g) ὁ ἐννοήσας ἑαυτόν. (h) τῶν ὅλων. (i) τυγχάνεις.

[1] "Darkness was upon the face of the deep" (Gen. i. 2.)

[2] The God that made the world and all things therein. He being Lord of Heaven and earth dwelleth not, &c. . . . seeing He Himself giveth to all life and breath and all things; and He made of one every nation of men for to dwell on all the face of the earth," &c., . . . "that they should seek God, if haply they might feel after Him and find Him, though He is not far from each one of us: for in Him we live and move and have our being, as certain even of your own poets have said: For we are also His offspring" (Acts xvii. 24, 28).

[3] "And The God said, Let us make man after our own image, after our likeness" (Gen. i. 26). "So The God created (ἐποίησεν, Septuagint) the man in His own image (after the image of God—Sept.), male and female created He them" (ἐποίησεν αὐτούς, ibid. 28).

unto life again."[1] These things Poemandres said. "But, further," said I, "tell me how shall I pass unto life, O Mind?" Mind, The God, saith, "The man of mind (a), let him recognise himself." "Not all men then," I say, "have mind."

22. "Say well, O Thou! speaking such things. I myself, The Mind, am present with the holy and good, and pure and merciful, with those living piously; and my presence becomes a help;[2] and forthwith they are cognizant of all things,[3] and lovingly propitiate the Father, and give thanks, praising, and sing hymns to Him in ranks (b), from affection; and before delivering over the body to its own death, they detest (c) the senses, knowing their operations (d); or rather I, The Mind, will not suffer the operations of the body which happen (e), to be accomplished; for being doorkeeper, I will shut out the incomings of the evil and base operations, cutting off the desires.

23. But from the fools and evil, depraved, and envious, and covetous, and murderers, and impious, I am afar off, delivering them to the avenging demon, who, applying the sharpness of the fire, attacks them sensibly (f), and prepares (g) them still more for wickednesses, that they may

(a) ὁ ἔννους.   (b) τεταγμένοι.   (c) μυσάττονται.   (d) ἐνεργήματα.
(e) προσπίπτοντα.   (f) αἰσθητικῶς.   (g) ὁπλίζει.

[1] "In Him was Life, and the Life was the Light of (the) men." "But as many as received Him, to them gave He the right to become children of God" (Revised Version, John i. 4, 12).

[2] "Thus saith the High and Holy One that inhabiteth eternity, whose Name is Holy: I dwell in the high and holy place, with him also that is of an humble and contrite spirit" (Isaiah lvii. 15). "Thus saith The Lord, the Heaven is my throne, and the earth is my footstool . . ., but to this man will I look, even to him that is poor and of a contrite spirit (ταπεινὸν καὶ ἡσύχιον, Septuagint), and that trembleth at my word" (ibid. lxvi. 1, 3). "He that loveth me shall be loved of my Father, and I will love him and will manifest myself unto him." "If a man love me he will keep my word; and my Father will love him, and we will come unto him and make our abode with him" (John xiv. 21, 23).

[3] "If any man loveth God, the same is known of Him" (1 Cor. viii. 3). "Then shall we know, even as we are known."

meet with a greater vengeance,[1] and he ceases not from insatiably moving their concupiscence to unbounded appetites, as in a battle in the dark, and so tortures, and augments the fire more and more upon them."

24. "You have well taught me," I said, "all things as I desired, O Mind! But tell me further about the ascent that is to be." (a) To these things Poemandres said: "First, indeed, in the dissolution of the body material, it delivers up the body itself unto alteration (b), and the form which thou hadst becomes invisible, and delivers the character (c) deprived of energy to the demon, and the senses of the body return back to their respective sources, becoming portions (d), and again united together with the energies (e). And passion and desire depart unto the irrational nature.

25. And thus the residue (f) hastens upward through the Harmony, and gives up to the first zone the energy of increase and that of decrease, and to the second the machination of the evils and the fraud de-energized (g); and to the third the concupiscent deception de-energized; and to the fourth, the pride of domineering, without means of satisfaction (h); and to the fifth, the unholy boldness and the rashness of the audacity; and to the sixth, the evil covetings after wealth, de-energized; and to the seventh zone, insidious falsehood.

26. And then, denuded from the operations (i) of the Harmony, it becomes energizing at the eighth nature, having its proper power, and along with the Entities (k) hymning The Father. Those being present at this his coming there, rejoice together, and being made like to those who are with him (l), he hears also the powers who are above the eighth nature in a certain sweet voice hymning The

(a) ἀνόδου τῆς γινομένης.   (b) ἀλλοίωσιν.   (c) τό ἦθος.
(d) μέρη γινόμεναι   (e) συνιστάμεναι εἰς τὰς ἐνεργείας.
(f) λοιπὸν, sine artic.   (g) ἀνενέργητον.   (h) ἀπλεονέκτητον.
(i) ἐνεργημάτων.   (k) ταῖς οὖσι.   (l) συνοῦσιν.

[1] Compare the parable of the Unclean Spirit (Matt. xii. 44; Luke xi. 24).

God. And then in order they mount upward to the Father and they deliver themselves up to Powers, and becoming Powers they become in God.[1] This is the good ending of those attaining knowledge, to be made divine (*a*). For the rest, why delayest thou? Is it not that having accepted (*b*) all things, thou mayest become guide to those who are worthy; so that the race of mankind through thee may be saved by God?"

27. Saying this to me, Poemandres mingled himself with the Powers; but I having given thanks, and blessed the Father of the Universals (*c*), rose up, empowered by Him and instructed as to the nature of everything (*d*), and the grandest vision; and I began to proclaim to the men the beauty of the piety and that of the knowledge. "O peoples, earthborn men, ye having given yourselves up to drunkenness and sleep and to the ignorance of God, be sober, cease being gluttons (*e*), allured by irrational sleep."

28. But they having heard, approached with one consent, and I say, "Why, O earthborn men, have ye given yourselves over to death, having power (*f*) to partake of immortality? Repent (*g*) ye who have walked together with the error, and who have intercommuned with the ignorance; depart from the dark light, partake ye of the immortality, having abandoned the corruption."

29. And some of them having jeered, stood off, having given themselves up to the way of the death; but some requested to be taught, casting themselves before my feet. But I raising them up became a guide of the human race, teaching the words how and in what way they shall be saved. And I sowed upon them the words of the Wisdom, and they were nourished with the Ambrosial

(*a*) θεωθῆναι. (*b*) παραλαβών. (*c*) τῶν ὅλων. (*d*) τοῦ παντός.
(*e*) κραιπαλῶντες. (*f*) ἐξουσίαν. (*g*) μετανοήσατε.

[1] The doctrine of Plato as to the life hereafter of the pious who had vanquished evil and the desires of the flesh is explained in Timæus (42): "He who has lived well the time belonging to him, having again proceeded to the habitation of his consociate star, shall lead a happy and familiar (συνήθη) life therein."

Water.¹ And it becoming evening, and the splendour of the sun beginning to be wholly set, I called upon them to give thanks to The God; and having fulfilled the thanksgiving, each returned to his own couch.²

30. But I inscribed within myself the beneficence of Poemandres, and fulfilled with the things which I wished, I was exceedingly rejoiced, for the sleep of the body became sobriety of the soul (*a*), and the closing of the eyes true vision, and my silence pregnant with the good, and the utterance of speech productions (*b*) of good things. But this happened to me receiving from my Mind, that is of the Poemandres, the Word of the supreme authority(*c*), whence becoming God-inspired (*d*),³ I arrived at the truth. Wherefore I give from soul and whole strength blessing to The Father God.

31. Holy The God, The Father of the Universals (*e*), whose counsel is perfected by His own powers. Holy The God Who willeth to be known and is known by His own. Holy Thou art Who by Word hast constituted the Entities. Thou art Holy, of Whom all nature was born—image (*f*).⁴ Thou art Holy Whom the nature formed not (*g*). Thou art Holy Who art stronger than all power. Thou art Holy Who art greater than all excellence. Thou art Holy Who

(*a*) νῆψις τῆς ψυχῆς. (*b*) γεννήματα. (*c*) τῆς Αὐθεντίας.
(*d*) θεόπνους. (*e*) τῶν ὅλων. (*f*) εἰκὼν ἔφυ. (*g*) ἐμ᾽ ὀρφωσεν.

¹ "Except a man be born of water and the Spirit, he cannot enter into the kingdom of God" (John iii. 5). "Jesus answered and said, If thou knewest the gift of God, and who it is that saith to thee, Give me to drink, thou wouldest have asked of Him and He would have given thee living water." "The water that I shall give him shall become in him a well of water springing up unto eternal life" (*ibid*. iv. 10, 14). See ch. iii., κρατήρ, *post*.

² From this passage some have surmised that this Hermes might have been one of the Therapeutæ, whose custom it was to worship and sing praises thus at sunsetting.

³ The meaning is doubtful. (Q.) If not θεόπνευς α πνέω. In Parthey's edition, the νους is not circumflexed. Here, by anticipation, are propounded the tenets of the Egyptian Mystics, and indeed of the Mystics of all ages of Christendom.

⁴ See *ante*, 8, and notes.

art superior to praises. Accept rational (*a*) sacrifices pure from soul and heart intent upon Thee, O unspeakable, ineffable, invoked (*b*) by silence! To me, beseeching that I stray not from the knowledge that is according to our essence assent; and strengthen me, and with this grace enlighten those who are in ignorance, brethren of my race, but sons of Thee! Wherefore I believe Thee, and bear witness; I pass into Life and Light. Blessed art Thou, Father! Thy Man wisheth to be sanctified with Thee, as Thou hast delivered to him the whole power (*c*) (*i.e.*, to be so).

CHAPTER II.

Of Hermes the Trismegistus, to Asclepius. Catholic Discourse.[1]

1. EVERYTHING that is moved, O Asclepius, is it not moved in something and by something?

Asclepius.—Most certainly.

Hermes.—Is there not necessity that that be greater in which it is moved than that moved?

Asclepius.—There is necessity.

Hermes.—Stronger therefore the motor[2] than that moved?

(*a*) λογικὰς.   (*b*) φωνούμενε.   (*c*) ἐξουσίαν.

[1] This chapter is extracted by Stobæus. (Physica, 384; Meineke, i. 104).

[2] See *post*, ch. ix. 9. The question of motion was important with the Platonists. In Phædrus (245), Plato had written: "Every soul is immortal, for the ever-moveable is immortal; but that moving other and moved by other, having cessation of motion, has cessation of life. But the self-moving alone, since not failing itself, never ceases being moved; but to the other things, as many as are moved, is fountain and beginning of motion. But a beginning (or principle, ἀρχή) is ingenerate."

Asclepius.—Stronger indeed.

Hermes.—There is necessity that that in which it is moved have a contrary nature to that which is moved?

Asclepius.—And altogether so.

2. *Hermes.*—Great then is this the World,[1] than which there is not any body greater?

Asclepius.—It is confessed.

Hermes.—And solid, for it hath been filled with many other great bodies, or rather with all as many bodies as there are?

Asclepius.—Thus it is.

Hermes.—A body then is the World?

Asclepius.—A body.

Hermes.—And moved?

Asclepius.—Most certainly.

3. *Hermes.*—Of what size (*a*) then must be the place[2] in which it is moved, and of what kind the nature? Is it not much greater that it may be able to receive the continuity of the forward course (*b*), and that that moved may not, impeded by the narrowness, retard (*c*) its motion?

(*a*) πηλίκον. (*b*) τῆς φορᾶς. (*c*) ἐπισχῇ.

[1] Κόσμος, *i.e.*, the order of the Universe.

[2] The question of motion is discussed by Plato in "Theætetus," 152, 181: "Motion is both change of place and revolution in itself. It is motion also when change takes place from youth to age, from black to white, from soft to hard. Two forms then of motion, change and revolution." "All things are generated from forward course (φορᾶς), and movement, and mixture; for nothing by no means ever is, but always is becoming." "Motion affords that seeming to be and that becoming. Inactivity (ἡσυχία) is the not being, and destruction. Heat and fire producing and preserving all things is of forward course and motion. Living animals are produced by the same. The health of the body is injured by sloth, restored by exercise; the health of the soul is improved and preserved by learning and care being motions, and acquires knowledge. By inactivity, carelessness, and want of instruction it learns nothing, and forgets what it may have learnt. Motion, then, is good both for soul and body; and Homer teaches that so long as there be the circulation in movement and the sun, all things are, and are preserved with gods and men. But if that stood still, all things would perish, and become, as it were, upside down."

Asclepius.—Some very great thing, O Trismegistus!

4. *Hermes.*—But of what kind of nature, whether of the opposite, O Asclepius? But to body, opposite nature is the incorporeal.

Asclepius.—It is confessed.

Hermes.—Incorporeal then is the place. But the incorporeal is either Divine or God. But the Divine I now speak of is not the generated but the ingenerate (*a*).

5. If, then, it be Divine, it is essential (*b*); but if it be God it becomes superessential (*c*). But otherwise it is intelligible (*d*) thus. For intelligible is the first God to us, not to Himself, for, the intelligible falls under the understander (*e*) by sense. The God then is not intelligible to Himself; for not being something else than that understood is He understood by Himself (*f*).

6. But to us he is something else, and because of this He is intelligible to us. But if the place is intelligible, it is not therefore God but place; but if also God it is so, not as being place, but as capacious energy (*g*). But everything moved is not moved in the thing moved, but in the stable, and that moving it therefore is stable. For it is impossible for it to be moved along with it.

Asclepius.—How then, O Trismegistus, are things here moved along with those being moved? for the spheres, thou saidst, those errants, are moved by the inerrant (*h*) sphere.[1]

Hermes.—This is not, O Asclepius, motion together (*i*), but countermotion; for they are not moved similarly, but contrary wise to each other; and the contrariety (*k*) has the resistance of the motion constant (*l*).

7. For the reaction (*m*) is arrest of progress (*n*). Wherefore, also, the errant spheres being moved contrary wise to that inerrant by the contrariant opposition, because of

(*a*) τὸ ἀγέννητον.   (*b*) οὐσιώδης.   (*c*) ἀνουσίαστον.
(*d*) νοητός.   (*e*) τῷ νοοῦντι ὑποπίπτει.   (*f*) ὑφ' ἑαυτοῦ.
(*g*) ἐνέργεια χωρητική.   (*h*) ἀπλανοῦς.   (*i*) συγκίνησις.
(*k*) ἐναντίωσις.   (*l*) ἑστῶσαν.   (*m*) ἡ ἀντιτυπία.   (*n*) φορᾶς.

[1] See ch. i. 14, and note there.

POEMANDRES. II.

the very opposition (a), are moved amongst each other (b) by the stable (c). And it is impossible that it should be otherwise; for those arctic (spheres) which thou seest neither setting nor rising, revolved about the same point, dost thou think to be moved or to stand still?

Asclepius.—To be moved, O Trismegistus.

Hermes.—What sort of motion, O Asclepius?

Asclepius.—That being turned always about the same point.

Hermes.—But the circulation about the same point is motion restrained by stableness (d). For what is around the same hinders that exceeding the same; but that in excess being hindered, if it stand in that which is around the same, so also the contrary course stands firm, being always maintained (e) by the contrariety.[1]

8. But I will mention to you a terrestrial example meeting the eye about this. Contemplate terrene animals, such as the man, I say, swimming. For the water flowing onwards, the resistance of the feet and of the hands becomes stability to the man, that he be not carried along with the water, nor be sunk by it.

Asclepius.—Thou hast spoken a very apposite example, O Trismegistus!

Hermes.—All motion then is moved in stability (f) and by stability. The motion therefore of the World, and of every material animal, does not happen to be generated by things without the World, but by those within to that without, either by soul or spirit, or something else incorporeal; for body does not move a thing with soul (g), not even the entire body, if it be without soul.

9. *Asclepius.*—How sayest thou this, O Trismegistus? Woods then and stones, and all other without soul, are they not bodies that are movers?

(a) περὶ τὴν ἐναντιότητα αὐτήν. (b) ὑπ' ἀλλήλων. (c) ὑπὸ τῆς ἑστώσης. (d) ὑπὸ στάσεως. (e) στηριζομένη. (f) ἐν στάσει. (g) ἔμψυχον.

[1] The same attempt to explain the relative motions of the planets and stars is to be found in the "Timæus" of Plato. See also *ante*, ch. i. 14, note.

Hermes.—By no means, O Asclepius! for that within the body, that moving the soulless, is it not that body moving both, that of the carrying (*a*) and that of the carried? Wherefore soulless will not move soulless (*b*), but that moving has soul, because it does move. Thou seest therefore the soul weighed down when alone it carrieth two bodies; and that, indeed, things moved are moved in somewhat, and by somewhat is plain.

10. *Asclepius.*—Then the things moved must be moved in a void, O Trismegistus!

Hermes.—May'st thou say well, O Asclepius! but none of the Entities is void, for alone nonentity is void, and alien from the existence (*c*); but that being, cannot be being, unless it were full of the existence; for that existing never can become void.

Asclepius.—But are there not some things void, O Trismegistus! as an void measure, or a void cask, and a void well and wine press, and the other suchlike things?

Hermes.—Alas! for this great error, O Asclepius! Those fullest and most replete, dost thou consider to be void?

11. *Asclepius.*—How sayest thou, O Trismegistus?

Hermes.—Is not the air a body?

Asclepius.—A body it is.

Hermes.—And does not this body permeate through all beings, and permeating fill all things? And body does it not consist mingled of the four?[1] Full then are all things which thou sayest are void, of the air and if of the air then of the four bodies. And it happens that the converse

---

(*a*) βαστάζοντος.   (*b*) ἄψυχον.   (*c*) τῆς ὑπάρξεως.

[1] Fire, Water, Air, and Earth, according to the Pythagoreans and Plato. Plato himself, in the "Timæus," says: "But as to that nature which was before the generation of heaven, of Fire, Water, Air, and Earth, we must consider that, and what occurred (τὰ πάθη) before this; for no one hath ever indicated their origin (γένεσιν). We call them beginnings or principles (ἀρχάς), placing them as elements of the Universe." Also, "of these four the existence of the World took each one whole. For He having established it, established it out of all fire, and water, and air, and earth, having left no part of any, nor power without."

expression is evidenced (*a*), that those things which thou callest full, all these are void of the air, these being narrowed of room by other bodies, and not being able to receive the air into their locality. Those things then which thou sayest are void, one must call hollow, not void, for they subsist, and are full of air and spirit (*b*).

12. *Asclepius.*—The saying is uncontradictable, O Trismegistus! The air is body, and this is the body which permeates through all the Entities, and permeating fills all things. But the locality then in which the Universe is moved—What should we call it?

Hermes.—Incorporeal, O Asclepius!

Asclepius.—The incorporeal then, what is it?

Hermes.—Mind and reason (*c*), whole out of whole (*d*), comprehending itself; free from all body, inerrant, impassible from body, intangible itself, stablished (*e*) in itself, having capacity (*f*) for all things, and conservative of the Entities, of which are, as it were, rays, the Good, the Truth, the archetype Light (*g*), the archetype of the Soul.[1]

Asclepius.—The God then, what is He?

Hermes.—He subsisting (*h*) One, not of these things, but being also cause to these things that they are, as well as to all, and to each one of the Entities.

13. Neither hath He left anything over beside (*i*) that is not (*k*); for all things are those generate from the Entities, not from those not Entities. For things not Entities have not the nature to be able to become to be (*l*), but that of not being able to become anything; and again, the Entities have not the nature of never to be (*m*).

14. *Asclepius.*—Whatever then sayest thou The God to be?

Hermes.—The God then is not Mind but the cause that

(*a*) ἐκφαίνεσθαι. (*b*) πνεύματος. (*c*) λόγος.
(*d*) ὅλος ἐξ ὅλου. (*e*) ἑστώς. (*f*) χωρητικός.
(*g*) τὸ ἀρχέτυπον φῶς. (*h*) ὑπάρχων. (*i*) ὑπέλιπε πλέον.
(*k*) τὸ μὴ ὄν. (*l*) γενέσθαι. (*m*) μηδέποτε εἶναι.

[1] See *ante*, ch. i. 8, and note.

Mind is (*a*). Nor Spirit, but cause that Spirit is.[1] Nor Light, but cause that Light is. Whence one must venerate The God under these two appellations; these to Him alone appertaining, and to no other—for neither of others called Gods,[2] nor of men, nor of demons, can any one, even after a sort (*b*) be good, but The God alone; and this alone He is and nothing else. For all other things are separable from the nature of the Good, for they are body and soul, having no place able to receive the Good.

15. For the magnitude of the Good is so great as is the subsistence (*c*) of all the Entities, both bodies and without bodies, and sensible and intelligible.(*d*) This is the Good, this The God.[3] Thou shouldst not then call anything else good since thou wouldest be impious, nor anything else ever The God, since thou wouldest again be impious.

16. In speech then indeed the Good is spoken of by all; but whatever it is, is not understood (*e*) by all; wherefore neither is The God understood by all, but through ignorance they call the Gods and some of the men good, by no means able either to be or to become such. For they are very different (*f*) from The God; for the Good is inseparable from The God, The God Himself being The Good. All

(*a*) τοῦ εἶναι νοῦν.   (*b*) καθ' ὁποσονοῦν.   (*c*) ὕπαρξις.
(*d*) νοητῶν.   (*e*) νοεῖται.   (*f*) ἀλλοτριώτατοι.

[1] This doctrine seems to be consonant to the Creed of the orthodox Greek Church as to the Procession. See as to this *post*, Part III. Plato ("Timæus," 28) had written: "Everything beginning anew of necessity is generated by some causer. For to everything it is impossible to have generation apart from causer. When, then, The Creator ever looking to that being thuswise, using some such pattern, had effected the idea and the power of it, of necessity it was that everything should be completed beautiful (καλόν). For the production of which, using a generated pattern, it would not be beautiful."

[2] "There is no God but One; for though there be that are called Gods, whether in heaven or in earth, as there be Gods many and Lords many, yet to us there is One, God The Father, of Whom are all things, and we unto Him" (1 Cor. viii. 4, 7).

[3] "There is none Good but One, that is The God." See the subsequent sections, 16 and 17. (Mark x. 18; Luke xviii. 19; and ch. vi. *post*, and note).

the other Gods then are called immortals, being honoured with the appellation of Gods; but The God is The Good, not by honour (a) but by nature. For one is the nature of The God the Good, and one the kind of both these (b), from which are all the kinds (c). For the Good is giving everything, and receiving nothing. The God then gives all things and receives nothing. The God then is The Good, and the Good The God.

17. But another appellation is that of The Father; again because the Maker of all things; for it is of a father to make.[1] Wherefore also in life the greatest and most religious anxiety (d) of the prudent (e) is the generation of children (f), and the greatest misfortune and irreligon, is that any one should depart childless from among men. And this man renders justice after death to the demon, and the punishment is this that the soul of the childless should be condemned (g) to a body having the nature neither of man nor of woman, which is accursed under the Sun. Wherefore, O Asclepius! be mutually pleased (h) with no one being childless; but on the contrary pity the misfortune, knowing what punishment awaits him.[2] So many and such things be said to thee, O Asclepius! a precognition somewhat of the nature of all things.[3]

(a) κατὰ τιμήν. (b) ἕνος ἀμφοτέρων. (c) τὰ γένη πάντα.
(d) σπουδή. (e) εὐφρονοῦσιν. (f) παιδοποιία.
(g) καταδικασθῆναι. (h) συνησθῆς.

[1] This passage is quoted and otherwise referred to by Justin Martyr (Apolog. ii. 6), and Lactantius (Divin. Instit. i. 6). See Part III., and see a similar passage, *post*, ch. v. 8, 10.

[2] The dying childless was accounted a great misfortune among the Jews. "They shall bear their sin; they shall die childless" (Levit. xx. 20). "Thus saith the Lord, Write you this man childless" (Jer. xxii. 30). It is manifest that this latter portion of ch. ii. was written before the epoch of Monachism. This is the only passage in which Hermes propounds any kind of metempsychosis.

[3] Two portions of this chapter are extracted by Stobæus (Ecloga Physica, Meineke's Edition, vol. I., p. 105).

CHAPTER III.

Sacred Discourse.

1. GLORY of all things, The God and Divinity and Nature Divine. Beginning of the Entities,[1] The God, and Mind, and Nature, and Matter; being Wisdom for the manifestation of everything (*a*). Beginning is the Divinity, and Nature, and Energy (*b*), and Necessity, and End and Renovation. For there was darkness without limit in Abyss (*c*), and Water and Spirit, subtle, intelligent (*d*), with divine power being in Chaos.[2] Then issued forth (*e*) Holy Light, and there were collected (*f*) under an arena (*g*) elements from moist essence, and all Gods[3] distribute of Seminal Nature (*h*).[4]

2. And all things being indiscriminate and orderless (*i*), the light were separated off upwards (*k*), and the heavy were made a foundation under a moist arena, the whole

(*a*) ἁπάντων. (*b*) ἐνέργεια. (*c*) ἐν ἀβύσσῳ (Sept.)
(*d*) λεπτὸν νοερόν. (*e*) ἀνείθη. (*f*) ἐπάγη.
(*g*) ἄμμῳ. (*h*) καταδιαιροῦσι Φύσεως ἐνσπόρου.
(*i*) ἀδιορίστων. ἀκατασκευάστων (the same word as in the Septuagint).
(*k*) ἀποδιωρίσθη εἰς ὕψος.

[1] "I am the Alpha and the Omega, beginning and ending, saith The Lord God, Which is, and Which was and is to come, The Almighty" (Rev. i. 11). "I am the First and the Last and the Living One" (*ibid.* 18).

[2] "And the Earth was without form and void (ἀόρατος καὶ ἀκατασκεύαστος, καὶ σκότος ἐπάνω τῆς ἀβύσσου, Septuagint), and darkness was upon the face of the deep, and the Spirit of God moved upon the face of the waters (καὶ πνεῦμα Θεοῦ ἐπεφέρετο ἐπάνω τὸν ὕδατος, Sept.). And The God said, 'Let Light be, and Light was (Γενηθήτω φῶς, καὶ ἐγένετο φῶς, Sept.) And The God saw the Light that it was good (καὶ εἶδεν ὁ Θεὸς τὸ φῶς ὅτι καλόν, Sept.) And The God divided the light from the darkness" (διεχώρισεν ὁ Θεὸς ἀνάμεσον, Sept.) In the margin of the Hebrew and in the Septuagint, "Between the light and between the darkness" (Gen. i. 2-5). See *ante*, ch. i. 7, and the "Timæus" of Plato, 52, 53, for similar statements.

[3] It is clear that throughout this treatise by "Gods" is meant the superior Intelligences, whom we know as Principal Angels, respecting whom see below, and ch. i. 9 *ante*, and note.

[4] See *post* 3, and note there.

being divided apart[1] by fire, and suspended up to be carried onward (a) by Spirit.

3. But each[2] God by his proper power (b), set for-

(a) ὀχεῖσθαι. (b) διὰ τῆς ἰδίας δυνάμεως.

[1] The agency of Fire or Heat is not directly noticed in Holy Scripture; but it is clear that it must have formed part of the original creation. To this may be referred—"He maketh his angels spirits, and his ministers a flame of fire," or "flaming fire" (Psalm civ. 4; Heb. i. 7).

See a statement similar to that in the text in the "Timæus" of Plato, 52, 53.

The account of the Creation in Genesis proceeds thus: "And The God said, Let there be a firmament (στερίωμα, Sept.) in the midst of the water, and let it divide the water from the water (διαχωρίζον ἀνάμεσον ὕδατος καὶ ὕδατος, Sept.); and The God made the firmament, and divided the water which was under the firmament from the water which was above the firmament; and it was so. And The God called the firmament Heaven. . . . And The God said, Let the water under the heaven be gathered together unto one gathering (εἰς συναγωγὴν μίαν, Sept.), and let the dry land appear. And the water under the heaven was gathered together unto its own gatherings, and the dry land appeared; and The God called the dry land Earth; and the collections (τὰ συστήματα, Sept.) of the waters called He Seas" (from the Septuagint *in loco*).

See *ante*, ch. i. 11, and notes there; and the extract, Part II., by Stobæus, from "The Things to Ammon" (Physica, 741; Meineke, i. 203).

The account of the creation of the Sun, Moon, and Stars in Genesis runs thus (ch. i. 14):—"And ('The,' Sept.) God said, Let there be lights (φωστῆρες, Sept.) in the firmament of the Heaven to divide the Day from the Night ('between the Day and between the Night,' Heb. and Sept.), and let them be for signs and for seasons, and for days and for years; and let them be for lights in the firmament of the heaven to give light (ὥστε φαίνειν, Sept.) upon the earth, and it was so." And ('The,' Sept.), God made two great Lights" (τοὺς δύο φωστῆρας, Sept.), &c. "The stars also. And ('The,' Sept.), God set them in the firmament of Heaven to give light upon the earth, and to rule over the Day ('for the rule of the day,' Heb.), and over the night, and to divide the light from the darkness (ἀνάμεσον τοῦ φωτὸς καὶ ἀνάμεσον τοῦ σκότους, Sept.); and God saw that it was good."

[2] "Bless the Lord, ye his angels, that excel in strength, that do his commandments, hearkening unto the voice of his word. Ministers of his that do his pleasure" (Ps. ciii. 20, 21). See Heb. i. 14; Dan. vii. 9.

ward (*a*) that ordained to him, and these became (*b*) beasts, quadrupeds, and reptiles, and aquatics, and winged, and every fruitful seed (*c*), and grass and green herb of every flower, having the seed of the reproduction (*d*) in themselves.[1]

And the Heaven appeared in Seven Circles,[2] and Gods

(*a*) ἀνῆκε.   (*b*) ἐγένετο.   (*c*) σπορὰ ἔνσπορος.
(*d*) σπέρμα τῆς παλιγγενεσίας.

Plato (*Politicus*, 271) had written: "The God first with care ruled over all this globe, as now, according to places; the several parts of the world are everywhere instinct by ruling gods, and divine demons divided, like shepherds, the animals by races and herds, each for each, sufficing for all things to which He assigned them." In the "Timæus" (58), he says: "The God made the self-sufficing and most perfect Good, using the secondary causes as his ministers in the accomplishment of his work, but Himself fashioning the Good in all his creations." Again (69), "Of the Divine, He Himself was Creator, but the creation of the mortal He committed to his offspring."

[1] "And God said, Let the earth bring forth grass" ('tender grass,' Heb., βοτάνιον χόρτου, Sept.), "the herb yielding seed, and the fruit tree yielding fruit after his kind, whose seed is in itself upon the earth" (σπεῖρον σπέρμα κατὰ γένος καὶ καθ' ὁμοιότητα, καὶ ξύλον κάρπιμον ποιοῦν καρπὸν οὗ τὸ σπέρμα αὐτοῦ ἐν αὐτῷ κατὰ γένος, Sept.). "And the earth brought forth grass, and herb yielding seed after his kind, and the tree yielding fruit, whose seed was in itself after his kind" (Gen. i. 11, 12).

"And God said, Let the waters bring forth abundantly the moving creature" ('creeping,' Heb.) "that hath life" ('soul,' Heb.; Ἑρπετὰ ψυχῶν ζωσῶν, Sept.) "and fowl that may fly" ('Let fowl fly' Heb.; πετεινὰ πετόμενα, Sept.) "above the earth in the" ('face of the,' Heb.) "open firmament of Heaven. And God created great whales, and every living creature that moveth" (ψυχὴν ζώων ἑρπετων) "which the waters brought forth abundantly, after their kind, and every winged fowl after his kind." "And God said, Let the earth bring forth the living creature after his kind, cattle" (τετράποδα, Sept.), "and creeping thing, and beast of the earth" (θηρία τῆς γῆς, Sept.) "after his kind. And God made the beast of the earth after his kind, and cattle" (κτήνη, Sept.), "and everything that creepeth upon the earth after his kind" (*ibid.* 12, 13).

According to the Timæus of Plato (77), trees and plants were created, that man might continue, and animals also.

[2] See ch. i. 7, and note there.

Dante has appropriated this notion in the "Divina Commedia," though the number of circles does not correspond.

POEMANDRES. III. 27

in their stellar forms (*a*), being visible with all their signs, and the constellations [1] were severally enumerated (*b*), with the Gods in them, and the circumference was wrapped around (*c*) with air borne onward in a circular course by Divine Spirit.[2] And they sowed (*d*) also the generations of

(*a*) ταῖς ἐνάστροις ἰδέαις. (*b*) διηριθμήθη τὰ ἄστρα.
(*c*) περιειλίχθη τὸ περικύκλιον. (*d*) ἐσπερμολόγουν.

[1] "He telleth the number of the stars, and calleth them all by their names" (Ps. cvii. 4). "He that maketh the seven Stars and Orion" (Amos v. 8). "He had in his right hand seven Stars" (Rev. i. 16). "The mystery of the seven Stars. The Seven Stars are the Angels of the Seven Churches" (*ibid.* 20). "He that holdeth the Seven Stars in His right hand" (*ibid.* ii. 1). "He that hath the Seven Spirits of God and the Seven Stars" (*ibid.* iii. 1); and see *ante* and note, ch. i. 9. "And I saw an Angel standing in the Sun" (*ibid.* xix. 17).

The wide-spread belief in the East, that the stars had great influence on the earth probably arose from the idea that Angels or Divinities resided in them. Josephus mentions that Berosus attributed to Abraham great knowledge of astrology, in which he instructed the Egyptians. Diodorus speaks of Heliadæ (Easterns), who were great astrologers. One of them built Hieropolis, and the Egyptians became great astrologers, and were looked upon as its inventors, and, according to A. Tatius, the Egyptians taught it to the Chaldæans. In the dialogue between Hermes and Asclepius (perhaps not a genuine work of Hermes himself), in answer to a question of Asclepius, Hermes is represented as affirming that the stellar Angels, called Decans, have very great influence over men. (See Part II. xix., *post*.)

Compare "The Stars in their courses fought against Sisera" (Judg. v. 20, English Version). "From the heaven Stars from the array of them" (ἐκ τῆς τάξεως αὐτῶν) "made war" (ἐπολέμησαν) "with Sisera" (Sept.). "Canst thou bind the sweet influence of Pleiades" ('The Seven Stars,' Heb.), "or loose the bands of Orion? Canst thou bring forth Mazzaroth" ('The twelve Signs,' Jerome) "in his season? or canst thou guide Arcturus with his sons?" (Job xxxviii. 31, 32; see also *ibid.* ix. 9). The Septuagint differs: "Συνῆκας δὲ δεσμὸν Πλειάδος, καὶ Φραγμὸν Ὡρίωνος ἤνοιξας; Ἡ διανοίξεις Μαζουρὼθ ἐν καιρῷ αὐτοῦ, καὶ Ἕσπερον ἐπὶ κόμης αὐτοῦ ἄξεις αὐτά." "Hast thou fastened the bond of Pleiades, and hast thou opened the fence of Orion, or wilt thou set open Mazzaroth in his season, and wilt thou bring Hesper to his zenith?"

The Seven Stars are thus enumerated in a verse attributed to Hermes by Stobæus: "Μήνη, Ζεὺς, Ἄρης, Παφίη, Κρόνος, Ἥλιος, Ἑρμῆς." (Physica, 176; Meineke, i. 45).

[2] Plato ("Timæus," 37, Hermann's edition, iv. 340) thus writes:

the men, for knowledge of Divine works, and energizing testimony (a) of nature and multitude of men for the dominion of all things that are under heaven, and the cognition (b) of good things, for to be increased in increase, and to be multiplied in multitude, and every soul in flesh through course of encircling Gods (c), for contemplation of Heaven, and course of the heavenly Gods,[1] and divine works and energy of nature, and for signs of good things,

(a) ἐνεργοῦσαν μαρτυσίαν. (b) ἐπίγνωσιν. (c) θεῶν ἐγκυκλίων.

"From Reason then and this Providence of God for the generation of Time, that Time might be generated, Sun and Moon, and five others denominated Planet Stars, were generated for the division and protection of the numbers of Time. And The God having made bodies of each of them, placed them in the Orbits in which the period of the others went being Seven, the stars being seven. Moon, indeed, in the first around the earth, but Sun in the second above earth, but Hesper and that called sacred of Hermes going in the circle equal in swiftness with the Sun, but having the contrary force to it, whence the Sun and that of Hermes and Hesper both overtake and are overtaken in these by one another. When all the Stars then needed to fabricate Time, had attained the course suitable each to each, and had become living bodies bound by vital chains, and had learned that ordained to them according to the motion of the diverse being diagonal (πλαγίαν) and overruled by the same, they revolved, some in a larger, some in a lesser orbit; those in a lesser orbit revolving faster, but those which had the larger revolving more slowly. That there might be some measure of their relative swiftness in their eight courses, God kindled Light in the second of the orbits, that next the earth, which we call Sun, especially that it might shine over all the heaven, and that living creatures, such to whom it was suitable, might partake of number, learning it from the orbit of this and the like. Thus then became Night and Day, and the period of the one and most intellectual revolution," &c. "There is no difficulty in seeing that the perfect number of Time completes the perfect year, when all the eight periods having their relative degrees of swiftness are accomplished together, and begin again at their original points of departure." See *ante*, sec. 2, note 2.

[1] The Seven Stars, with their guardian angels (viz., the Sun, the Moon, Venus, Mercury, Mars, Jupiter, and Saturn), were by Hermes believed to revolve round the Earth, which remained unmoved in the midst. So also the remainder of the Stars, but these latter fixed in a solid firmament (στερέωμα, Septuagint). See *post*, ch. xi. 7, and note.

for knowledge of Divine power, to know parts (*a*) of good and evil things, and to discover workmanship (*b*) of all good things.

4. Their living and becoming wise beginneth according to portion (or degree) (*c*), of course of encircling Gods, and to be resolved into that; and there shall be great memorials of artificial works (*d*) upon the earth, leaving behind in renewal the wasting (*e*) of times. And every generation of animated flesh (*f*), and of the fruit of seed, and of all art energy (*g*); those which are diminished, shall be renewed by necessity, and by renewal of Gods, and by course of periodical circle of Nature. For Divine is the whole cosmical composition (*h*) renovated by Nature. For in the Divine has Nature also been constituted.[1]

(*a*) μοίρας, or degrees.   (*b*) δαιδαλουργίαν.   (*c*) μοίραν.
(*d*) τεχνουργημάτιον.   (*e*) ἀμαύρωσιν.   (*f*) ἐμψύχον σαρκὸς.
(*g*) τεχνουργιάς.   (*h*) κοσμικὴ σύγκρασὶς.

[1] The construction of this Chapter is in many parts obscure, and the text corrupt or incomplete. Plato ("Timæus," 30), after saying that The God had brought all things out of disorder into order, adds: "For it was not lawful for The Best to work out anything else but the most beautiful."

The account of the Creation of Man, and the purposes for which he was created, in the book of Genesis, which it will be instructive to compare with that of Hermes, is as follows:—

"And God said, Let Us make Man in Our Image, after Our Likeness: and let them have dominion over the fish of the sea, and over the fowl of the air, and over the cattle, and over all the earth, and over every creeping thing that creepeth upon the earth. So God created Man in His own image, in the image of God created He him; male and female created He them. And God blessed them, and God said unto them, Be fruitful, and multiply, and replenish the earth, and subdue it; and have dominion over the fish of the sea, and over the fowl of the air, and over every living thing that moveth (or 'creepeth,' Heb.) on the earth. And God said, Behold, I have given you every herb bearing seed ('seeding seed,' Heb.), which is upon the face of all the earth, and every tree in the which is the fruit of a tree yielding seed, to you it shall be for meat. And to every beast of the earth, and to every fowl of the air, and to every thing that creepeth upon the earth, wherein there is life ('a living soul,' Heb.), I have given every green herb for meat: and it was so. And God saw

CHAPTER IV.

To his own Son Tat. Discourse.
The Crater, or Monas.

1. The Creator (a), not with hands but by Word,[1] made(b) the whole World,[2] so that conceive of Him thuswise, as of the present and everbeing, and having made all things, and One and Only and by His own Will having created (c) the Entities. For this is the body of Him; not touchable, nor

(a) δημιουργός. (b) ἐποίησεν τὸν πάντα κόσμον. (c) δημιουργήσαντος.

everything that He had made, and, behold, it was very good" (Gen. i. 26-31).

The version of the Septuagint is as follows:—

"Καὶ εἶπεν ὁ Θεὸς ποιήσωμεν Ἄνθρωπον κατ᾽ εἰκόνα ἡμετέραν καὶ καθ᾽ ὁμοίωσιν; καὶ ἀρχέτωσαν τῶν ἰχθύων τῆς θαλάσσης καὶ τῶν πετεινῶν τοῦ οὐρανοῦ καὶ τῶν κτηνῶν καὶ πάσης τῆς γῆς καὶ πάντων τῶν ἑρπετῶν τῶν ἑρπόντων ἐπὶ τῆς γῆς. Καὶ ἐποίησεν ὁ Θεὸς τὸν ἄνθρωπον, κατ᾽ εἰκόνα Θεοῦ ἐποίησεν αὐτόν, ἄρσεν καὶ θῆλυ ἐποίησεν αὐτούς. Καὶ εὐλόγησεν αὐτοὺς ὁ Θεὸς λέγων Αὐξάνεσθε καὶ πληθύνεσθε καὶ πληρώσατε τὴν γῆν καὶ κατακυριεύσατε αὐτῆς, καὶ ἄρχετε τῶν ἰχθύων τῆς θαλάσσης καὶ τῶν πετεινῶν τοῦ οὐρανοῦ καὶ πάντων τῶν κτηνῶν καὶ πάσης τῆς γῆς καὶ πάντων τῶν ἑρπετῶν τῶν ἑρπόντων ἐπὶ τῆς γῆς. Καὶ εἶπεν ὁ Θεὸς Ἰδοὺ δέδωκα ὑμῖν πάντα χόρτον σπόριμον σπεῖρον σπέρμα ὅ ἐστιν ἐπάνω πάσης τῆς γῆς, καὶ πᾶν ξύλον ὃ ἔχει ἐν ἑαυτῷ καρπὸν σπέρματος σπορίμου ὑμῖν ἔσται εἰς βρῶσιν. Καὶ πᾶσι τοῖς θηρίοις τῆς γῆς καὶ πᾶσι τοῖς πετεινοῖς τοῦ οὐρανοῦ καὶ παντὶ ἑρπετῷ ἕρποντι ἐπὶ τῆς γῆς ὃ ἔχει ἐν ἑαυτῷ ψυχὴν ζωῆς καὶ πάντα χόρτον χλωρὸν εἰς βρῶσιν καὶ ἐγένετο οὕτως. Καὶ εἶδεν ὁ Θεὸς τὰ πάντα ὅσα ἐποίησε καὶ ἰδοὺ καλὰ λίαν" (*Field's Edition, Cantab.* 1665).

[1] The Chaldee paraphrast has "Memra." "By the Word of The Lord were the heavens made and all the host of them by the breath of His mouth" (Ps. xxxiii. 6). "He spake and it was done" (*ibid.* 9). "Through faith we understand that the worlds have been framed by the Word of God" (Heb. xi. 3). "For this they wilfully forget that there were heavens from of old, and an earth compacted out of water and amidst water, by The Word of God" (2 Pet. iii. 5). See also Gen. i. 6; John i. 3.

[2] The word "κόσμος" has been uniformly translated "World," but it must be understood to mean the entire cosmical "Ordo," or Universe.

visible, nor measurable, nor separable (*a*), nor like to any other body. For He is neither fire, nor water, nor air, nor Spirit; but all are from Him; for being good He willed to dedicate this to Himself alone, and to adorn the earth.[1]

2. But as ornament of Divine body, He sent down The Man, immortal animal, mortal animal. And the Man indeed excelled the animals and the world because of the Speech (*b*) and of the Mind. For the Man became spectator of the works of The God, and wondered, and acknowledged the Maker.

3. The Speech, then, O Tat! He hath imparted among all the men but by no means the Mind; not envying (*c*) any; for envy cometh not thence, but is conceived (*d*) below in the souls of those men who have not the Mind.

Tat. Wherefore, then, O Father! has not The God imparted The Mind to all men?

Hermes. He willed, O Child! this to be stationed (*e*) in the midst, as it were a prize for the Souls.

4. *Tat*. And where hath He stationed it?

Hermes. Having filled a great Cup (*f*), of this He sent down giving a herald (*g*), and commanded him to proclaim to the hearts of men these things; Baptize thyself who is able into this the Cup, who is believing that thou shall return to Him who hath sent down the Cup, who is recognizing for what thou wast generated (*h*). As many, then,

(*a*) διαστατόν.   (*b*) τὸν λόγον.   (*c*) φθονῶν, grudging.
(*d*) συνίσταται.   (*e*) ἰδρῦσθαι.   (*f*) κρατῆρα.
(*g*) δοὺς κήρυκα.   (*h*) γέγονας.

[1] See Plato in Stob. Physica (64 Meineke, i. 16): "The One, the only natured (μονοφυές), the singular (μοναδικόν), the really Being, the Good. But all these of such sort of names attach to The Mind. Mind, then, is The God, a separate form (εἶδος). But let the separate be heard of as the unmixed with all matter, and implicated with none of things corporeal, nor sympathetic with the passionate in nature. But of this Father and Maker, the other divine productions are indeed intelligible, and the World called intelligible, and are exemplars of the visible world; in addition to these certain ethereal powers (but they are irrational and corporeal) and aerial and of water, but the sensible productions (ἔκγονα) of the First God, Sun, Moon, Stars, Earth, and the World comprehending all things."

as understood the proclamation and were baptized with The Mind, these partook of the knowledge and became perfect men, having received the Mind. But as many as failed of (a) the proclamation, they having obtained the Speech, but not the Mind, are ignorant for what they were generated, and by Whom.[1]

5. But the senses of these are very like those of the irrational (b) animals, and having the temperament in cupidity (c) and passion (d), they admire not those things worthy of contemplation, but attaching themselves to the pleasures and appetites of the body, believe that the Man was generated for the sake of these. But as many as have partaken of the gift that is from The God, these, O Tat! according to comparison (e) of the works, are immortal instead of mortal, embracing (f) all things in their own Mind, those upon the earth, those in Heaven, and if there is anything above Heaven. So much having elevated themselves, they behold the Good, and having beheld, they have considered their sojourn here as misfortune, and having despised all things corporeal and incorporeal, they hasten to The One and Only.

6. This, O Tat! is the science (g) of the Mind, the inspection (h) of divine things, and the recognition (i) of The God—the Cup being Divine.[2]

(a) ἥμαρτον.   (b) ἀλόγων.   (c) τὴν κρᾶσιν θυμῷ.
(d) ὀργῇ.   (e) κατὰ συγκρίσιν.   (f) ἐμπεριλαβόντες.
(g) ἐπιστήμη.   (h) ἐντορία, looking into.   (i) κατανόησις.

[1] "He that believeth and is baptized shall be saved" (Mark xvi. 16). "Except a man be born anew, he cannot see the kingdom of God" (John iii. 3). "Except a man be born of water and the Spirit, he cannot enter into the kingdom of God" (ibid. 5).

[2] Here is enunciated the substance of what has been improperly called "Mysticism" (to be distinguished from Quietism),—viz.: "A sacred and secret knowledge of God and of Divine things." Hermes anticipates the sentiments of the Epistles and Homilies of the two Egyptian Macarii. In Homily vi. (Edit. Pritius, 1598), are found these expressions—"Ὁ θρόνος τῆς θεότητος ὁ νοῦς ἡμῶν ἐστι, καὶ πάλιν ὁ θρόνος τοῦ νοῦ ἡ Θεότης ἐστὶ καὶ τὸ πνεῦμα." "The throne of the Divinity is the Mind of us; and again, the throne of the Mind is The Divinity and The Spirit." See post, ch. x. 5, 6, and ch. xiii.

Tat.—I, too, wish to be baptized, O Father!

Hermes.—Unless, first, thou shalt hate the body,[1] O Child! thou canst not love thyself; but having loved thyself thou shalt have Mind, and having the Mind thou shalt obtain also (*a*) the science.

Tat.—How sayest thou these things, O Father?

Hermes.—For it is impossible, O Child! to be about both—about things mortal, namely, and things divine. For of Entities there being two, body and bodiless, in which the mortal and the Divine are understood (*b*), the choice of one or the other is left to him who wisheth to choose.[2] For it is not possible that both concur; but with whomsoever the selection (*c*) is left, the one being diminished hath manifested the energy of the other.

7. The choice, then, of the more excellent not only happens most fair to the chooser to deify (*d*) the Man, but also shows forth the piety towards God; but that of the inferior hath indeed destroyed the man, but he hath transgressed (*e*) nothing towards God but this only, that like as pageantries (*f*) pass on in the midst, not able themselves to energize anything, but are hindering them,—in the same way so these make a pageant (*g*) only in the world, being led away by the bodily pleasures.

8. These things being thus, O Tat! those which are from The God both have belonged to us, and will belong (*h*); let those from us follow and not lag behind; for The God is not the cause, but we are the cause of evil things, preferring these to the good.[3] Thou seest, O Child! how many

(*a*) μεταλήψῃ.   (*b*) νοεῖται.   (*c*) ἐξαίρεσις.
(*d*) ἀποθεῶσαι.   (*e*) ἐπλημμέλησεν.   (*f*) πομπαί.
(*g*) πομπεύουσι.   (*h*) ὑπῆρξέ καὶ ὑπάρξει.

[1] "This is life eternal, that they should know Thee the only true God" (John xvii. 3).

"I buffet my body, and bring it into bondage" (1 Cor. ix. 27).

"Love not the world, neither the things that are in the world. If any man love the world, the love of the Father is not in him" (1 John ii. 15).

[2] See the Excerpt from Stobæus, Ethica ii. 358, *post*, Part II. xviii.

[3] "Let no man say when he is tempted, I am tempted of God: for

bodies we must pass through, and how many choirs of demons, and continuity and courses of stars, that we may hasten to the One and only God. For The Good is insurpassable, interminable, and endless (*a*); in itself also it is without beginning; but to us seeming to have as beginning the knowledge (*b*). The knowledge then does not become a beginning to it, but to us it affords the beginning of that which should be known (*c*).

9. Let us lay hold of the beginning, and we shall make way with quickness through everything. For it is altogether perverse (*d*) the abandoning things accustomed and present, to revert to those ancient [1] and pristine. For the things appearing delight, but those appearing not cause difficulty in believing. But the evils are more apparent, but the good is obscure to the eyes; for there is neither form nor figure to it. For this reason it is similar to itself, but to all others dissimilar; for it is impossible for incorporeal to be apparent (*e*) to body.

10. This is the difference of the like from the unlike, and to the unlike is the shortcoming to the like (*f*).[2] For the Monas (Unit) being beginning (*g*) and root of all things, is in all things as it were root and beginning; for without beginning is nothing; but beginning is out of nothing but out of itself, since it is beginning of the others.[3] For it is this (beginning) since there happens not

(*a*) ἀτελές.   (*b*) τὴν γνῶσιν.   (*c*) τοῦ γνωσθησομένου.   (*d*) σκολιόν.
(*e*) Φανῆναι.   (*f*) ὑστέρημα πρὸς τὸ ὅμοιον.   (*g*) ἀρχή.

God cannot be tempted with evil, neither tempteth He any man; but every man is tempted, when he is drawn away of his own lust, and enticed" (James i. 14, 15).

[1] "Forgetting the things which are behind, and stretching forward to the things which are before" (Phil. iii. 13, Revised Version).

[2] This is extracted by Stobæus (Physica, 306; Meineke, i. 81).

[3] Plato enumerated three ἀρχάι or beginnings—"The God, The Matter, The Idea: By whom, out of which, to which: But the God is Mind of the world, but the Matter that subject to generation and destruction; and Idea incorporeal Essence in the intelligences and the phantasies of the God," Stobæus (Physica, 309; Meineke, i. 82).

being other beginning. Monad then being beginning, comprises in it (a) every number, comprised by none; and it engenders (b) every number engendered by no other number.

11. But everything engendered is imperfect and divisible, may be increased and diminished; but to that perfect nothing of these things happens; and what may be increased also is increased by the Monad, but is consumed (c) by its own weakness, when no longer able to receive the Monad.[1]

This then to thee, O Tat! as far as possible is described the Image of The God, which if thou contemplatest accurately, and shalt understand with the eyes of the heart, believe me, O Child! thou shalt find the way to the things above,—or rather, the Image itself will guide thee. For the spectacle hath something peculiar; those who shall attain to the contemplation it detains and attracts, just as they say the magnet-stone the iron.[2]

(a) ἐμπεριέχει.   (b) γεννᾷ.   (c) ἀναλίσκεται.

[1] Here is set forth the Pythagorean doctrine. He placed the principles (ἀρχὰς) of all things in numbers and their symmetries, which he calls harmonies, but these composed of both elements (στοιχεῖα). Again, he placed the Monad and the indefinite Duad in these principles. One of these principles he assigns to The creative and eternal Cause, which is Mind The God; but the other to the passive and material, which is the Visible World. "The nature of number is a Decade, for you count up to Ten, and then go back to the Monad; and of these Ten the power is in the Fours, for it is made up of the Tetrad and of its parts; and if any one exceeds the Tetrad, he will fall over out of the Ten." (See Stob., Physica, 300; Meineke, i. 80). The views of Leibnitz in his "Principia Philosophiæ and Theodicæ," nearly resemble the above.

[2] Here may be quoted the noble passage from the Wisdom of Solomon, wherein many of the expressions and ideas closely resemble what has preceded and what follows (ch. vii. 16, 17, 22-29).

The English version is this:—

"For in His hand are both we and our words; all Wisdom also, and knowledge of workmanship. For He hath given me certain knowledge of the things that are, namely, to know how the world was made, and the operation of the elements, &c. For Wisdom,

CHAPTER V.

*Of Hermes the Trismegistus, to his own Son Tat.
That the Invisible God is most Manifest.*

1. THIS discourse also, O Tat! I will go through with thee, in order that thou mayst not be uninitiate in the Name of The more excellent God; but do thou understand, how that seeming to the many nonapparent, shall become very apparent to thee. For it would not be, if it were nonapparent. For everything apparent is generated (*a*), for it hath appeared. But the nonapparent always is, for it has no need to appear. For it ever is, and makes all other things apparent. He being nonapparent, as ever being, Himself making manifest (*b*), is not made manifest; not Himself generated; but in imagination (*c*) imagining all things.[1] For imagination is of the things generated only. For imagination is naught but generation.

(*a*) γεννητὸν.   (*b*) Φανερῶν.   (*c*) Φαντασία.

which is the worker of all things, taught me: for in her is an understanding Spirit, holy, One only, manifold, subtile, lively, clear, undefiled, plain, not subject to hurt, loving the thing that is good, quick, which cannot be letted, ready to do good ; kind to man, stedfast, sure, free from care, having all power, overseeing all things, and going through all understanding, pure and most subtile Spirit. For Wisdom is more moving than any motion: she passeth and goeth through all things by reason of her pureness. For She is the breath of the power of God, and a pure influence flowing from the Glory of the Almighty: therefore can no defiled thing fall into her. For she is the brightness of the everlasting Light, the unspotted mirror of the power of God, and the Image of his Goodness. And being but one, she can do all things: and remaining in herself, she maketh all things new: and in all ages entering into holy souls, she maketh them friends of God, and prophets. For God loveth none but him that dwelleth with Wisdom. For she is more beautiful than the Sun, and above all the order of Stars: being compared with the Light she is found before It."

The Septuagint has no essential difference.

[1] Imagination, or Phantasy, seems here to be equivalent to the "Idea" previously spoken of.

POEMANDRES. V.

2. But the One ingenerate is plainly both unimaginable (*a*) and nonapparent; but imagining (*b*) all things, He appears through all things and in all things,[1] and especially in those in whom He may have wished to appear. Do thou then, O Child, Tat! pray first to the Lord and Father, and Only and One and from Whom the One, to be propitious (*c*), that thou mayst be able to understand The God so great (*d*), if that but one ray of Him may shine forth upon that thine understanding. For understanding (*e*) alone discerns the nonapparent (*f*) as being itself nonapparent; if thou art able, it will appear to the eyes of thy mind, O Tat! for the Lord is without envy (*g*); for He appeareth throughout the whole World. Thou mayst be able to take understanding, to see it, and lay hold of it with thine own hands, and to contemplate the image of The God. But if that within thee is nonapparent to thee, how shall He in Himself through thine eyes appear to thee?

3. If, however, thou wishest to see Him, consider the Sun, consider the course of the Moon, consider the order of the Stars; who is He maintaining this order?[2] for the whole order is determined (*h*) by number and place.[3] The Sun is the greatest god of the gods in heaven, to whom all the heavenly gods yield as if to a king and dynasty. And this the so vast (*i*), the greater than earth and sea, sub-

(*a*) ἀφαντασίαστος.   (*b*) φαντασιῶν.   (*c*) ἵλεω(ς).   (*d*) τηλικόντον.
(*e*) νόησις (the passage is corrupt).   (*f*) τὸ ἀφανές.
(*g*) ἄφθονος (ungrudging).   (*h*) περιώρισται.   (*i*) τηλικοῦτος.

[1] "For of Him, and through Him, and to Him, are all things" (Rom. ii. 36). See to the same effect 1 Cor. viii. 6; Coloss. i. 16.

[2] "Which commandeth the Sun, and it riseth not, and sealeth up the Stars; which alone spreadeth out the heavens, and treadeth upon the waves of the Sea ('ὡς ἐπ᾽ ἐδάφους,' as if upon floors,' Sept.); which maketh Arcturus, Orion ("Εσπερον, Sept.), and Pleiades, and the chambers of the South" (Job ix. 7-9). "The Moon and the Stars, which Thou hast ordained" (Ps. viii. 3). "He telleth the number of the Stars; He calleth them all by their names" (Ps. cxlvii. 4).

[3] See *ante*, ch. i. 14, and note there.

mits (*a*), having above itself stars revolving smaller than itself. Whom reverencing or whom fearing, O Child? And each of these the Stars being in Heaven, make not alike or equal course. Who is He having defined to each the way and the magnitude of the course?

4. This Bear (*b*) which turned about itself, and carrying round along with it the whole World order (*c*): who is He having fabricated that organism? Who is He having cast bounds about the Sea? Who He having stablished (*d*)[1] the Earth?

For there is some One, O Tat! the Maker and Lord of all these things. For it is impossible that either place or number or measure be conserved apart from the Maker.[2] For all order (*e*) cannot be made (*f*) without place and

(*a*) ἀνέχεται. (*b*) Ἄρκτος. (*c*) τὸν πάντα κόσμον.
(*d*) ἱδράσας. (*e*) τάξις. (*f*) ἀποίητος.

[1] "The Lord made the Sea and all that therein is" (Exod. xx. 11). "The Sea is His and He made it, and His hands formed the dry land" (Ps. xcv. 5). "Thou hast founded the world and its fulness" (Ps. lxxxix. 11). "The world also shall be established that it shall not be moved" (Ps. xcvi. 10. See also Ps. xxiv. 2, xxxv. 6; Jonah ix. 9; Acts iv. 24, xiv. 15; Rev. x. 6). "Where wast thou when I laid the foundations of the earth? Declare, if thou hast understanding. Who hath laid the measures thereof, if thou knowest? or who hath stretched out the line upon it? Whereupon are the foundations thereof fastened? or who laid the corner-stone thereof? Or who shut up the Sea with doors, when it brake forth as if it had issued out of the womb? and brake up for it my decreed place, and set bars and doors, and said, Hitherto shalt thou come, and no further; and here shall thy proud waves be stayed?" (Job xxxviii. 4. See Isaiah li. 10). "The Lord which hath placed the land for the bound of the sea, by a perpetual decree that it cannot pass it" (Jer. v. 22, and see Neh. ix. 6). "The Lord possessed me in the beginning of His ways before His works of old," &c., "when He gave to the Sea His decree that the waters should not pass His commandment; when He appointed the foundations of the earth, then I was by Him" (Prov. viii. 22-29).

[2] "Ποιητής," Maker, "Creator." In this Hermes rises beyond Plato, whose God may seem to some to be rather a constructor and arranger of material already existing. In his Timæus he speaks of Fire, Water, Air, and Earth as beginnings or first principles (ἀρχάς), and asserts that no one hath ever indicated what was their origin. Yet, in other places, he speaks of The God as Ποιητής.

without measure, but without Master (*a*), neither this, O Child! For if the unordered is defective (*b*), in that it doth not keep the way of the order, yet it is under a Master, Him having not yet ordained the order to it.[1]

5. I wish it were possible for thee becoming winged to fly up into the air, and being lifted up in the midst between the Earth and Heaven to behold the solidity of the Earth and the fluidity of the Sea, the flowings of rivers, the looseness of the air, the vehemence of fire, the course of stars, the very swift circling (*c*) of heaven around these. O most fortunate spectacle that, Child! at one glance to behold all these, the immovable in movement, and the invisible apparent; by means of which is effected the very order of the World, and this the World of the order.

6. If thou wouldest behold the Creator also through the things mortal, those upon the earth and those in depth, consider, O Child! the man fabricated (*d*) in the belly, and examine accurately the art of the fabricator (*e*), and learn who it is fabricating this beautiful and divine image of the Man. Who is He having circumscribed (*f*) the eyes, who He having perforated the nostrils and the ears, who He having opened the mouth, who He having stretched out and bound together the nerves, who He having formed in channels the veins, who He having hardened the bones, who He having cast the skin about the flesh, who He having separated the fingers and the limbs, who He having widened a basis for the feet, who He having opened the pores, who He having extended the spleen, who He having formed the heart pyramidwise, who He having put together the sides, who He having widened the liver, who He having hollowed out (*g*) the lung, who He having made the stomach

---

(*a*) ἀδέσποτος. (*b*) ἐνδεές. (*c*) περίβασιν. (*d*) δημιουργούμενον.
(*e*) τοῦ δημιουργήσαντος. (*f*) περιγράψας. (*g*) σηραγγώσας.

[1] Plato (Timæus, 30), "For The God having willed that all things be good, and nothing according to His might, be bad (φαῦλον), thus taking up everything as much as was seen, not being at rest but moved confusedly and disorderly, brought it into order from this disorder."

capacious, who He having fashioned the most honourable parts for being evident, but having concealed the base.[1]

7. Behold how many arts of one material! how many works in one circumscription (*a*), and all exceedingly beautiful and all measured, yet all in difference. Who made all these things? What mother, what father? If not alone The invisible God, by The will of Himself having created all things?[2]

8. And a statue indeed or an image apart from a sculptor or painter (*b*), no one says can become to be (*c*); and hath this creation become to be (*d*), apart from a creator? O this much blindness! O this much impiety! O this much ignorance! Never ever, O Child, Tat! shouldst thou deprive the Creator of His creations. Better and superior it is—[3]. As much as is according to God in name, so much is He the Father of all things, for He is Only (*e*), and this is the function for Him to be, Father.

9. But if you compel me to speak something more bold, it is His Essence to be pregnant (*f*) of all things, and to make (*g*). And since apart from the Maker it is impossible that anything be generated, so also it is impossible that He ever be not, unless ever making all things in Heaven, in air, in earth, in depth, in every part of the world, in every part of the Universe (*h*), in that being and in that not being; for there is nothing in the universal world which is not Him. He is both the Entities (*i*) and

(*a*) περιγραφῇ. (*b*) ζωγράφου. (*c*) γεγονέναι. (*d*) γέγονεν.
(*e*) μόνος. (*f*) κύειν. (*g*) ποιεῖν. (*h*) τοῦ παντός. (*i*) τὰ ὄντα.

[1] "God set the members every one of them in the body, as it hath pleased Him. . . . Our uncomely parts have more abundant comeliness. For our comely parts have no need: but God hath tempered the body together, having given more abundant honour to that part which lacked" (1 Cor. xii. 22-24).

[2] "First of all believe that there is One God, Who created and framed all things of nothing into a Being. He comprehends all things, and is Only, immense, not to be comprehended by any."—Shepherd of Hermas, Lib. II., Mandat. I.; Wake's Apostolical Fathers.

[3] Here occurs a lacuna, and the text is corrupt.

those nonentities; for the Entities He hath manifested, but those nonentities He hath in Himself.

10. This the God is superior to a name; This the unmanifest, *This* the most manifest, to be contemplated by the mind; This visible to the eyes; This incorporeal, multicorporeal—yea, rather of every body (*a*); for there is nothing which This is not. For This is alone all things. And because of this He has all names, that He is One Father, and because of this He has not a name[1] that He is Father of all. Who, then, is able to bless (*b*) Thee concerning Thee, or to Thee? Looking whither shall I bless Thee, above, below, within, without? for there is no condition (*c*), no place about Thee, nor anything else of the Entities; for all things are in Thee, all things from Thee, having given all things and receiving nothing; for Thou hast all things, and nothing that Thou hast not.[2]

11. When, O Father! shall I hymn Thee? for neither thine

(*a*) παντὸς σώματος. (*b*) εὐλογῆσαι. (*c*) τρόπος.

[1] "But proper name for the Father of all things Who is unbegotten there is none; for whoever is called by a name has the person older than himself who gives him that name. But the terms, Father, God, and Creator, and Lord and Master, are not names, but terms of address derived from His benefits and His works" (Just. Martyr, Apolog. ii. 6).

This passage is cited with the highest approbation by Lactantius (Divin. Instit., i. ch. 6), and again in a different sense (*ibid.* iv. 7). See *post*, Part III.

[2] "For of Him, and through Him, and unto Him are all things" (Rom. xi. 38). It is impossible to lay down in stronger terms the doctrine of the all-pervading and particular providence of God, and of His being the actual and present prompting author of every thing and event. (See Psalm cxxxix. 1-12). Cudworth, in the Intellectual System (ch. iv. 33), ascribes these sentiments to the old Egyptian Theology, apparently quoting this and other passages of the Poemandres and "the Asclepian dialogue," where it is repeated from the Poemandres; and Wilkinson (Ancient Egyptians, iii. 178), and after him Rawlinson (History of Egypt, i. 314), reiterate this statement. Without denying that the ancient Egyptians were Monotheists, such a statement cannot be proved from the above-named authorities which were both posterior to the Christian era.

hour nor time is it possible to ascertain (*a*), concerning what also shall I hymn? concerning what things Thou hast made, or concerning those Thou hast not made? concerning those Thou hast made manifest, or concerning those Thou hast concealed? Wherefore also shall I hymn Thee? As if being of myself, as if having something mine own? (*b*) as being another? For Thou art what I may be, Thou art what I may do, Thou art what I may speak, for Thou art all things, and there is nothing else that Thou art not. Thou art everything generated (*c*). Thou that art not generated; Mind also, intelligent (*d*). Father too creating, God also energizing; good moreover, and making all things. For of matter, indeed, the lightest in parts (*e*) is air; but of air, Soul (*f*); of Soul, Mind; but of Mind, The God.

CHAPTER VI.

That in The God alone is The Good, and by no means anywhere else.

1. THE Good, O Asclepius! is in nothing excepting The God alone. Rather, indeed, the Good is The God Himself evermore. But it is thus, He must be Essence, destitute (*g*) of all movement, and of generation (but naught is destitute of this), but having around Itself a stable energy wanting nothing, without superfluity, most copious provider (*h*). One thing is the beginning of all things; for that providing (*i*) everything is Good. When I say also in all respects, it is ever Good. But this belongs to no one else except to The God only. For neither is He wanting of anything, so that coveting to possess it He should become

(*a*) καταλαβεῖν.   (*b*) ἴδιον.   (*c*) γενόμενον.
(*d*) νοούμενος.   (*e*) λεπτομερέστερον.   (*f*) ψυχή.
(*g*) ἔρημον.   (*h*) χορηγόν.   (*i*) πᾶν γὰρ τὸ χορηγοῦν.

POEMANDRES. VI.

evil; nor is any of things being to be lost by Him, having lost which He should be grieved; for grief is part of evil. Nor is anything superior to Him by which He might be assailed, nor is anything compeer (*a*) with Him so that He be injured, and for this reason should be in love (*b*) with it; nor disobedient with which He should be angry; nor wiser which He might envy.

2. These things then not existing in His Essence, what remains beside but The Good only? for as none of the evil things in such an Essence, so in none of the others will the Good be found. For in all, things are otherwise, both in the small and in the great, and in those individually, and in this the animal the greater and most powerful of all. For things generated (*c*) are full of passions, the generation itself being subject to passion (*d*). But where passion is there nowhere is The Good; but where The Good there nowhere is even one passion. For where day is, nowhere night, but where night, nowhere day. Wherefore impossible is it that in generation there be The Good, but in the nongenerate (*e*) only. For as the common being (*f*) of all things is bound up in the Matter, so is it also of The Good. In this way the world is good so far as it also makes all things, so as in the part of the making to be good; but in all other things not good. For also it is passible (*g*), and moveable, and maker of passible things.

3. In the Man indeed the good is ordered according to comparison with the evil. For here that which is not very evil is the good, and that here good is the least particle of the evil. It is impossible then to purify the good here from the evil; for here the good grows evil (*h*), and being grown evil no longer remains good, and not having remained becomes evil. In The God alone, therefore, is The Good, or The God Himself is The Good. Only, therefore, O Asclepius! is the name of The Good among men, but the fact itself nowhere, for it is impossible. For the material body

(*a*) σύζυγον.   (*b*) ἐρασθήσεται.   (*c*) γεννητά.   (*d*) παθητής.
(*e*) τῷ ἀγεννήτῳ.   (*f*) μετουσία.   (*g*) παθητός.   (*h*) κακοῦται.

is not capable (a)[1], that on all sides restricted (b), by evil, and labours, and griefs, and desires, and anger and errors, and mindless opinions. And the worst of all, O Asclepius! is that each of these the aforesaid is believed here to be the greatest good.[2] That more than unsurpassable evil, the gluttony (c), the error, the provider of all the evils, is the absence here of the Good.

4. And I also give thanks to The God, to Him Who hath instilled into my mind respecting the knowledge of The Good; that it is impossible for that to be in the world. For the world is the plenitude of the evil (d),[3] but The God of the Good, or the Good (the plenitude) of The God. For the excellencies of the beautiful are around this very Essence, and perhaps these His Essences appear thus, both more pure and more distinct. For we may dare to say, O Asclepius! that the Essence of The God, if indeed He have Essence, is the Beautiful, but the Beautiful is also Good. No good thing is to be comprehended among those in the world. For all things falling under the eye are images, and as it were adumbrations (e), and those who fall not under it,[4] and specially that of The Beautiful and of The Good. And as the eye is not able to behold The God, so neither The Beautiful nor The Good; for these are integral parts of The God, properties (f) of Himself only, familiars (g), inseparables, most lovely, which either God Himself loveth or they love The God.

(a) ὸυ χωρεῖ. (b) πάντοθεν ἐσφιγμένον.
(c) μᾶλλον ἀνυπέρβλητον ἡ γαστριμαργία.
(d) κόσμος πληρωμά τῆς κακίας. (e) εἴδωλά σκιαγραφίαι.
(f) ἴδια. (g) οἰκεῖα.

[1] "For I know that in me, that is in my flesh, dwelleth no good thing" (Rom. xx. 18).

[2] "For that which is exalted among men is an abomination in the sight of God" (Luke xvi. 15).

[3] "This present evil world" (ἐνεστῶτος αἰῶνος πονηροῦ, Greek) (Gal. i. 4). "The whole world" (κόσμος ὅλος) "lieth in wickedness" (1 John v. 19). "All that is in the world, the lust of the flesh and the lust of the eyes, and the pride of life, is not of the Father" (*ibid.* ii. 16), "but of the world" (ἐκ τοῦ κόσμου).

[4] Here is a lacuna in the text which mars the sense.

5. If thou art able to understand (a) The God, thou wilt understand The Beautiful and Good, the exceeding bright, the exceeding radiant, from The God. For that is the Beauty incomparable, and that the Good inimitable, just as also God Himself. As then thou understandest The God, thus also understand The Beautiful and Good; for these are incommunicable to the others of the animals, because of being inseparable from The God. If Thou inquirest about The God, thou inquirest about The Beautiful.

6. For the way leading to it is one, the piety with knowledge; hence the ignorant, and they not having journeyed the way, which is concerning this piety, dare to speak of the Man as beautiful and good, not having even beheld a dream whether anything is good, but preimplicated (b) with every evil, and having believed the evil to be good, and thus using it insatiably, and fearing to be deprived of it, and striving in every way that, not only he may have, but also may augment it. Such are the human gods and The Beautiful, O Asclepius! which we are neither able to fly nor to have hated. For that, of all things, is most difficult, because we have need of them, and without these we cannot live.

CHAPTER VII.

That the Greatest Evil among Men is Ignorance of The God.

1. WHITHER are ye carried, O men, intoxicated! drinking up the unmixed wine of ignorance, which yet ye cannot bear, but already are even vomiting it? Stop, be sober; look again with the eyes of the heart, and if ye all cannot,

(a) νόησαι, to conceive in mind.　　(b) προείλημμενον.

at least ye that are able. For the vice (*a*) of ignorance inundates all the earth, and corrupts therewith the soul enclosed in the body, not suffering it to be harboured in the havens of the salvation.

2. Be not therefore borne along together by the much current, but ye that are able, having made use of reflux to attain the haven of the salvation, having been harboured therein, seek a guide, who shall lead you in the way to the gates of the knowledge, where is the shining Light, that pure from darkness, where not one is drunken, but all are sober, looking on in the heart to Him willing to be seen. For He is not audible, nor effable, nor visible to the eyes, but to Mind and Heart. First, however, it is necessary that thou shouldest tear off[1] the garment which thou bearest, the web (*b*) of ignorance, the support of wickedness, the bond of corruption, the dark enclosure, the living death, the sentient corpse, the tomb carried about with thee, the domestic robber, him hating through the things he loves, and grudging (*c*) through the things he hates.

3. Of such sort is the hateful garment which thou hast put on,[2] drawing thee down to itself, that not having looked back and beheld the beauty of The Truth, and the

---

(*a*) κακία.   (*b*) ὕφασμα.   (*c*) φθονοῦντα.

[1] Plato had written in Phædo (66, 67)—"If, whilst in the company of the body, the soul cannot have pure knowledge, one of two things must follow; either that knowledge is not to be attained at all, or if at all, after death. In the present life we make the nearest approach to knowledge when we have the least possible communion or fellowship with the body, and are not infected with the bodily nature, but remain pure until the hour when God Himself is pleased to release us; and then the foolishness of the body shall be cleared away, and we shall be pure and hold converse with other pure souls from below, which is no other than the light of Truth, for no impure thing is allowed to approach the pure."

Compare 1 Cor. xiii. 12—"Now I know in part, but then shall I know even as I am known." Also Rev. xxi. 27—"There shall nowise enter into it anything unclean," &c.

[2] "I know that in me, that is, in my flesh, dwelleth no good thing" (Rom. vii. 18). "I buffet my body and bring it into bondage" (1 Cor. ix. 27). It is instructive to compare with the text the language of

indwelling Good, thou shouldest hate its vileness, having understood the snare, which it hath laid in wait for thee, making those things seeming to us and being considered objects of sense (a), insensible, having obstructed them with much matter, and filled them with abominable pleasure,[1] so that thou shouldest neither hear those things about which it behoves thee to hear, nor discern those about which it behoves thee to discern.

CHAPTER VIII.

That none of the Entities perish, but mankind erroneously call the changes, destructions and deaths.

1. CONCERNING Soul and body, O Son! now is to be discoursed; in what way verily the soul is immortal, and of what quality (b) is energy in constitution and dissolution of body. For concerning naught of these is the death, but it is intellectual notion (c) of an appellation "immortal," either as vain work (d), or by deprivation of the first letter;

(a) αἰσθητήρια.   (b) ἐνέργεια δὲ ποταπή.   (c) νόημά.   (d) κενὸν ἔργον.

William Law, in his "Spirit of Prayer" (Part I., Works vii. 84):— "Our own life is to be hated, and the reason is plain: it is because there is nothing lovely in it. It is a legion of evil, a monstrous birth of the Serpent, the World, and the Flesh. It is an Apostasy from the Life and Power of God in the Soul—a life that is death to Heaven, that is pure unmixed Idolatry, that lives wholly to self and not to God, and therefore all this own life is to be absolutely hated, all this Self is to be denied, and mortified, if the Nature, Spirit, Tempers, and Inclinations of Christ are to be brought to life in us."

[1] "I see a different law in my members, warring against the law of my mind, and bringing me into captivity under the law of sin which is in my members. O wretched man that I am! Who shall deliver me out of the body of this death?" (Rom. vii. 23). "The mind of the flesh is enmity against God" (*ibid.* viii. 7). "They that are in the flesh cannot please God" (*ibid.* viii. 8). See also Galat. v. 17.

that being called θάνατος instead of the ἀθάνατος.[1] For the death is of destruction; but naught of those things in the world is destroyed, for if the World is second God and immortal animal, it is impossible for any part of the immortal animal to die; for all the things in the world are parts of the world, and especially the Man, the rational animal.

2. For first of all really (*a*), and eternal, and nongenerate, The Creator of The Universe (*b*), God. But the second that after His image the World by Him engendered,[2] and by Him held together and nourished and immortalized, as by its own father, everliving as immortal. For the everliving (*c*) differs from the eternal (*d*). For The One was not generated by another, and if it be generate, it was yet not generated by itself but always is generate. For the eternal in that it is eternal, is the Universe (*e*). And The Father Himself, of His Own Self, is eternal, and the World became (*f*) eternal and immortal by The Father.

3. And so much of matter as was set apart by Him The Father having embodied and swelled out (*g*) the Whole, formed this sphere like,[3] placing around it such quality (*h*),

(*a*) ὄντως.	(*b*) τῶν ὅλων.	(*c*) ἀείζωον.	(*d*) ἀιδίου.
(*e*) τὸ πᾶν.	(*f*) γέγονε.	(*g*) ὀγκώσας.	(*h*) τό ποῖον.

[1] See the doctrine of Plato as to what death is (Phædo, 67).

[2] Plato enunciates the same views in the Phædon and in Timæus (33 and 41): "For The God in His power willed that all things should be good, and nothing bad, and brought the Universe fully out of disorder; for it neither was nor is possible that He should do aught else but what is most beautiful; thus having completed a work that might be something most beautiful and perfect in its nature. So then, according to the right reason, it behoves one to say that this the κόσμος became through the Providence of The God a living creature (ζῷον), endued in very truth with Soul and Mind." (See Stobæus, Florilegium, Meineke, iv. 105).

[3] Plato thought that the κόσμος was spherical in form. In the Timæus (33 and 62) he says: "He gave it figure (σχῆμα), the becoming, and the convenient; for when about to encompass all living beings in it, with living being (ζῷῳ), a figure would be becoming, that comprehending in it all such like figures; wherefore also He described it circular, spherelike from the centre, distant every way so far to

being both itself immortal and having the material eternal. But full of the Ideas (*a*) The Father having sown in the qualities,[1] inclosed them in the sphere as if in a cave,[2] willing for every quality to adorn that of quality with itself; but with this immortality having encompassed the whole body, lest the matter having wished to secede from the constitution thereof, should be dissolved into its own disorder (*b*). For when the matter was unincorporate, O Child! it was without order; but it has even here that revolution (*c*)[3] in respect of the other small qualities, that of the increase and that of the diminution, which men call death.

4. But this the want of order exists (*d*) around earthly animals; for the bodies of the heavenly have one order, which they have allotted from the Father at the beginning; and this is maintained, by the restoration (*e*) of each,[4] indissoluble;

(*a*) ἰδεῶν.   (*b*) τὴν ἑαυτῆς ἀταξίαν.   (*c*) τὴν εἰλουμένην.
(*d*) γίνεται.   (*e*) ἀποκαταστάσεως.

the extremities." "So all the heaven being spherelike, and the World thus brought into being every part being equidistant from the centre, to speak of above or below is neither just nor accurate. If any one were to go round this in a circle, often, standing at the antipodes, he would speak of the same part of it as above and below. As I said, to talk of the spherical as having one part above and another below, is not wise."

[1] Referring to the "Ideas" or "Forms" which Plato held to be the originals of all things, Plutarch defined the "Idea" thus (quoted by Stobæus, Physica, ch. xii. 6*a*; Meineke, i. 87):—"Idea is Incorporeal Essence, cause of such like beings as itself is, and pattern (παραδείγμα) of the subsistence (ὑποστάσεως) of the objects of sense (αἰσθητῶν) having themselves (ἐχόντων) according to nature; it indeed sustained of itself, and imaging (ἐνεικονίζουσα) shapeless materials, and becoming cause of the arrangement (διατάξεως) of these, applying order of a father to the objects of sense."

Plato, in "Parmenides," says:—"It appears to me that the matter stands thus: that these Forms (εἴδη) stand in the Nature as if patterns, and that other things resemble these, and are likenesses, and the participation of the Forms with the others, becomes nothing else than the being assimilated to them."

[2] This simile of the cave is borrowed from Plato's Republic, lib. v. 28, 517, *et seq.*; Hermann, iv. 202.

[3] Parthey suggests "confusion," p. 38.

[4] Referring to the return of each to its own place in the heavens. See *ante*, ch. iii. and note 3 there.

but the restoration of the earthly bodies is constitution (a), and the dissolution itself restores (b) to the indissoluble bodies; that is to say, the immortal; and thus there becomes deprivation of the sense, not destruction of the bodies.

5. But the third animal, The Man, generated after the image of the World, but having Mind, according to the will of the Father beyond other earthly animals, not only has sympathy with the second God, but also intelligence (c) of the first; for of the one it is sensible as of body, but of the other it receives intelligence as of an incorporeal and of the Good Mind (d).

Tat.—This animal, then, does not perish?

Hermes.—Speak well (e), O Child! and understand what God is, what the World, what an immortal animal, what a dissoluble animal, and understand that the World indeed is from The God, and in The God, but the Man from the world, and in the world, but the beginning and comprehension (f) and constitution of all things is The God.[1]

CHAPTER IX.

Concerning Understanding and Sense (g), *and that in The God only is The Beautiful and The Good, but elsewhere not at all.*

1. YESTERDAY, O Asclepius! I delivered the perfect Discourse; but now I consider necessary, consequential to that, to go also through the discourse respecting Sense. For sense and understanding seem indeed to have differ-

(a) σύστασις. (b) ἀποκαθίστατai. (c) ἔννοιαν.
(d) νοῦ τοῦ ἀγαθοῦ. (e) εὐφήμησον. (f) περιοχή.
(g) νοήσεως, understanding; αἰσθήσεως, sense.

[1] It seems evident from the contents of this Chapter, connected with what precedes and what follows, that Poemandres, in mystical

ence, because that is material (*a*), but this essential (*b*); but to me both seem to be united, and not to be separated among men, by Reason (*c*). For in the other animals the sense is united to the nature, but in men understanding (*d*). But Mind differs from understanding as much as The God from Divinity (*e*). For the Divinity indeed is generate by (*f*) God, but understanding by the Mind, being sister of the speech and organs of each other. For neither is the speech uttered apart (*g*) from understanding, nor is the understanding shown without speech.

2. The Sense then and the Understanding, both together, have influence (*h*) upon the Man, as it were, connected with each other. For neither apart from Sense is it possible to understand,[1] nor to have sensation apart from understanding. But it is possible to understand Understanding (*i*) apart from Sense, as those fancying (*k*) visions in their dreams; but it seems to me that both the energies are generated in the vision of the dreams, and that the sense is aroused to wakefulness out of sleep. For the Man has been divided both into the body and into the Soul, and when both the parts of the Sense shall concord one with another, then that the understanding is spoken out and brought forth (*l*) by the Mind.

3. For the Mind conceives all the thoughts (*m*); good indeed when it shall have received the seeds from The God, but the contrary when from any of the demons; no

(*a*) ὑλική.	(*b*) οὐσιώδης.	(*c*) λόγῳ.
(*d*) νόησις, or intellect.	(*e*) Θειότης.	(*f*) ὑπό.
(*g*) χωρίς.	(*h*) συνεπεισρέουσιν.	(*i*) νόησιν νοεῖσθαι.
(*k*) φαντάζόμενοι, imagining.	(*l*) ἀποκυηθεῖσαν.	(*m*) κύει νοήματα.

language, means to teach the future immortality of the human body (see Philippians iii. 21), after a renovation of the same after death. He seems also to hold the future eternity of created matter. Plato, in Timæus, had declared that the κόσμος was perishable, so far as its nature was concerned, for it was an object of sense, because corporeal, but that it will never perish by the providence and continuous coherence (συνοχῇ) of God.

[1] See Locke, "No Innate Ideas." "Nihil in intellectu quod non prius fuit in sensu."

part of the world being vacant from the Demon; that Demon to be separated from The God; who entering in unawares (a) sowed the seed of his own energy, and the Mind conceived what was sown :[1] adulteries, murders, parricides, sacrileges, impieties, stranglings, hurling down from precipices, and all other such the works of evil demons.[2]

4. For the seeds of The God are few, but great and both beautiful and good: Virtue, and Temperance, and Piety. But Piety is Knowledge of God,[3] which he who recogniseth (b), becoming full of all the good things, possesses (c) the divine thoughts, and not like the many. Because of this, those being in knowledge, neither please the many, nor the many them; they seem to be mad, and occasion laughter, and being hated and despised, and perhaps also murdered. For we have said that wickedness (d) must dwell here, being in its own region; for its region is the earth (e), not the World (f) as some may say blaspheming. But the Godfearing man will contemn all things, perceiving the Knowledge. For all things to such an one, although to others the evil, are good; and taking counsel he refers all things unto the Knowledge, and what is wonderful, alone renders the evils good (g).[4]

5. I return again to the discourse of Sense. Human, then, is the common Union (h) in man, of sense with understanding. But not every man, as I said before, enjoys

(a) ὑπεισελθών. (b) ἐπιγνοὺς. (c) ἴσχει.
(d) κακίαν. (e) ἡ γῆ. (f) κόσμος.
(g) ἀγαθοποιεῖ. (h) τὸ κοινωνῆσαι.

[1] See the parable of the Sower, Matthew xiii. 39. "Out of the heart of men proceed evil thoughts, adulteries" (Mark vii. 21). "When lust hath conceived, it bringeth forth sin" (James i. 15). See also Galat. v. 19.

[2] See Lactant., Div. Instit., ii. 15, 16, where these sentiments are quoted as from Hermes.

[3] Quoted by Lactant., *ibid*. 16. See John xvii. 3. "And this is life eternal, that they might know Thee the only true God, and Jesus Christ whom Thou hast sent." That this wisdom and knowledge is identical with piety, St Augustine maintains in his Eucheiridion.

[4] It is superfluous to refer to the numerous passages of Holy Scripture which enunciate the same doctrines as those here set forth.

this understanding, but one is material, another essential. For the one along with wickedness (material, as I said), from the demons possesses (a) the seed of the understanding; but these along with the essentially good are saved by The God. For The God is the Creator of all things; creating all things He makes all things like to Himself; but these good things generated, in the use of energy are barren: for the worldly course rubbing against (b) these generations (c), makes them qualities, soiling these indeed with the evilness, but purifying those with the Good. For the World also, O Asclepius! has its proper sense and understanding, not like to the human nor as various, but as superior and simpler.

6. For the sense and understanding of the World is one, in the making all things, and unmaking them into itself, organ of the will of The God; and so organised, that, having received all the seeds unto itself from The God, conserving them in itself, it might manifestly (d) make all things, and dissolving might renew all things; and when thus dissolved, as a good agriculturist of life it imparts by the change a renewal to these its offspring (e). There is nothing that it does not engender alive (f). But bearing it makes all things alive, and it is at once the place and the creator of life.

7. But the bodies from matter are in difference. For some indeed are from earth, some from water, some from air, and some from fire; but all are composite (g), and some are more so, some more simple; more so indeed are the heavier, the lighter less so. But the velocity (h) of its course effects the variety of the generations of qualities (i). For breath (k) being very dense stretches forth the qualities (l) over the bodies with one fulness, that of the life.

8. The God indeed then is Father of the World, but the World of things in the world. And the World indeed is

(a) ἰσχει.
(b) ἡ κοσμικὴ φορὰ τρίβουσα, wearing away.
(c) τὰς γενέσεις.
(d) ἐναργῶς.
(e) Φυομένοις.
(f) ζωογονεῖ.
(g) σύνθετα.
(h) i.e., τοῦ κοσμου.
(i) τῶν ποιῶν γενέσεων.
(k) πνοή.
(l) προτείνει τὰ ποιά.

son of The God; but things in the World are from the World, and properly was it called "World" (κόσμος), for it adorneth all things by the variety of the generation (a) and by the indefectibility (b) of the life, and the unweariedness of the energy, and the quickness of the necessity, and the combination (c) of the elements, and the order of the things generated. The same then should be called "World" both necessarily and fittingly. Of all animals therefore both the Sense and the Understanding comes in upon them from without, inspired (d) by that circumambient; but the World having once received this along with the being generated, has it, having received it from The God.

9. But The God is not, as it seems to some, insensible and mindless. For through superstition (e) they blaspheme. For all things as many as are, O Asclepius! these are in The God, and generated by The God, and thence dependent (f); some indeed energizing through the bodies, and others moving through animated Essence (g), others making life through spirit, and others undertaking those defunct; and that suitably. But I rather say, not that He has these things, but I show forth the Truth, He is all things, not receiving them from without but giving them forth outwards (h). And this is the Sense and the Understanding of The God, the moving all things always, and there shall be never a time when any of the Entities shall be deficient (i); but when I say the Entities, I speak of The God. For the Entities The God has, and neither is anything without (k) Him, nor is He without anything.[1]

10. These things to thee, O Asclepius! being intel-

(a) γενέσεως, or production.   (b) ἀδιαλείπτῳ.   (c) συστάσει.
(d) εἰσπνέουσα.   (e) δεισιδαιμονίας.   (f) ἐκεῖθεν ἠρτημένα.
(g) διὰ οὐσίας ψυχικῆς.   (h) ἔξω.   (i) ἀπολειφθήσεται.   (k) ἐκτός.

[1] The foregoing passages may be possibly taken in a Pantheistic sense; but they surely may be better understood of the particular superintending Providence of a Deity which pervades and guides all things, and on which all things are dependent. They are almost the exact words of Malebranche in his *Recherche de la Vérité* (lib. iii. ch. vi., part 2).

ligent (a) will seem true, but being without intelligence incredible. For the understanding is the believing, and the disbelieving is the not understanding. For my discourse attains even up to the truth. For the Mind is great, and being brought on the way by the discourse up to a certain point, is able to attain the Truth; and having considered all these things, and found them consonant, it believed those interpreted by the discourse, and hath rested (b) in that beautiful belief. To those then having understood the aforesaid from The God they are credible, but to those not having understood incredible. Let these things and so much be discoursed concerning Understanding and Sense.

CHAPTER X.

The Key. To his Son Tat.

1. THE Discourse of yesterday, O Asclepius! I addressed to thee, but that of to-day it is just to address to The Tat, since moreover it is an epitome of the generic discourses which have been spoken to him. The God then and Father and The Good, O Tat! has the same Nature, or rather also Energy. For the appellation of Nature (c) is also that of increase, which is concerning things changeable and unchangeable, and moveable and immoveable, that is things Divine and things human, of which He wills each to be. But Energy is otherwise (d), as we have taught also respecting other things Divine and human; what one must understand about this.

2. For the Energy of Him is The Will, and His Essence the Willing all things to be. For what is God and Father and the Good, than the being of all things not yet in being? But the very existence (e) of the Entities, that is

(a) ἐννοοῦντι.   (b) ἐπανεπαύσατο.   (c) i.e., φύσις.
(d) ἀλλαχοῦ.   (e) ὕπαρξις.

The God, that is The Father that is The Good, to Whom none of other things belong (*a*). For the World indeed and the Sun itself also father of things according (*b*) to their common being, is not moreover equally the cause of the good to the animals nor of their living. But if this thus be the case, it is nevertheless entirely as being compelled by The Good Will; apart from which it will be possible neither to be, nor to be generated.

3. For the father is the cause of the children, and of the seed, and of the nutriment, having taken the appetite of the Good from the Sun. For The Good is The making power (*c*). But this is not possible to be ingenerate (*d*) in any other but in Him only; Him receiving indeed nothing, but willing all things to be.[1] I will not say, O Tat! making (*e*); for a maker is defectible in much time, in that he sometimes makes, sometimes does not make, both in quality and quantity (*f*). At one time they are so many and of such quality, at another the contrary. But The God is Father and The Good, in that He is all things.[2]

(*a*) πρόσεστι. (*b*) κατὰ μετουσίαν, participation.
(*c*) τὸ ποιητικόν, making. (*d*) ἐγγενέσθαι. (*e*) ποιοῦντι.
(*f*) ποιότητος καὶ ποσότητος.

[1] Here, as in other places, the writer wholly differs from the notion of the Deity being a mere constructor or arranger of formless matter; an opinion attributed by some to Plato. See *ante*, note to ch. v. 4. Malebranche energetically maintained that there was no other immediate principle, no other efficient reason, no other real mover than the Grace and the Will of God. See his *Premotion Physique*, p. 93; *Recherche de la Vérité* (1712), last part; *Meditations Chretiennes*, vi.; *Traité de Morale*, 94.

The doctrine of this Chapter is energetically and luminously set forth by William Law in his "Way to Divine Knowledge" (Works, vii. p. 146).

[2] "God derives not His being from creatures, but all creatures are but imperfect participations of the Divine Being" (Malebranche, *Recherche de la Vérité*, lib. 3, pt. 2, c. vi.). "God is so far all Being that He has all the being of each of His creatures, retrenching their bounds. Remove this boundary and difference and you remain in the Universality of Being, and consequently in the infinite perfection of Self-existence" (Fenelon, *Existence de Dieu*, part 2, v. 1). "I believe that there is no substance purely Intelligible but that of

4. Thus verily are these things to him who is able to perceive. For indeed this (a) wills to Be, and is also Itself, especially for Itself. For verily all other things are because of This. For it is proper to the Good to become known. This is The Good, O Tat!

Tat.—Thou hast filled us, O Father! with the good and most beautiful spectacle, and the eye of my mind hath been little short of sanctified by such kind of spectacle. For not as if a ray of the Sun, being fiery, does it dazzle and make the eyes close, is thus the spectacle of The Good. On the contrary, it shines forth and augments the light of the eyes to so much as he who is able can receive the influx of the intellectual (b) splendour.[1] For it is rather sharp in penetrating (c), but not injurious and replete with all immortality.

5. They who are able to drink in somewhat more of this spectacle oftentimes fall asleep from the body into this most beauteous vision. As Uranus and Kronos our forefathers experienced.[2] Would that we also, O Father!

Hermes.—Would it may be so, O Child! But now as yet we are not intent upon the vision, and we are not yet strong enough to open the eyes of our mind, and to contemplate the beauty of that The Good,[3] the incorruptible, the incomprehensible. For then thou will perceive it when thou mayest have nothing to say about it. For the know-

(a) i.e., ἀγαθόν.   (b) νοητῆς λαμπηδόνος.   (c) εἰς τὸ καθικνεῖσθαι.

God, that we can discover nothing but in His Light, and that we shall be unintelligible to ourselves until we see in God. Still He presents to ourselves the Idea perfectly intelligible which He has of our being comprehended in His Own " (Malebranche, *Recherche de la Vérité*, lib. 3, part 2, ch. i.).

[1] "In thy light shall we see Light" (Ps. xxxvi. 9). "The Lord shall be unto thee an everlasting light" (Is. lx. 19). "To give the light of the knowledge of the glory of God" (2 Cor. iv. 6). "God is Light, and in Him is no darkness at all" (1 John i. 5; and see John viii. 12, 9, 5). "Who only hath immortality dwelling in light unapproachable" (1 Tim. vi. 16), &c., &c.

[2] Lactantius (Div. Instit., i. 11) alludes to this passage as a proof that both were men, and never really Divinities.

[3] "Now we see in a mirror darkly" (1 Cor. xiii. 12).

ledge of It is both divine silence and repose (*a*) of all the Senses.

6. For he having understood this is neither able to understand any other thing, nor he having beheld this to behold any other thing, nor to hear of any other thing, neither to move his entire body. For seizing hold of all his bodily senses and motions he moves not (*b*); but shining around all the mind and the whole soul, it enlightens and abstracts from the body, and transforms the whole of it into the Essence of God.[1] For it is possible, O Child! that the soul be deified (*c*), placed in body of Man, having beheld the beauty of The Good.

7. *Tat.*—To be deified how sayest thou, O Father?

Hermes.—Of every soul divisible, O Child! there are changes.

Tat.—How again divisible?

Hermes.—Hast thou not heard in the Generics (*d*) that from one soul that of the Universe (*e*) are all souls themselves which are rolled about (*f*) in all the world, as if distributed? Of these the souls then, many are the changes; of these indeed into a happier, of those into the opposite. Some then indeed being reptile, are changed into watery beings, but some of the watery into terrestrial, but those terrestrial into winged, those aerial into men, and those of humankind possess the beginning of immortality changing into demons. Whence thus they pass into the choir of the unerring Gods. But there are two choirs of Gods;

(*a*) καταργία. (*b*) ἀτρεμεῖ. (*c*) ἀποθεωθῆναι.
(*d*) ἐν τοῖς γενικοῖς. (*e*) τῆς τοῦ παντός. (*f*) κυλινδούμεναι.

[1] "We all with unveiled face reflecting as a mirror the glory of the Lord, are transformed into the same image from glory to glory" (2 Cor. iii. 18, Revised Version). "That by these" (promises) "ye may become partakers of the Divine Nature" (2 Pet. i. 4. See 1 John iii. 2). As remarked above (ch. iv. 6), Hermes here enunciates the sentiments and objects of the real Christian Mystics of all ages, especially those of the Fathers of the desert, and of the two Macarii Egyptii, of St Augustine, Fenelon, Malebranche, and many others, especially of the author of the "Imitation of Christ." See *ante*, ch. iv. 1 and 6, and note there.

one indeed of those erring,[1] the other of those unerring, and this is the most perfect glory of the Soul.

8. For Soul entering into the body of a man if it remain Evil, neither tastes immortality nor partakes of the Good, but retrograde turns its way back to that of the reptiles. And this is the condemnation of an evil soul; ignorance is the vice of soul. For a soul nothing acquainted with the Entities, nor the nature of them, nor with The Good, being blind, is entangled with the bodily passions; and the unfortunate, not having known itself, serves bodies alien and depraved (a), carrying the body as if a burthen,[2] and not ruling but ruled over. This is Vice of Soul.

9. Contrariwise, Virtue of Soul is Knowledge. For he knowing is both good and pious and already Divine.

Tat.—But who is this, O Father?

Hermes.—He neither speaking many things, nor hearing many things; for he listening (b) to two discourses and hearings, fights with a shadow. For The God and Father and the Good is neither spoken nor heard. But this having itself thus, in all the Entities are the Senses; because of its not being possible to be, apart from them. Knowledge differs much from Sense. For Sense is generate from that overpowering (c), but Knowledge is the end of Science (d), but Science gift of The God. For all Science is incorporeal, using for an organ the Mind itself, but the Mind using the body.

10. Both then enter (e) into bodies, things mental and material; for from antithesis and contrariety must all things consist (f), and it is impossible that this should be otherwise.

Tat.—Who then is this material God?

Hermes.—The beautiful World, but it is not good. For it is material and easily passible, and it is indeed the first of the passibles, but second of the Entities and wanting (g)

(a) μοχθηρῶις. (b) σχολάζων. (c) γίνεται τοῦ ἐπικρατοῦντος.
(d) ἐπιστήμης. (e) χωρεῖ εἰς. (f) δεῖ τὰ πάντα συνεστάναι. (g) αὐτοδεής.

[1] "The Angels which kept not their first Estate" (Jude 6).
[2] "The body of this death" (Rom. vii. 24).

to itself, and itself sometime generated, but ever in being; being too in generation and ever generated. Generation is of qualities and quantities; for it is moveable.

11. For every material movement is generation. The mental state (a) moves the material movement in this manner, since the world is a sphere, that is a head; but above head there is nothing material; just as neither is there anything mental beneath the feet, but all material. But Mind, head itself is moved spherically, that is similarly to a head. As many things then as are united to the membrane (b) of this the head wherein is the soul, are by nature(c) immortal, as if [of the body formed in Soul]; and having the Soul full (d) of [or fuller than][1] the body. But things distant from the membrane, in which the body possesses more than the soul, are by nature mortal; but all is a living animal; so that the universe is composed both of material and mental.

12. And the World indeed is first,[2] but the Man second animal after the World, but first of the things mortal; and indeed of the other animals he has the living quality (e) in him. Not, moreover, is he only not good, but also evil, as mortal. For the World is not good as moveable, but not evil as immortal, but the Man both as moveable and as mortal is evil.

13. But the Soul of man is carried on (f) in this way: The Mind in the Reason, the Reason in the Soul, the Soul in the Spirit, the Spirit in the Body. The Spirit penetrating through the veins and arteries and blood moves the animal, and as it were, after a certain manner, supports it. Wherefore also some have thought the Soul to be blood; being mistaken as to the nature, not knowing that first must the Spirit return back into the Soul, and then the

(a) νοητὴ στάσις. (b) τῷ ὑμένι. (c) πέφυκε.
(d) πλήρη. (e) τὸ ἔμψυχον. (f) Ὀχεῖται.

[1] Menard reads πλείω (more of soul than body), which is doubtless the meaning. The passage is probably corrupt.

[2] This and the next section are extracted by Stobæus (Physica, 770; Meineke, i. 215).

blood be coagulated, and the veins and the arteries be emptied, and then the animal perish (*a*), and this is the death of the Body.[1]

14. From one beginning have all things depended (*b*), but the beginning is from The One and Only. And the beginning indeed is moved, that beginning may again become (*c*), but The One stands abiding, and is not moved. And three therefore are these, The God and Father and The Good, and the World and the Man. And The God hath indeed the World, but the World the Man. And the World indeed is generated Son of The God; but the Man as it were offspring of the World.

15. For The God ignoreth not the Man, but moreover thoroughly knoweth him and desires to be known. This alone is saving for Man, The knowledge of The God.[2] This is the ascent to the Olympus. By this alone the Soul becometh Good, and not sometimes Good, sometimes Evil; but becomes so of necessity.

Tat.—How sayest thou this, O Trismegistus?

Hermes.—Contemplate a Soul of a boy, O Child! not having yet received its distribution (*d*), his body being yet small and not yet fully amplified (*e*).

Tat.—How?

Hermes.—Beautiful to look upon everywhere, and not yet defiled by the passions of the body, still almost dependent from the Soul of the world; but when the body has been amplified (*f*) and shall have drawn it out, into the masses (*g*) of the body, having distributed (*h*) itself, it engenerates oblivion, and partakes not of the beautiful and

(*a*) καθελεῖν.　　(*b*) τὰ πάντα ἤρτηται.　　(*c*) γένηται.
(*d*) διάλυσιν.　　(*e*) ὠγκωμένου.　　(*f*) ὀγκωθῇ.
(*g*) ὄγκους.　　(*h*) διαλύσασα.

[1] So far as in Stobæus (Eclog. Physica; Meineke, i. 212). As to the subject of death, see Part II., Excerpts by Stobæus in the Florilegium, ch. ii.; Meineke, iv. 106, and *ante*, ch. viii. 1, 2, and *post*, xi. 15.

[2] "This is life eternal, that they should know Thee The Only True God" (John xvii. 3). "And hath given us an understanding (διάνοιαν), that we may know Him that is true. . . . This is the true God, and eternal life" (1 John v. 20).

good. And the oblivion becomes vice. And the same thing happens to those departing out of the body.

16. For the Soul recurring back into itself,[1] the Spirit is contracted into the blood, and the Soul into the Spirit, but the Mind becoming pure from its garments being divine by nature, taking a fiery body, circulates in every place, having abandoned the Soul to judgment and to the punishment according to desert.

Tat.—How speakest thou this, O Father?[2] The Mind is separated from the Soul, and the Soul from the Spirit, thou having said the Soul to be garment of the Mind, but of the Soul the Spirit?

17. *Hermes.*—It behoves the hearer to agree in mind, O Child! with the speaker, and to consent, and to have his hearing more acute than the voice of the speaker. The composition of these garments, O Child! is generate in an earthly body. For it is impossible that the Mind should establish itself by itself naked in an earthly body, for neither is any earthly body able to bear (a) so great immortality nor to endure (b) this such virtue, a body with passions being under the same skin with it. It hath taken then as it were an envelope (c) the Soul. But the Soul also itself being something divine uses the Spirit as if an envelope. But the Spirit pervades the Animal.

18. When then the Mind has departed from the earthly body, it forthwith puts on its own the fiery tunic, which it could not, having to dwell in the earthly body. For earth sustains not fire, for all is enflamed even by a small spark. And because of this the water is diffused around the Earth as rampart and wall resisting against the flame of the fire. Mind however being the most swift of all divine thoughts, and swifter than all the elements, has its body the Fire. For The Mind being Creator of all things, uses the Fire as

(a) ἐνεγκεῖν.   (b) ἀνέχεσθαι.   (c) περιβολήν.

[1] See *post*, sec. 21, and note.
[2] The following is extracted by Stobæus (Physica, 775; Meineke, i. 219).

an instrument towards that Creation.[1] That Mind indeed [Creator] of the Universe uses all things, but that of the Man things upon earth only. For the mind upon earth being destitute of the Fire is unable to create the things Divine, being human in the administration.

19. But the human soul, not every one but the pious, is a kind of demonhood (*a*) and divine; and such a soul after the departure from the body, having striven the strife of this piety (but strife of piety is having known The God[2] and to have wronged no man) becomes wholly Mind. But the impious Soul remains in that its proper Essence (*b*), punished by itself and seeking an earthly body into which it may enter, being human (*c*). For other body[3] does not yield place (*d*) to a human soul; nor is it justice (*e*) that a human soul should degrade (*f*) into a body of an irrational animal. For of God is this law, to guard a human Soul from this so great disgrace.[4]

(*a*) δαιμονία τίς.   (*b*) ἰδίας οὐσίας.   (*c*) ἀνθρώπειον.
(*d*) χωρεῖ.   (*e*) θέμις.   (*f*) κάταπεσεῖν.

[1] See *ante*, ch. i. The following section 19 is extracted by Stobæus (Physica, 1007; Meineke, i. 307).

[2] Quoted by Lactantius (Divin. Instit., ii. 16, and v. 15; see also iii. 9). "This is Life eternal, that they should know Thee The Only True God" (John xvii. 3).

[3] It has been surmised from this passage that Hermes (with Plato) held that the souls of the dead generally might pass into other human bodies. But as to this point, see *post contra*.

[4] Hermes here dissents from Platonism. Plato, speaking as from Socrates (Phædo, 80), says: "The Soul, the very likeness of the Divine and immortal, and intellectual and uniform, and indissoluble and unchangeable; the Body the likeness of the human, mortal, unintellectual, multiform, dissoluble, and changeable. Must we suppose that the Soul which is invisible, passing to the true Hades, which like her is invisible, and pure and noble, and on her way to the True and Wise God, whither if God will my soul is also soon to go: that the Soul, if this be her nature and origin, is blown away and perishes immediately on quitting the body as the many say? That can never be. The truth rather is that that soul which is pure at departing and draws after her no bodily taint, having never voluntarily been connected with the body, which she is ever avoiding, herself gathered into herself which has been the study of her life,

20. *Tat.*—How then is the human soul punished, O Father?

Hermes.—And what is a greater punishment of a human Soul, O Child! than the impiety? and what sort of fire has so great a flame as this impiety? and what kind of devouring wild beast thus maltreats the body so much, as this impiety the very Soul? Or seest thou not, how many evils the impious Soul suffers? shouting and crying out, " I am burned, I am consumed; what I may say, what I

---

meaning that she has studied true philosophy, the practice of death; that soul herself invisible, departs to the invisible world, to the Divine, immortal, and rational. Thither arriving she is secure of bliss and is released from the errors and follies of men, their fears and wild passions and all other human ills, and ever dwells, as they say of the initiated, in company with the Gods. But the soul, which has been polluted and impure at the time of her departure and always the servant of the body, enamoured and fascinated by it and by its desires and pleasures, until she believes that Truth exists only in a bodily form which a man may use for the purposes of his lusts, and is accustomed to hate and fear and avoid the intellectual principle, which to the bodily eye is invisible and can only be attained by philosophy,—do you suppose that such a soul will depart pure and unalloyed? She is held fast by the corporeal, which is heavy and earthy. They are dragged down again to the visible, to the tombs and sepulchres, compelled to wander about such places in payment of the penalty of their former evil ways. The craving after the corporeal never leaves them, and they are imprisoned finally in another body, imprisoned in the same natures which they had in their former lives. Men who have followed after gluttony and wantonness and drunkenness pass into apes and animals of that sort: those who have chosen injustice and tyranny into wolves and hawks and kites, according to their several natures and propensities. Some may be happier than others who have practised civil and social virtues, such as temperance and justice, although not acquired by philosophy. They may pass into some quiet and social nature like their own, such as bees, wasps, or ants, or back into the form of men. But he who is a philosopher and lover of learning, who is entirely pure at departing, is alone permitted to attain to the Divine nature. This is why the true votaries of philosophy abstain from all fleshly lusts, and refuse to give themselves up to them. They who have any care of their own souls, say farewell to all this; they will not walk in the ways of the blind, and when philosophy offers purification and relief from evil, they turn and follow it."

shall do, I know not. I am eaten up, the unfortunate, by the ills enclosing me! I neither see nor, the miserable, do I hear!" These are the voices of the soul being punished, not as the many suppose and thou opinest, O Child! that a soul going forth from the body becomes a wild beast (a), which is a very great error.[1]

21. For the Soul is punished after this manner. But the Mind when it becometh demon, is ordained to acquire a fiery body for the ministries (b) of The God, and entering into the very impious soul chastises it with the scourges of the sins; by which being scourged, the impious soul turns itself to murders, and injuries, and blasphemies, and various violences, and other things by which men are wronged; but the Mind entering into the pious Soul guides it to the light of the Knowledge. And the such like Soul never ever experiences satiety, hymning and blessing all men, and in words and deeds doing all things well, imitating its own Father.[2]

22. Wherefore, O Child! giving thanks to The God, it behoves to pray to obtain the beautiful Mind. The Soul then passes on to the superior, but to the inferior it is im-

(a) θηριάζεται.   (b) ὑπερησίας.

[1] See *ante* xix., sec. 4, note.

Plato in Timæus (42) had also spoken thus : " Those who are dominated by bodily passions shall be avenged by justice; but he that has passed well the proper time, living again, proceeding to the dwelling of the associate (ξυννόμου) star, will lead a happy life; but failing of these he will in his second birth change into the nature of a woman; but not ceasing then from the way of evil by which he was debased, he changes into some beastly nature, and shall not cease from labours, until by reason having conquered the great tumult and debasement, and being other, he return to the form of the first and best habitude (ἕξεως).

[2] Compare Wisdom, iii. 1-10:—" The souls of the righteous are in the hand of God, and there shall no torment touch them. In the sight of the unwise they seemed to die. . . Yet is their hope full of immortality. . . . But the ungodly shall be punished according to their own imaginations, which have neglected the righteous and forsaken the Lord."

passible.[1] For there is a community of Souls, and those of the Gods hold communion with those of the men, and those of the men with those of the irrationals. But the superior take care of the inferior, Gods of men,[2] but men of the irrational animals, but The God of all. For He is Superior to all, and all are inferior to Him. The World then is subject to The God; but the Man to the World, and the irrational to the Man; but The God is over all things and about all things. And of The God indeed the Energies are like as rays, and of the World the natures are rays, but of the Man the arts and sciences are rays. And these Energies indeed energize throughout the world, and upon the Man through the physical rays of the World, but the natures through the elements, but the men through the Arts and Sciences.

23. And this is the administration of the Universe (*a*), dependent from the Nature of The One and pervading it through the Mind of One.[3] Than which nothing is more divine and more energetic, or more unitive (*b*) of Men indeed to the Gods, or of Gods to the Men. This is the Good demon. Blessed the Soul which is fullest of this; unfortunate the Soul which is void of this.

Tat.—How sayest thou thus again, O Father?

Hermes.—Dost thou think then, O Child! that every soul has the good Mind? for it is of this that our discourse is about, not concerning the servile one (*c*), concerning whom we have just before spoken, him sent downwards (*d*) because of the judgment.

24. For Soul apart from the Mind can neither say any-

(*a*) διοίκησις τοῦ παντός. (*b*) ἑνωτικώτερον.
(*c*) ὑπηρετικοῦ. (*d*) καταπεμπομένου.

[1] The following, down to the end of this chapter, is extracted by Stobæus (Physica, 766; Meineke, i. 213).

[2] "Are they" (*i.e.*, Angels) "not all ministering Spirits, sent forth to do service for the sake of them that shall inherit salvation?" (Heb. i. 14). "When The Most High divided the nations, when He separated the Sons of Adam, He set the bounds of the nations according to the number of the Angels of God" (Deut. xxxii. 8, Septuagint Version).

[3] Or "through the One Mind."

thing nor do anything. For, oftentimes the Mind hath departed out of (*a*) the Soul; and in that hour the Soul neither discerns nor hears, but is like an irrational animal. So great is the power of the Mind; but neither does it endure an inert (*b*) Soul, but relinquishes the Soul of such sort attached to the body, and by it drawn downwards. The Soul of this sort, O Child! has not Mind. Wherefore neither ought one to call such an one Man. For Man is a Divine Animal, and is not comparable with the other animals, those upon earth, but with those above in Heaven called Gods,[1] or rather, if it behoveth one boldly to speak the truth, the Man really is above them, or, they are altogether equipollent with each other.

25. For no one indeed of the heavenly Gods shall descend unto earth, having left the boundary of Heaven, but the Man ascends unto the Heaven, and measures it, and knows what kind of things of it are on high, and what kind below, and learns all other things accurately; and what is greater than all, without leaving this earth he becomes on high. So great is the grandeur to him of this (*c*) extension. Wherefore it is to be dared to say that the Man upon earth is a mortal God, but the Heavenly God an immortal Man. Wherefore through (*d*) these the Two are all things administered, World and Man; but by (*e*) The One all things.[2]

(*a*) ἐξέστη.   (*b*) νωτρᾶς.
(*c*) ἐκτάσεως; in Stobæus the word is ἐκστάσεως.
(*d*) διά.   (*e*) ὑπό.

[1] "I have said, Ye are Gods; and all of you are children of the Most High" (Ps. lxxxii. 6). "They are equal with the Angels; and are Sons of God" (Luke xx. 36). "But are as Angels in Heaven" (Mark xii. 25).

[2] Five portions of this Chapter are extracted by Stobæus (Eclog. Physica). See *supra* and Meineke, vol. i., and index.

CHAPTER XI.

Mind to Hermes.

1. *Mind.*—Restrain then the discourse, O thrice greatest Hermes! and call to remembrance the things said. But as it has occurred to me to speak, I will not delay.

Hermes.—Many speaking many things, and those different, concerning the Universe and The God, I learnt not the truth; Do thou, Master, make plain (*a*) to me concerning this, for to thee only would I confide the explanation concerning these things.

2. *Mind.*—Hear, O Child! how The God and the Universe have themselves. God, The Eternity, the World, the Time, the Generation. The God makes Eternity (*b*), The Eternity the World, The World the Time; but The Time the Generation. But of The God is as it were Essence, The Good, The Beautiful, The Happiness, The Wisdom; of the Eternity the Identity (*c*); of the World the Order; of the Time the Change; but of the Generation, The Life and the Death. The Energies of The God Mind and Soul, but of the Eternity permanence and immortality, but of the World, restitution and redestruction, but of the Time augmentation and diminution, and of the Generation quality. The Eternity then is in The God, The World in the Eternity; but the Time in the World, and the Generation in the Time. And the Eternity indeed is stationed (*d*) around The God, and the World is moved in the Eternity, the Time is accomplished (*e*) in the World, but the Generation takes place in the Time.

3. The fountain then of all things is The God, but Essence the Eternity, Matter the World; Power of The God the Eternity, Work of the Eternity the World, not sometime (*f*) generated, but always generated by the Eternity; neither therefore will it ever be corrupted, for

(*a*) διασάφησον. (*b*) αἰῶνα ποιεῖ. (*c*) ἡ ταυτότης.
(*d*) ἕστηκε. (*e*) περαιοῦται. (*f*) οὔποτε.

Eternity is incorruptible, nor does any of things in the World perish, the World being encompassed by the Eternity.

Hermes.—But the Wisdom of The God, what is it?

Mind.—The Good and the Beautiful and the Happiness and the whole of Virtue and The Eternity. The Eternity then provides (*a*) the Immortality, imparting also permanence to the Matter.

4. For the generation of that is dependent from the Eternity, as also the Eternity from The God. For the Generation and the Time in Heaven and in Earth are beings double in nature: in Heaven indeed unchangeable and incorruptible, but in earth changeable and corruptible. And of the Eternity indeed the Soul is The God, but of the World the Soul is the Eternity, but of the Earth the Heaven. And The God indeed is in the Mind but the Mind in the Soul, but the Soul in the Matter, but all these through the Eternity. But this the Universal Body, in which are all the bodies, is full of Soul, but the Soul full of the Mind and of The God; within it fills but without encircles it, vivifying the Universe. Without indeed this the great and perfect Animal the World (*b*)[1], but within, all the animals; and above indeed in the Heaven abiding in the identity, but below upon the earth changing the generation.

5. But the Eternity keeps together (*c*) this, whether through necessity, or through providence, or through nature, and if anything else any one thinks or shall think. This Universe The God is energizing; but the Energy of God being a power insuperable, with which one could compare neither things human nor things divine. Wherefore, O Hermes! by no means of things below nor of things above shouldst thou think any like to The God, since thou

(*a*) κοσμεῖ.   (*b*) ζῶον τὸν κόσμον.   (*c*) συνέχει.

[1] Plato (Timæus, 92): "This the World having thus received animals, mortal and immortal, and having been fulfilled, became a visible animal, containing the visible, sensible God, Image of The Intelligible, the greatest the best, the most beautiful and most perfect, one Heaven; This being only begotten."

wouldest fall from the truth. For nothing is like to The without like and Only and One; and not to any other one shouldst thou think that He yields in the power. For who beside Him is either Life and [1] Immortality, and change of quality? And what else should He do? For The God is not inert, else all things would become inert; for everything is full of God, for neither in the world is inertness (a) anywhere, nor in any other. For inertness is an empty word, both as to the maker and the thing generated.

6. For all things must be generate, both always and according to the preponderance (b) of each place. For the Maker is in all things, not settled (c) in any, nor Making in something, but all things.[2] For Power being energizing, is not self sufficient (d) in the things generated, but the generated are under Him. Contemplate through me the World subjected to thy view, and consider accurately the beauty of it, a body indeed undecayable (e), and than which nothing is more ancient, and throughout the whole in full vigour (f) and new, and still more vigorous.

7. Behold also those subject Seven Worlds arranged in eternal order and in different course fulfilling the Eternity, and all things full of light, but fire no where, for the friendship and the combination of things opposite and those dissimilar became Light, shining forth through the energy of The God,[3] Generator of all Good, and Prince (g) of all order and guide of the Seven Worlds; a Moon, the precursor of all these, Organ of the Nature changing the Matter below;

(a) ἀργία. (b) ῥοπήν. (c) ἱδρυμένος. (d) αὐτάρκης.
(e) ἀκήρατον. (f) ἀκμαῖον. (g) ἄρχοντος.

[1] "Who only hath immortality, dwelling in Light unapproachable" (1 Tim. vi. 16).

[2] "However destitute Planets, Moons, and rings may be of inhabitants, they are at least vast scenes of God's presence and of the activity with which He carries into effect everywhere the laws of nature; and the glory of creation arises from its being not only the product but the constant field of God's activity and thought, wisdom, and power" (Whewell's "Plurality of Worlds," ch. xii., Fourth Edit., 382. See sec. 12, *post*).

[3] "And God said, Let Light be, and Light was" (Gen. i. 3).

and the Earth in the midst of the Universe, established as support (*a*) of this beautiful World,[1] nourisher and nurse of those upon Earth. Behold also the multitude of the immortal animals how large it is, and of the mortal; in the midst of both as well of the immortal as of the mortal, the Moon revolving around.

8. All things then are full of Soul, and all things properly (*b*) moved by that; some indeed around the Heaven, but others around the Earth, and neither the right towards the left, nor the left towards the right; nor those above downwards, nor those below upwards. And that all these are generate, O most beloved Hermes! thou dost not still need to learn of me; for they are bodies, and have soul, and are moved. But for these to concur (*c*) in one is impossible apart from the gatherer (*d*).

9. This then must be some one and such altogether One. For different and many being the motions and the bodies not similar, yet but one velocity ordered throughout all, it is impossible that there be two or more Makers; for the one order is not preserved with many. For in the feebler, emulation will ensue of the superior, and they will contend. And if other was the Maker of the mutable animals and mortals, he would have desired to make immortals also; just as also he of the immortals, mortals. Suppose then if also there be two; one being the Matter and one the Soul, with which of them would be the conducting of the making (*e*)? and if somewhat also with both, with whom the larger portion?

10. But think thus, as of every living body having the constitution (*f*) of Matter and Soul, and of the immortal and of the mortal, and of the irrational. For all living

(*a*) ὑποστάθμην.   (*b*) Ἰδίως.   (*c*) συνελθεῖν.
(*d*) χωρὶς του συνάγοντος.   (*e*) χορηγία τῆς ποιήσεως.   (*f*) σύστασιν.

[1] See *ante*, ch. iii. 4, and note there. Mr Proctor, in his work, "Our place among Infinities," states that the Egyptians held that the Sun and Moon revolved round the Earth, but the five other planets round the Sun. But this passage proves the general belief to have been that the whole system revolved round the Earth, which remained stationary in the midst.

bodies are animated (*a*), but those not living are again matter by itself. And Soul likewise by itself approached to (*b*) the Maker is cause of the life; but cause of all the life is that which is (cause) of the immortals.

Hermes.—How then are also the mortal animals different from the mortal? And how is it that the immortal and making immortality, makes not the animals (so)?

11. *Mind.*—And that there is some One who is making these things is plain, and that He is also One is most manifest; for also there is one Soul and one Life and one Matter.

Hermes.—Who then is He?

Mind.—Who may it be other than The One God? For to whom can it belong to make animated animals but to the God only?[1] One then is God. Most ridiculous then if having acknowledged the World to be One and the Sun One and the Moon One and The Divinity One, but The God Himself to be as multiple (*c*) as you wish.[2]

12. He then makes everything in many ways. And what great thing is it for The God to make life and soul and immortality and change, thou doing such many things. For thou seest, and speakest, and hearest, and smellest, and tastest, and touchest, and walkest, and understandest, and breathest, and it is not another who is seeing, and another who is hearing, and another who is speaking, and other who is touching, and other who is smelling, and other who is walking, and other who is understanding, and other who is breathing, but one who is doing all these things. But neither are these possible to be apart from The God. For just as, shouldest thou become inert (*d*) of these, thou art no longer animal; so neither, should The God become inert of them, what it is not lawful to say, no longer is He God.

13. For if it is demonstrated that nothing is possible to

(*a*) ἔμψυκα. (*b*) παρακειμένη. (*c*) πόσον. (*d*) καταργηθῆς.

[1] Quoted by Lactant. (Divin. Instit., i., vi.).

[2] This passage disconnects the author from all complicity with the Egyptian or Greek Mythology.

be¹ [apart from The God or inert], by how much rather The God. For if there is anything that He does not make, if it be lawful to say it He is imperfect. But if He is not inert but perfect, then He makes all things. For a little give thyself up to me, *O Hermes!* thou wilt the more easily understand the work of The God as being one: that all the things generate be generate, whether those once generated, as those about to be generated. But this, O most beloved! is Life, this is The Beautiful; this is The Good, this is The God.

14. If thou wishest also to understand this in operation, see what would happen to thee wishing to engender. But this is not like to Him, for He indeed is not delighted, nor has He another co-operator. For being selfworking (*a*) He is always in the work, being Himself what He makes. For if He should be separated from it, of necessity all things must collapse, all things be deathstruck as there not being life; but if all things are living, and One also the Life, One then also is The God. And again, if all things are living, both those in the heaven and those in the earth, and one Life throughout all things is generate by The God, and this is The God, then all things are generate by The God. But Life is the Union (*b*) of Mind and Soul. Death however not the destruction of the compounds but dissolution of the union.²

15. ³[Eternity then is the image of The God but of the eternity the world, of the world the Sun, of the Sun the man]. But this transmutation the people say to be death, because that the body indeed is dissolved, but the life, it being dissolved, departs to the obscure (*c*). But in this dis-

(*a*) αὐτουργός.   (*b*) ἕνωσις.   (*c*) εἰς τὸ ἀφανές.

¹ Parthey's note (p. 92) here is:—" Post εἶναι, excidisse videtur χωρὶς τοῦ θεοῦ." But query whether not "καταργήμενον," "inert." (See a similar argument, Lactant., de Irâ Dei, ch. 11).

² See *ante*, sec. 14, and note. Also ch. viii. 1, 2; ch. x. 13; and *post*, Part II., Excerpt II. by Stobæus, and notes there.

³ It seems probable, as suggested by L. Ménard (p. 76), that this phrase has been interpolated here by some copyist or scholiast, it being out of place with what precedes and follows.

course, O Hermes! most beloved to me I say, as thou hearest, the World also to be transformed because of part of it becoming each day in the obscure, but by no means to be dissolved. And these are the passions (a) of the World, revolutions and occultations (b). And the revolution is conversion (c), but the occultation, renovation.

16. For the World is of all manner of forms (d), not having the forms lying without, but itself changing them in itself. Since then the World was generated of all forms, He having made it, what should He be? for without form (e) indeed He cannot be, and if He be also of all forms He will be like to the World. But having one form so far He will be inferior to the World. What then may we say Him to be? lest we reduce the discourse into doubtfulness; for nothing doubtful is to be understood about The God. He has then one Idea (f), which is His proper own (g), which incorporeal, may not be subject of (h) the sight; and shows all [ideas] by means of the bodies. And be not astonished if there be some incorporeal idea.

17. For it is as if that of the discourse, and margins (i) in the writings (k). For they are seen being wholly outside, but smooth in the nature, they are also entirely even. But consider what is said more boldly, but yet more truthfully. For just as a man cannot live apart from life, so neither can The God live without doing the Good. For this is as it were Life and as it were motion of The God, to move all things and to vivify.

18. But some of the things spoken ought to have peculiar consideration; understand as such what I say. All things are in The God; not as if lying in place; for the place indeed is both body and immoveable, and things lying have not motion. For they lie otherwise (l) in incorporeal, otherwise in appearance. Understand Him comprising all things, and understand, that than the incorporeal,

(a) πάθη.
(b) δινήσεις καὶ κρύψεις.
(c) στροφή.
(d) παντόμορφος.
(e) ἄμορφος.
(f) ἰδέαν.
(g) ἰδία.
(h) ὑποσταίη.
(i) ἀκρώρειαι.
(k) ἐξέχουσαι.
(l) ἄλλως.

there is nothing more comprehensive (*a*), nor quicker nor more powerful, but it of all things is the most comprehensive and quickest and most powerful.

19. And understand thus of (*b*) thyself, and command the Soul of thine to proceed to India, and quicker than thy command it will be there; command it to proceed to the Ocean, and there again it will quickly be, not as if having passed on from place to place, but as if being there. Command it also to fly up to the Heaven, and it will not be in want of wings; nor will anything be hindrance to it, neither the fire of the Sun, nor the atmosphere, nor the revolution (*c*), nor the bodies of the other stars, but, piercing through all, it will fly up even to the last body. And if thou shouldest wish even to break through this Universe (*d*), and to behold the things without (if indeed there be anything without the World), it is possible for thee.

20. See how much power, how much speed thou hast! Art thou able for all these things together, but The God not? After this manner then understand The God as if that He had all understandings (*e*) in Himself, the whole World itself. If then thou wouldest not compare (*f*) thyself with The God, thou canst not understand The God; for like is understandable by like. Augment thyself to an immeasurable magnitude, having got rid of all body, and having surpassed all time, become eternity; and thou wilt understand The God. Having supposed (*g*) in thyself nothing impossible, think thyself immortal and able to understand all things: every art indeed, every science, the habit of every animal. Become more lofty than every height and lower than every depth. Collect in thyself all the sensations (*h*) of the things made, of fire, water, dry and moist, and at the same time to be everywhere in earth, in sea, in heaven, not yet to have been born, to be in the womb, young, old, to have died, things after the death, and

(*a*) περιεκτικώτερον. (*b*) ἀπὸ. (*c*) ἡ δίνη.
(*d*) αὐτὸ ὅλον. (*e*) νοήματα. (*f*) ἐξισάσῃς.
(*g*) ὑποστησάμενος. (*h*) αἰσθήσεις.

having understood all these things together, times, places, affairs, qualities, quantities, thou wilt be able to understand The God.

21. But if thou shouldest shut up the Soul of thee in the body and debase it, and say, I understand nothing, I can nothing, I fear the sea, I am not able to ascend into the Heaven, I know not who I (*a*) have been, I know not who I shall be; what with thee, and with The God? for thou canst understand nothing of things beautiful and good, being a lover of the body, and evil. For the complete evil is the being ignorant of the Divinity (*b*); but the being able to have known and to will and to hope, is the (*c*) right way, peculiar (*d*) of the good, and smooth and easy; journeying He will meet thee everywhere, everywhere will He be seen, where and when thou dost not expect; watching, sleeping, sailing, journeying by night, by day, speaking, silent; for there is nothing which is not image (*e*) of the Divinity.

22. *Hermes.*—Is The God invisible?

Mind.—Speak well! And who is more manifest than He? For this very thing He made all things that thou mayest discern Him throughout all things. This is The Good of The God, this is His virtue, that He is apparent throughout all things. For nothing is invisible, not even of the incorporeal. Mind is seen in the understanding, The God in the making. These things have to thee as to so much been explained, O Trismegistus! But all the other things likewise consider with thyself and thou shalt not be deceived.

(*a*) ἤμην. (*b*) τὸ θεῖον. (*c*) εὐθεῖα.
(*d*) ἰδία. (*e*) εἰκών.

CHAPTER XII.

Respecting Common Mind.
To Tat.[1]

1. *Hermes.*—The Mind, O Tat! is of the very essence of The God; if indeed there is any essence of God, and of what quality this may be He alone hath accurately known. The Mind then is not cut off from the Essentiality of The Godhead (*a*) but united, just as the light of the Sun. But this the Mind in men indeed is God. Wherefore also some of men are Gods,[2] and their humanity is nigh to the Deity. For also the Good Demon hath called the Gods immortal men, but the men mortal Gods. But in irrational animals the Mind is the nature.

2. For where Soul, there also is Mind, as where life there also is Soul. But in the irrational animals the soul is life, void of the Mind; for the Mind is benefactor of the souls of men, for it works on them (*b*) to their proper good; and in the irrational indeed it co-operates with the nature of each, but it practises against (*c*) those of the men. For every Soul generate in body is forthwith depraved, both by

(*a*) οὐσιότητος θεότητος.   (*b*) ἐργάζεται αὐτὰς.   (*c*) ἀντιπράσσει.

[1] According to Ménard (Pref., p. 73), the author of this chapter is some obscure disciple of Plotinus; and the Good Demon mentioned therein, Ammonius Saccas, the reputed founder of the Neo-platonists in the beginning of the 3d century; but the translator does not accept this view. The whole chapter is a metaphysical amplification of the Divine truth so energetically set forth (amongst others) by Malebranche in his *Recherche de la Vérité*, and *Traité de la Morale*. "For in Him we live, and move, and have our being" (Acts xvii. 28). "And in Him all things consist" (Col. i. 17). "Upholding all things by the Word of His power" (Heb. i. 3). See *ante*, ch. x. 4, note 1; and hereafter sec. 14, for what is meant by the Good Demon.

[2] "I have said ye are Gods" (Ps. lxxxii. 6). "Partakers of the Divine nature" (2 Peter i. 4). "Is it not written in your law, I said, Ye are Gods? If He called them Gods unto whom the word of God came, and the Scripture cannot be broken; say ye of Him," &c. (John x. 34).

the grief and the pleasure. For of the composite body both the grief and the pleasure seethe (*a*), just as humours, into which the Soul having entered is immerged (*b*).

3. In whatsoever souls then the Mind presides—to these it shows its own light, practising against their proclivities (*c*); just as a good physician pains the body pre-occupied by disease, burning or cutting for the sake of health. In the same way also the Mind pains the Soul, extricating it from pleasure, by which every disease of Soul is generate. A great disease of the Soul is Atheism (*d*), since thereupon follows opinion (*e*), unto all things that are evil and nothing good. Thus then the Mind counteracting this, procures the Good for the Soul, as also the physician the health for the body.

4. But as many human Souls as have not obtained The Mind as pilot, suffer the same with those of the irrational animals. For becoming co-operator with them and letting loose the desires to which they are borne, tending together (*f*) by the force of the appetite to the irrational, like as the irrationality of the animals, irrationally enraged and irrationally desiring, they cease not, nor have satiety of the evils. For angers and irrational desires are excessive vices. But for these, as it were avenger and convicter, The God hath set over them the law.[1]

5. *Tat.*—There, O Father! the discourse concerning the Fate, that previously uttered to me, is in danger of being overthrown. For if it is altogether fated to this some one to fornicate or commit sacrilege, or to do any other evil something, why is he punished, he from necessity of Fate having done the deed?

(*a*) ζέουσιν.   (*b*) βαπτίζεται.   (*c*) προλήμμασιν.
(*d*) ἀθεότης.   (*e*) δόξα.   (*f*) συντεινούσας.

[1] "What then is the law? It was added because of transgressions" (Gal. iii. 19).

Plato in "Laws" (716) says: "The God then, as is also the ancient saying, having the beginning and the end and the mean of all Entities, terminates things directly, proceeding according to Nature. But with Him ever follows on Justice, avenger of those who depart from the Divine Law" (Hermann's Edit., v. 118).

Hermes.—Of Fate indeed are all the works, O Child! and apart from that not anything of corporeal things, neither good nor evil happens to be. It is fated too that he having done the evil to suffer. And for this he does it, that he may suffer what he does suffer, because he hath done it.

6. But at the present let be (*a*) the discourse concerning Vice and Fate; for elsewhere we have spoken concerning these, but now the discourse with us is concerning Mind, what the Mind can, and how it is different; in men indeed of such kind, but in the irrational animals changed; and again that in the irrational animals indeed, it is not beneficent, but in men extinguishing both the irascible and the concupiscent (*b*). And of these one must understand some indeed as persons with reason (*c*), but others without reason.

7. All men are subject to fate and to generation and to change; for these are the beginning and end of Fate; and all men indeed suffer things fated, but those with reason of whom we have said that the Mind is Guide, suffer not in like manner with the others, but having departed from Vice, not being evil, suffer not evil.

Tat.—Again how sayest thou, Father? A fornicator not evil? a murderer not evil? and all the rest?

Hermes.—But he with reason (*d*), O Child! not having fornicated will suffer but as having fornicated; neither having murdered but as having murdered. And the quality of change it is not possible to escape from, just as also of generation; but it is for him having Mind, to escape Vice.

8. Wherefore also I have heard[1] the good Demon, O Child! saying always . . . . and if he had given it in

(*a*) ἐχέτω. (*b*) τὸ θυμικὸν καὶ τὸ ἐπιθυμητικόν.
(*c*) ἐλλογίμους ἄνδρας. (*d*) ὁ ἐλλόγιμος.

[1] This is apparently peculiarly Socratic; but that the meaning of Hermes did not stop there is manifest from his afterwards denominating the good Demon The "First begotten God," and identifying it afterwards with the Mind or Wisdom of God. This passage, however, has lacunæ, and is clearly partially corrupt.

writing he would altogether have profited the race of men, for He alone, O Child![1] as First begotten God having viewed (a) all things pronounced Divine words. . . . . I have heard then Him sometime saying that One are all things, and especially the bodies intelligible (b), for we live in power and in energy and eternity. And the Mind then is good . . . which is the Soul of it; but this being of such kind, there is nothing separable of things intelligible (c). Thus then it is possible that Mind ruling (d) over all things and being the Soul of The God, do whatever it wishes.

9. But do thou understand and refer this discourse to the enquiry which thou enquiredst of me in what is before : I speak concerning the Fate of The Mind. For if thou wouldest accurately put away the contentious words, O Child! thou wilt find that truly The Mind, the Soul of The God, dominates over all things, both Fate and Law and all other things; and nothing impossible for it, neither the placing the human Soul up above (e) Fate, nor, having neglected things which happen, to place it beneath The Fate.[2] And let these things indeed, as to so much be spoken, the best of the good Demon.

Tat.—And divinely, O Father! and truly and helpfully these things.

10. But this further explain to me. For thou saidest that the Mind in the irrational animals energized according to Nature (f), working together with their appetites (g).

(a) κατιδών. (b) τὰ νοητὰ σώματα. (c) οὐδὲν διαστατόν τῶν νοητῶν.
(d) ἄρχοντα. (e) ὑπεράνω. (f) δίκην Φύσεως. (g) ὁρμαῖς.

[1] "The image of The invisible God, the Firstborn of all creation" (Coloss. i. 15). "The beginning of the creation of God" (Rev. iii. 14). "The Firstborn" (Heb. i. 6). "The Firstborn of the dead Jesus Christ" (Rev. i. 5). For "Only begotten," see John i. 14, 18; iii. 16, 18; 1 John iv. 9.

[2] Lactantius (Divin. Instit., lib. ii. ch. 16) writes:—"Hermes affirms that those who have known God are not only safe from the attacks of demons, but that they are not even bound by fate. The only protection," he says, "is piety; for over a pious man neither evil demon nor fate has any power."

But the appetites of the irrational animals as I think are passions; and if also the Mind co-operates with the appetites and the appetites of the irrationals are passions, then the Mind also is passion, commingling (*a*) with the passions.

Hermes.—Well done, O Child! thou enquirest nobly. It is just for me also to answer.

11. All things, O Child! incorporeal in body are subject to passion (*b*), and peculiarly (*c*) are they passions; for everything moving is incorporeal, and everything moved, body. And incorporeals are moved by the Mind, and movement is passion. Both then have passion (*d*), both the moving and the moved; the one indeed ruling, the other ruled. Having departed from the body, departure is also from the passion. But rather perhaps, O Child! nothing is passionless, but all are subject to passion. But passion differs from what is subjected to passion. For the one energizes, the other is passive. But the bodies also energize of themselves; for either they are immoveable or are moved; but whichever it may be it is passion. But incorporeals always energize, and because of this they are subjects of passion. Let not then appellations disturb thee, for both the energy and the passion are the same thing, but to have used the more honourable (*e*) name is not grievous.

12. *Tat.*—Most clearly, O Father! hast thou delivered the discourse.

Hermes.—And see this, O Child! that these two things The God hath bestowed on the Man beyond all the mortal animals, both the Mind and the Reason, equivalent (*f*) to immortality; and in addition to these he has the enunciative Reason (*g*).[1] Of these if any one make use for what he ought, he will differ nothing from the immortals; but rather moreover going forth from the body, he will

(*a*) συγχρωτίζων.   (*b*) παθητά.   (*c*) κυρίως.   (*d*) πάσχει.
(*e*) εὐφημοτέρῳ.   (*f*) ἰσότιμα.   (*g*) τὸν προφορικὸν λόγον.

[1] *i.e.*, Language, λόγος, that word being here used in a double sense for both Speech and Reason.

be guided by both unto the choir of the Gods and blessed.

13. *Tat.*—Do not however the other animals use language (*a*), O Father!

Hermes.—No! Child, but voice; for language differs altogether much from voice. For language indeed is common to all men, but voice is peculiar to each kind of animal.

Tat.—But also of the Men, O Father! according to each nation the language is different.

Hermes.—Different indeed, O Child! but one the Man, and so the language is one, and is mutually interpreted, and the same is found both in Egypt and Persia and Greece. But thou seemest to me, O Child! to be ignorant of the virtue and magnitude of Language. For the blessed God, Good Demon,[1] declared Soul to be in Body, but Mind in Soul, Reason (*b*) in the Mind, The Mind in The God, but The God Father of these.

14. The Reason then is the image of the Mind, and Mind of The God, and the Body indeed of the Idea (*c*) and the Idea of the Soul.[2] Of Matter now the most subtle (*d*) is Air, of Air the Soul, of Soul Mind, and of Mind God. And The God indeed is around all things and through all things.[3] But the Mind around the Soul, and the Soul around the Air, and the Air around the Matter. Of necessity both the Providence and the Nature are instruments (*e*) of the World, and of the order of the Matter; and of things intelligible each indeed is essence, but essence of them is the identity (*f*). Of the bodies of the Universe each is many. For the composite bodies having the identity, and making

(*a*) λόγον. (*b*) λόγον, *i.e.*, προφορικόν. (*c*) τῆς ἰδέας.
(*d*) λεπτομέριστατον. (*e*) ὄργανά. (*f*) ταυτότητα.

[1] Who is meant by the Good Demon is here plainly stated.

[2] What is here meant by "Idea" is difficult to determine. Whether the "Idea" of Plato, or the form of the manner and mode of existence and species.

[3] "Of Him, and through Him, and to Him, are all things" (Rom. xi. 36).

the change into one another, always conserve the incorruption of the identity.

15. But in all the other composite bodies there is number of each. For apart from number it is impossible for constitution or composition or dissolution to become. But the Unities (a) generate and augment the number, and again dissolved receive [it] (b) into themselves. And the Matter is One. But this entire World, the great God, and image of the Greater, and united to Him and conserving the order and will of The Father is plenitude (c) of the Life. And there is nothing in this throughout all the eternity of the paternally given (d) revolution,[1] neither of the whole, nor of them in part, which is not living. For not one thing neither hath become, nor is, nor shall be in the World, dead. For the Father hath willed Life to be in it, whilst it be constituted. Wherefore also it must be God.

16. How then, O Child! in The God, in the Image of the Universe,[2] in the plenitude of the Life, can there be dead things? For deadness is corruption, and the corruption destruction. How then can any part of the incorruptible be corrupted or anything of The God be destroyed?

Tat.—The animals in it die not then, O Father! being parts of it?

Hermes.—Speak well, O Child! erring in the appellation of the [thing] generate. For they do not die, O Child! but as composite bodies are dissolved, and the dissolution is not death, but the dissolution of the mixture (e). And they are dissolved not that they may perish, but that they may become new. For what is the energy of Life? Is it not motion? What then in the World is immoveable? Nothing, O Child!

(a) ἑνάδες.　　　(b) *i.e.*, number.　　　(c) πλήρωμά.
(d) πατρῴας.　　　　　　　　　　　　(e) κράματος.

[1] ἀποκαταστάσεως; Latine, "Reditus Solis Lunæ, &c., anno vertente ad eadem signa."

[2] παντός. Parthey (p. 109) translates "patris," πάτρός; the sense rather requires this latter word. Ménard translates as in the text.

17. *Tat.*—Does not the earth seem to thee immoveable, O Father?

Hermes.—No, Child! but also multimoveable, and it alone also stable. For how would it not be ridiculous the nurse of all to be immoveable, her producing (*a*) and generating all things; for it is impossible apart from motion that the producer produce anything. Thou hast asked the most ridiculous thing, whether the fourth portion shall be inert. For the immoveable body signifies nothing else but inertness.

18. Know then universally, O Child! that the whole Entity (*b*) in the World is moved either by way of diminution or augmentation; but what is moved also lives, but there is no necessity that the whole (*c*) living animal should be the same. For the entire World, being collective (*d*), is, O Child! unchangeable, but the parts of it are all changeable; but nothing corruptible or destroyed. But the appellations confuse mankind. For the generation is not Life, but the Sense, nor the change death, but oblivion. These things then having themselves thus, immortal are all things, the Matter, the Life, the Spirit, the Soul, out of which every animal has been constituted.

19. Every animal therefore is immortal through the Mind; but of all especially The Man, who is susceptible of God, and joint in Essence (*e*) with God. For with this animal alone God holds converse (*f*), by night through dreams, by day through symbols (*g*), and through all He predicts to him things future through birds, through entrails, through spirit (*h*), through an oak;[1] wherefore also The Man professes to be acquainted with things antecedent and present and future.

20. And see this, O Child! that each of the other animals frequents one part of the world, the aquatics indeed

(*a*) Φύουσαν. (*b*) πᾶν τὸ ὄν. (*c*) τὸ ζῶον πᾶν.
(*d*) ὁμοῦ ὤν. (*e*) συνουσιαστικός. (*f*) ὁμιλεῖ.
(*g*) συμβόλων, possibly presages. (*h*) πνεύματος.

[1] The foregoing seems to prove that the author wrote under the Roman domination.

the water, the terrestrial the earth, and those aloft the air; but the Man makes use of all these: earth, water, air, fire. He beholds also heaven, and he touches this also with his sense. But The God is around all and throughout all; for He is Energy and also Power, and it is nothing difficult to understand The God, O Child!

21. But if thou wishest also to contemplate (*a*) Him, behold the order of the World and the fair symmetry (*b*) of this order, behold the Necessity of things apparent, the Providence of those having been generated (*c*) and are generate, behold the Matter being very full of life, The so great God moved along with all Good, and beautiful Gods, and Demons, and Men.

Tat.—But these, O Father! are altogether Energies?

Hermes.—If then they are altogether Energies, O Child! by whom then are they energized unless by God? Or art thou ignorant that just as parts of the World (*d*) are Heaven and Earth and Water and Air, the same way parts of God, are Life and Immortality, Energy, and Spirit, and Necessity, and Providence, and Nature, and Soul, and Mind, and the permanence of all these, that called Good? and there is not anything beside of things generate or those having been generated where there is not The God.

22. *Tat.*—In the Matter then, O Father?

Hermes.—Matter, O Son! is apart from God,[1] that to it thou mayest set apart a peculiar place. But what, being but a Mass (*e*), dost thou think it to be, not being energized? But if it be energized, by whom is it energized? for these energies we have said to be parts of The God. By whom then are all the animals vivified? By whom are things immortal made immortal? By whom are unstable things changed? But whether thou sayest Matter, or Body, or Essence, know that these same are energies of

(*a*) θεωρῆσαι. (*b*) εὐκοσμίαν. (*c*) γεγονότων.
(*d*) τοῦ κόσμου μέρη. (*e*) σωρὸν.

[1] The doctrine of Plato about Matter is enunciated, Timæus, 30. See *post*, Part II., Excerpts from Stobæus (Physica, 319; Meineke, i. 84).

The God, and of Matter energy the Materiality, and of Bodies energy the Embodiment (*a*), and energy of the Essence the Essentiality, and this is The God the Universe.[1]

23. But in the Universe there is nothing which is not The God, whence neither magnitude, nor place, nor quality, nor figure, nor time is about The God; for He is Universe (*b*), and the Universe is throughout all things and around all things. This The Word (*c*), O Child! venerate and worship (*d*). But worship of The God is one, not to be evil.[2]

(*a*) σωματότητα. (*b*) πᾶν.
(*c*) τὸν λόγον. (*d*) προσκύνει καὶ θρήσκευε.

[1] See above, that this does not include Matter.

[2] In the First Epitome of Clement (Dressel's Edit. 17), according to that Editor put together in the time of Jerome, the following is stated to have been the teaching of St Peter:—"Let them believe in One Father Almighty, and in His only-begotten Son, generated from Him in an unspeakable manner before the worlds, and in The Holy Spirit from Him ineffably proceeding; and let them acknowledge One God in Three Subsistences, without beginning, without end, everlasting, eternal, increate, irreversible, unchangeable, simple, incomposite, incorporeal; invisible, untouchable, uncircumscribed, incomprehensible, infinite, not understandible; good, just, all-powerful Creator of all creations, Autocrat of all things, all-seeing, all-providing Supreme Lord and Judge." The words of Newton as to the Deity are as follows:—"Æternus est et infinitus omnipotens et omnisciens; id est durat ab æterno in æternum, et adest ab infinito in infinitum. Non est æternitas et infinitas, sed æternus et infinitus; non est duratio et spatium, sed durat et adest. Durat semper et adest ubique, et existendo semper et ubique durationem et spatium constituit." The same doctrine is laid down, Lact. Div. Instit., vi., ch. v.; and (quoting Hermes), vi., ch. 25, totidem verbis.

CHAPTER XIII.

To his Son Tat on a Mountain. Secret Discourse about Regeneration and Profession (a) *of Silence.*

1. *Tat.*—In the Generalities, O Father! thou hast spoken enigmatically and not lucidly, discoursing concerning Deity, and hast not revealed, having said that no one can be saved before the Regeneration (b); and I having become suppliant of thee on the descent from the mountain after that thou hadst conversed with me, and desiring to learn the discourse of the Regeneration, because that, beyond all things this alone I know not, thou promisedst when thou shouldest become alienated (c) from the World, to deliver it to me. Wherefore I became prepared, having alienated also the thought in me from the deceit of the World. But do Thou fulfil to me also the last residues (d) in which thou promisedst to deliver to me Regeneration, propounding them with voice or privily. I am ignorant, O Trismegistus! from what matter and womb Man hath been generated, and from what kind of seed.

2. *Hermes.*—O Child! intellectual Wisdom (e) is in Silence, and the Seed the truthful Good.

Tat.—Of whom sowing, O Father? for as to the whole I am in doubt.

Hermes.—Of the Will of The God, O Child!

Tat.—And of what kind (f) the engendered, O Father? Being destitute of the Essence that intelligible (g) in me, other will be the engendered (h) God Son of God.

Hermes.—The All in all, constituted of all Powers.[1]

Tat.—Thou speakest enigma to me, O Father! and dost not converse as father with son.

(a) ἐπαγγελίας.
(b) τῆς παλιγγενεσίας.
(c) μέλλης ἀπαλλοτριοῦσθαι.
(d) ὑστερήματα.
(e) σοφία νοερά.
(f) ποταπός.
(g) τῆς οὐσίας τῆς νοητῆς.
(h) ὁ γιννώμενος.

[1] See Colossians i. 15, 16, &c., before cited.

Hermes.—This kind, O Son! is not taught; but when He may wish is brought to remembrance by The God.

3. *Tat.*—Thou tellest me things impossible, O Father! and forced. Whence I wish to reply to them correctly. Have I been produced (*a*) stranger Son of the paternal race? Grudge me not, O Father! I am a genuine (*b*) Son; relate to me the mode of the Regeneration.

Hermes.—What can I say, O Child! I have not what to speak except this. I perceive a certain unfeigned (*c*) spectacle generated in me; from the mercy of God I have also gone forth from myself into an immortal body, and I am now not what formerly, but have become generated (*d*) in Mind. This fact is not taught neither by that fictile (*e*) element by which it is possible to see, and because of this the first composed form is neglected by me; nor that I am coloured and have touch and measure; I am alien now from these things. Thou lookest at me verily, O Child! with eyes, when with fixed attention thou considerest with body and sight; I am not beholden (*f*) with those eyes now, O Child![1]

4. *Tat.*—Thou has cast me into no small madness and irritation of mind, O Father! For now I do not see myself.[2]

Hermes.—Would, O Child! that thou also wouldest come out of thyself, as those who in sleep perceive dreams apart from sleep.

Tat.—Tell me this too. Who is the generator (*g*) of the Regeneration?

Hermes.—The Son of The God One Man by the Will of God.[3]

(*a*) πέφυκα.   (*b*) γνήσιος.   (*c*) ἄπλαστον.   (*d*) ἐγεννήθην.
(*e*) πλαστῷ.   (*f*) θεωροῦμαι.   (*g*) γενεσιουργός.

[1] The parallel between this passage and 1 Cor. ii. 14 is remarkable. "Now the natural man receiveth not the things of the Spirit of God; for they are foolishness unto him: and he cannot know them, because they are spiritually judged" ("discerned," Authorised Version).

[2] This in the dialogues of Plato is a reply of his auditors to some of the paradoxes propounded by him.

[3] See *ante*, ch. i. 12, note, where the quotation of that passage and

5. *Tat.*—Now for the rest, O Father! thou hast brought me to silence, abandoned by previous thoughts; for I behold thy magnitude the same, O Father! with the character (*a*).

Hermes.—And in that thou art deceived; for the form of mortals is changed day by day: for by time it is turned to augmentation or diminution, as falsity.

6. *Tat.*—What then is true, O Trismegistus?

Hermes.—That not perturbed (*b*), O Child! that not limited (*c*), the colourless, the formless, the invariable, the naked, the luminous, the comprehensible in itself, the unalterable, the good, the incorporeal.[1]

Tat.—I am really maddened, O Father! for seeming to have become wise through thee, my senses have been closed up by this cogitation (*d*).

Hermes.—Thus it holds, O Child! for [sense perceives that] this is borne upwards as fire, that borne downwards as earth, and moist as water, and blowing together as air; but how wilt thou understand this by sense, that not hard, that not moist, the unconstrainable, the not dissolved, that understood solely in power and energy? Thou wantest Mind alone able to understand the generation in God.

7. *Tat.*—I am then unable, O Father!

Hermes.—Let it not be, O Child! Draw to thyself and it will come; wish and it becomes. Lay to rest (*e*) the senses of the body, and it will be the generation of The Deity; purify thyself from the irrational avengers (*f*) of the Matter.

(*a*) τῷ χάρακτῆρι. (*b*) θολούμενον. (*c*) διοριζόμενον.
(*d*) νοήματος. (*e*) κατάργησον. (*f*) τιμωρῶν.

this is extracted by Lactantius (Divin. Instit., iv. 6, vii. 4, *post*, Part III.). Here we find a distinct assertion of the Incarnation of the Son of God. This passage and the remainder of the Chapter is almost a repetition of John iii. 3-21. For after having said, "Except a man be born anew;" "Except a man be born of water and the Spirit, he cannot enter into the kingdom of God;" "Ye must be born anew;" he subjoins, "So God loved the world, that He gave His only begotten Son, that whosoever believeth on Him should not perish, but have eternal life." "That the world should be saved through Him."

[1] See Excerpt from Stobæus, Part II. v., "Of Truth," *ad fin.*

Tat.—Avengers I have then in myself, O Father!

Hermes.—Not few, O Child! but both fearful and many.

Tat.—I am ignorant, O Father!

Hermes.—This is one Avengeress, O Child! Ignorance; but the second Grief, the third Intemperance, the fourth Concupiscence, the fifth Injustice, the sixth Covetousness, the seventh Deceit, the eighth Envy, the ninth Cheatery, the tenth Wrath, the eleventh Rashness, the twelfth Malice (*a*); these are in number twelve; but under these are more others, O Child! and through the prison of the body they compel the within placed (*b*) man to suffer in his senses.[1]

8. But these stand off, not forthwith (*c*), from him who is pitied by The God; and thus is composed (*d*) both the way and reason of the Regeneration. Henceforward, O Child! be silent and speak well; and through this the mercy will not cease to us from The God. Rejoice henceforward, O Child! being purified by the powers of The God unto comprehension (*e*) of the discourse. Knowledge of The God hath come to us, and that coming, O Child! the ignorance is banished. Knowledge of joy hath come to us; this having arrived, O Child! Grief will fly to those who give place to it. I call the Temperance (*f*) power for joy,[2] O sweetest power! Let us assume it, O Child! most readily. How along with the arrival hath it expelled the intemperance.

9. But the fourth now I call Endurance (*g*), the power adverse to the concupiscence. This degree, O Child! is the fixed seat of Justice (*h*); for without contention behold how it hath banished the injustice. We are justified, O Child! injustice being absent. The sixth power coming

(*a*) κακία.   (*b*) ἐνδιάθετον.   (*c*) ἀθρόως.
(*d*) συνίσταται.   (*e*) συνάρθρωσιν.   (*f*) ἐγκράτεια.
(*g*) καρτερίαν, continence.   (*h*) ἵδρασμα δικαιοσύνης.

[1] "The works of the flesh are manifest, which are fornication, uncleanness, lasciviousness, idolatry, sorcery, enmities, strife, jealousies, wraths, factions, divisions, heresies, envying, drunkenness, revellings, and such like" (Galat. v. 19).

[2] Temperance was considered the greatest virtue by the Platonists, and to include almost every other.

to us that contrary to covetousness I call Communication (*a*). That departing, I call moreover upon the Truth; and the deceit flies and Truth becomes present. Behold how the Good is completed, O Child! the Truth becoming present. For envy hath departed from us, and with The Truth, The Good also hath become present along with Life and Light, and no more hath supervened any vengeance of the darkness, but they have fled away vanquished by assault.

10. Thou hast learnt (*b*), O Child! the way of the Regeneration. The Decade[1] becoming present, O Child! the intelligent generation (*c*) has been constituted and expels the twelfth (*d*); and we are made contemplators by the generation.[2] Whosoever then hath obtained according to the mercy, the generation according to God, having relinquished the bodily sense, recognises himself constituted of Divine things and is rejoiced.

11. *Tat.*—Become stable (*e*) by The God, O Father! I imagine (*f*), not with vision of eyes, but with that intellectual energy through Powers. I am in heaven, in earth, in water, in air. I am among animals, among plants, in the womb, before the womb, after the womb, everywhere. But still tell this to me how the vengeances of darkness being in number twelve, are expelled by ten powers? What is this way, O Trismegistus!

12. *Hermes.*—This the tabernacle (*g*), O Child! which we have passed through, is constituted out of the zodiacal circle and that consisting of animal signs (*h*), being twelve in

(*a*) κοινωνίαν. (*b*) ἔγνωκας. (*c*) νοερὰ γένεσις.
(*d*) scilicet, κακίαν. (*e*) ἀκλινής.
(*f*) φαντάζομαι. (*g*) σκῆνος. (*h*) ζωδίων.

[1] The Decade was one of the perfect numbers of Pythagoras and Plato.

[2] "Adding on your part all diligence, in your faith supply virtue; and in your virtue knowledge, and in your knowledge temperance, and in your temperance patience, and in your patience godliness, and in your godliness love of the brethren, and in your love of the brethren love" (2 Pet. i. 5; and see Matt. v.).

number, of one nature indeed, but of all shaped form (*a*). For error of the Man there are distinctions in them (*b*), O Child! united in the operation. Temerity (*c*) is inseparable from Wrath, and they are also indistinguishable. Suitably then according to the right reason they make the departure, as if also eliminated by ten powers, that is by the Decade. For the Decade, O Child! is soul generative (*d*); for life and light are united there where the number of the Unit hath been born of the Spirit. The Unit (*e*) therefore according to reason hath the Decade and the Decade the Unit.

13. *Tat.*—Father! I behold the Universe and myself in The Mind.

Hermes.—This is the Regeneration, O Child! the no longer employing imagination upon the Body, that triply divided (*f*), through this discourse concerning the Regeneration on which I have made comment; that we may not be calumniators of the Universe towards the many, to whom God Himself does not will to reveal it.[1]

14. *Tat.*—Tell me, O Father! has this the Body, that constituted of Powers, ever dissolution?

Hermes.—Speak well! and utter not impossibles, since thou willest sin, and the eye of thy mind be made impious. The sensible body of the Nature is far off from the essential generation (*g*). For that is dissoluble but this indissoluble, and that mortal, but this immortal; knowst thou not that thou hast been born God [2] and Son of the One, which also I?

(*a*) παντομόρφου δε ιδέας.   (*b*) εις πλάνην του ανθρώπου.
(*c*) προπέτεια.   (*d*) ψυχογόνος.   (*e*) ή ενάς.
(*f*) το τριχή διαστατόν, *i.e.*, Body, Soul, Spirit.   (*g*) ουσιώδους γενέσεως.

[1] This passage is doubtful in meaning, with various readings, some of which omit the negative. (See Parthey, 122, note).

[2] " I said ye are gods, and ye are all the children of the Highest. The Sons of God," applied to men (Gen. vi. 2, 41; John x. 34, quoting Psalm lxxxii. 6). " The Sons of God came to present themselves before the Lord" (Job i. 6, ii. 1). " Ye are the Sons of the living God" (Hos. i. 10). " To them gave He right to become children of God" (John i. 12). " For as many as are led by the Spirit of God,

15. *Tat.*—I was wishing, O Father! the praise through the hymn, which thou saidst when I had become at the Ogdoad (*a*) I should hear of the Powers.[1]

Hermes.—According as the Poemandres prophesied of the Ogdoad (*b*), thou hastest well, Child! to loose the tabernacle; for thou hast been purified. The Poemandres, the Mind of the Supreme Power (*c*), hath not delivered to me more than the things written, knowing that from myself I shall be able to understand all things, and to hear those which I wish, and to see all things; and he hath charged me to do things beautiful. Wherefore also all the Powers that are in me sing.

16. *Tat.*—I wish, Father, to hear and desire to understand these things.

Hermes.—Be still, O Child! and now hear the harmonized praise, the hymn of the Regeneration which I judged not fit so easily to speak forth, unless to thee at the end of the whole. Whence this is not taught but is hidden in silence. Thus then, O Child! standing in a place open to the sky (*d*) looking toward the South wind about downgoing of the setting sun bow the knee; and likewise also at the return towards the sunrise quarter.[2] Be at rest then, O Child!

Secret Hymnody.

17. Let all Nature of World receive the hearing of this hymn! Be opened, O Earth! Let every vehicle (*e*) of rain be opened to me. The trees wave ye not! I am about to hymn The Lord of the creation, and the Universe and The One. Open ye Heavens and Winds be still!

(*a*) ἐπὶ τὴν ὀγδοάδα. (*b*) ὀγδοάδα.
(*c*) τῆς αὐθεντίας, see ch. i. 3, and note there.
(*d*) ἐν ὑπαίθρῳ. (*e*) μοχλός.

these are Sons of God" (Rom. viii. 14). "Now are we children of God" (1 John iii. 1, 2).

[1] As to the Eighth or Ogdoad, see ch. i. 25, 26.

[2] From this and a former passage it has been conjectured that Hermes might have been one of the Therapeutics, whose custom it was to worship thus kneeling and at these periods of the day.

Let the immortal circle of The God receive my discourse. For I am about to hymn Him having founded (*a*) all things, Him having fixed the Earth, and suspended Heaven, and commanded from the Ocean the sweet water to become present (*b*) unto the earth inhabited and uninhabitable, for the nourishment and use of all men; Him having commanded fire to shine for every action on gods and men. Let us all together give the praise to Him, The Sublime above the heavens, to the Founder of all Nature. This is the Eye of the Mind, and may He receive the praise of these my powers.

18. Ye powers that are in me hymn The One and the Universe; sing along with my will all the powers which are in me. Holy Knowledge, enlightened from thee, through thee hymning the intelligible (*c*) Light, I rejoice in joyfulness of Mind. All ye powers hymn together with me, and do thou my Temperance (*d*) hymn; my Justice hymn the just through me. My Communionship (*e*) hymn the Universe; through me Truth hymn the Truth; The Good hymn Good. Life and Light; from us to you the praise passes. I give thanks to Thee, O Father! Energy of the Powers, I give thanks to Thee, O God! power of these energies of mine. Thy Word through me hymneth Thee. Through me receive the Universe in speech, rational sacrifice (*f*).

19. The Powers that are in me shout these things. They hymn Thee the Universe; they perform Thy Will. Thy Counsel is from Thee; to Thee the Universe. Receive from all rational sacrifice. The Universe that is in us, Life preserve! Light enlighten! O Spirit God! For The Mind Shepherdeth (*g*) Thy Word, O Spirit-bearing Creator! (*h*)

20. Thou art The God. Thy Man shouteth these things through Fire, through Air, through Earth, through Water, through Spirit, throughout the works of Thee. From the

(*a*) κτίσαντα. (*b*) ὑπάρχειν. (*c*) νοητόν.
(*d*) ἐγκράτεια. (*e*) κοινωνία. (*f*) τὸ πᾶν λόγῳ λογικὴν θυσίαν.
(*g*) ποιμαίνει. (*h*) πνευματοΦόρε δημιουργέ.

Eternity of Thee I have found praise; and what I seek by that Thy counsel I acquiesce in (a). I know that by Thy will, this the Praise is said.

Tat.—O Father! I have placed thee in my World.

Hermes.—In the intelligible (b) say, O Child!

Tat.—In the intelligible, O Father! I am able; from the hymn of thee and this thy praise my Mind hath been enlightened. Moreover I also wish from my own thought to send praise to The God.

21. *Hermes.*—O Child! not incautiously.

Tat.—In the Mind, O Father! What I contemplate I Tat say to Thee, O Patriarch of the generative energy (c); to God I send rational sacrifices. O God! Thou Father! Thou the Lord! Thou the Mind! Receive the rational sacrifices which Thou wishest from me; for Thou being willing, all things are performed.

Hermes.—Thou, O Child! send an acceptable sacrifice to The God, Father of all things. But add also, O Child! through the Word (d).[1]

(a) ἀναπέπαυμαι.

(b) ἐν τῷ νοητῷ.

(c) γενάρχα τῆς γενεσιουργίας.

(d) διὰ τοῦ λόγου.

[1] It is manifest that in this Chapter Hermes mystically yet unmistakeably enunciates the doctrine of the Holy Trinity, "God The Father," "Thy Word," and The "Spirit God." See Cyrill. Alexand. contr. Julian. 33, and Suidas (*post*, Part III.). Cudworth (Intell. System, ch. iv., cxxxvi.) writes:—"Since all three, Orpheus, Pythagoras, and Plato, travelling into Egypt, were there initiated into the arcane theology of the Egyptians, called Hermaical, it seemeth probable that this doctrine of a Divine Triad (ἡ τῶν τριῶν θεῶν παράδοσις) was also part of the arcane theology of the Egyptians." He proceeds further to show at length that the Pagan philosophers above named and their followers "called this their Trinity, a Trinity of Gods." This opinion, so far as Greek philosophers and the ancient Egyptians are concerned, has been controverted by Mosheim in the notes to his Latin translation of Cudworth's work and by others, on the ground that this philosophical creed was in a Trinity not of persons, but of attributes. (See Rawlinson's "Egypt," vol. i. p. 320). But this objection by no means applies to our Hermes, whose Trinity is that of Three Persons who were in Union, each actively employed in the Creation, in sustaining the cosmical system, and in conducting Man to Heaven.

Tat.—I give thanks to Thee, Father! having prayed for me to assent (*a*) to these things.

22. *Hermes.*—I rejoice, O Child! at thy having gathered in fruit from the Truth, the good things, the immortal productions. Having learnt this from me, announce silence of the Virtue; to no one, Child, revealing the tradition of the Regeneration, that we may not be reckoned as calumniators. For sufficiently each of us hath meditated, I indeed as speaking, and thou as hearing. Mentally (*b*) hast thou known thyself and The Father that is ours.

CHAPTER XIV.

To Asclepius. To be Rightly Wise (c).

1. Since the son of mine Tat, in thine absence, wished to learn the nature of the Entities, but did not permit me (*d*) to pass over any, as son and junior but lately arriving at the knowledge of the particulars respecting each one, I was compelled to speak more fully, in order that the theory might become to him easy to follow. But to thee I, having selected the principal heads of the things spoken, have wished to commit them to thee in few words, having interpreted them more mystically, as to one of such an age, and scientific of their nature.

2. If the things apparent have all been generated and are generate, but those generated are generate, not of themselves but by other; but many are the generated, rather all the apparent and all the different and dissimilar, and the generate are generate by other: there is some One Who is doing these things, and He ingenerate and older than those generated. For the generated I say are gene-

(*a*) μοι αἰνεῖν.   (*b*) νοερῶς.   (*c*) εὖ Φρονεῖν.   (*d*) ὑπερθίασθαι.

rate by other; but of the generated beings it is impossible that any be older than all, except only the Ingenerate.

3. But this is both Superior and One and Only, really wise as to all things, as not having anything older. For He rules both over the multitude, and the magnitude and difference of things generate, and over the continuity (a) of the making and the energy. Then the generated are visible but He invisible. On account of this He makes, that He may be *in*visible (b). He always then is making, wherefore He is invisible. Thus He is worthy to understand, and for the understander to wonder at, and the wonderer to bless Himself, having recognised his own kindred Father (c).

4. For what is sweeter than an own kindred Father? Who then is He, and how shall we recognise Him? Whether is it just to ascribe to Him the appellation of The God or that of The Maker, or that of The Father, or also the three? God indeed because of the Power, Maker because of the energizing, Father because of the Good. For Power is different from things generate, but energy is in this, that all things are generated. Wherefore having cast away the much speaking and vain speaking, we must understand these two, That Generate, and The Maker; for between these is naught, nor any third thing.

5. Understanding then all things and hearing all things, remember these Two; and consider these to be the All, placing nothing in ambiguity (d), neither of those above nor of those below, nor of those divine, nor of those changeable, nor of those in secrecy. For Two are all things; That Generate, and The Maker, and that the one be separated from the other is impossible; for neither is it possible for the Maker to be apart from the Generate, nor the Generate apart from the Maker; for both of them are the very same; wherefore it cannot be that the one be separated from the other, as neither self from itself.

(a) τῇ συνεχείᾳ τῆς ποιήσεως.   (b) ἵνα ἀόρατος ᾖ; another reading adopted by Patricius is ἵνα ὁρατὸς ᾖ.

(c) γνήσιον πατέρα.   (d) ἀπορίᾳ.

6. For if the Maker is nothing else beside that making, only, simple, incomposite, it is of necessity that He make this same for Himself; since generation is the making by the Maker, and every the generate it is impossible to be generate by itself. Generate must be generated by another. Without Him making, the generated neither is generated, nor is. For the one without the other hath lost its proper nature by deprivation of the other. If then the Entities are acknowledged to be Two,[1] That Generate and That Making, One are they by the Union (*a*); this indeed preceding but that following. Preceding indeed God The Maker but following That Generate, whatever it may be.

7. And because of the variety of those generate thou shouldst not be scrupulous, fearing to attribute meanness and dishonour to The God. For His Glory is One—The Making all things, and this is of The God as it were body, The Making; but to Him The Maker nothing evil or base is to be imputed. For these are the passions following upon the generation, as rust on the brass and dirt on the body. For neither did the brass worker make the rust, nor those having generated the dirt, nor The God the evilness; but the vicissitude (*b*) of the generation makes them as it were to effloresce (*c*); and because of this The God made the change, as it were a purgation of the generation.

8. Besides indeed to the same limner (*d*) it is allowed both to make Heaven, and Gods, and earth, and sea, and men, and all the brutes (*e*), and the inanimate, and the trees; but to The God is it impossible to make these? O the much silliness and ignorance, this about The God! For such sort suffer the most dreadful of all things. For affirming that they both reverence and praise The God, by not ascribing (*f*) to Him the making of all things they neither know The God, and in addition to the not knowing, also in the greatest degree are they impious towards

(*a*) τῇ ἑνώσει.   (*b*) διαμοιβή.   (*c*) ἐξανθεῖν.
(*d*) ζωγράφῳ.   (*e*) ἄλογα.   (*f*) ἀνατιθέναι.

[1] See Cyrill. Alex. Contr. Jul., 63 E, (*post*, Part III.).

Him, having attributed to Him as passion, contempt (*a*), or impotence, or ignorance, or envy; for if He makes not all things, in pride (*b*) He makes them not, or not being able, or being ignorant, or grudging, which is impious.

9. For The God has one only Passion, The Good; but The Good is neither proud nor impotent, nor the rest; for this is The God The Good, with Whom is every power of making all things; but everything that is generated hath been generated by The God; that is by The Good and Him able to make all things.

10. But if, how then He makes and how the generate are generated thou wishest to learn it is permitted thee. Behold a very beautiful and very similar figure; an agriculturist casting down seed into the earth, sometimes wheat, sometimes barley, sometimes some other of the seeds. Behold the same planting a vine, and an apple, and fig, and the others of the trees. Thus The God indeed in Heaven sows immortality, but in Earth change, but in the Universe life and motion. These things then are not many but few, and easily numbered. For all of them are four,[1] both The God Himself and the Generation in which the Entities (*c*) consist.[2]

(*a*) ὑπεροψίαν.   (*b*) ὑπερηφανῶν.   (*c*) τὰ ὄντα ἐστίν.

[1] *viz.*, Earth, Air, Fire, Water.
[2] See the first line of ch. i., *ante*.

FINIS POEMANDRES.

HERMES TRISMEGISTUS.

PART II.

EXCERPTS MADE BY STOBÆUS (5TH OR 6TH CENTURY) FROM THE WORKS OF HERMES.

I.—OF TRUTH.

FROM THE THINGS TO TAT (*Florilegium*, xi. 23; *Meineke*, i. 248).

"RESPECTING Truth, O Tat! it is impossible for Man, being an imperfect being, and composed of imperfect members, and the tabernacle (*a*) consisting of various bodies and many, to speak with boldness. But what is possible and just that I affirm, that Truth is in eternal (*b*) bodies only, of which also the bodies themselves are true. Fire is very fire, and nothing else; Earth very earth itself, and nothing else; Air itself air, and nothing else; Water very water, and nothing else; but these bodies of ours are constituted of all these; for they have of fire, they have also of earth, they have also of water, also of air; and it is neither fire, nor earth, nor water, nor air, nor anything true; but if, at the beginning, the constitution (*c*) of us had not Truth, how then can it either see or speak Truth? but only to understand if God will. All things, then,

(*a*) τὸ σκῆνος.   (*b*) ἀιδίοις.   (*c*) σύστασις.

those upon earth, O Tatius! are not Truth, but imitations of the Truth, and not all but these few, but others falsehood and error, O Tatius! and semblances of phantasy (*a*), just like images standing together. But when from above the phantasy has this influx, there Truth becomes imitation of the Truth; but apart from the energy from above, there remains falsehood. Just as also the image shows the body indeed in the drawing (*b*), but it is not body according to the phantasy of the thing seen. And it looks indeed having eyes, but it sees nothing, and hears nothing at all. And the drawing has indeed all the other things, but they are falsehoods, deceiving the eyes of the beholders, of some indeed supposing to see truth.[1] If, then, we thus understand and see each of these as they are, we both understand and see a true thing; but if beside the Entity (*c*), we shall neither understand nor shall know anything true.

Is there, then, O Father! Truth even in the earth?

And thou hast not blindly erred, O Tatius! Truth is by no means in the earth, nor can be; but that some of the men understand concerning Truth, to whom The God shall have given the God-discerning (*d*) power. Thus I understand and say, nothing is true on the earth; all are phantasies and semblances. I understand and speak true things.

To understand and speak true things, then, ought we not to call this Truth?

But, what?

Ought one to understand and speak the Entities? Yet there is nothing true upon the earth? This is true, the not

(*a*) δόξαι Φαντασίας.
(*b*) τῇ γραφῇ.
(*c*) παρὰ τὸ ὄν.
(*d*) θεοπτικήν.

[1] Here is a manifest lacuna. Plato had written (Laws E, 730*b*), "Truth is esteemed by Gods as of all good things, by men of all things, of which he about to be born may be immediately partaker, blessed and fortunate from his beginning, so that he live through the most time being true, for he is faithful; but he is faithless by whom falsehood is willingly loveable, to whomsoever unwillingly he is mindless; neither of which is enviable, for every one, both whoso is faithless and foolish, is unloveable."

knowing anything true; how also can it possibly be, O Child? Truth is most perfect Virtue; it is the unmixed Good; that neither perturbed (a) by matter, nor encompassed by body, naked, lucid, irreversible (b), holy, unalterable, good; but things here, O Child! such as they are, thou seest incapable of receiving (c) this Good, corruptible, subject to passion, dissoluble, reversible, ever interchanged (d), becoming other from others. What things, then, are not true, even to themselves—how ever can they be true? For everything that is altered is falsehood, not abiding in what it is, but veering about, exhibits to us phantasies, others and others.

Is not Man then true, O Father?

According to (e) man he is not true, O Child! For The True is that having its constitution from itself only, and abiding according to it, such as it is. But the Man is constituted of many things, and does not abide according to himself, but is turned and changed, age from age, form from form (f), and this being still in the tabernacle. And many have not known their children, a short time intervening, and again children likewise parents. That then which is so changed about as not to be recognised—can it be true, O Tatius? Is not that, on the contrary, a falsehood, becoming in various phantasies of changes? But do you understand to be something true, the abiding and eternal; but Man is not always, wherefore neither is he a true thing. For the Man is a certain phantasy, but the phantasy would be extremest (g) falsehood.

Neither these, then, O Father! the eternal bodies—since they change—are true?

Everything, then, that is gendered and changeable is not true; but being generate by the forefather, as to the matter it is possible to esteem (h) them true. But even these have some falsehood in the change, for nothing not abiding of itself (i) is true.

(a) θολούμενον.   (b) Φανόν ἄτρεπτον.   (c) ἄδεκτα.
(d) ἐναλλοιούμενα.   (e) καθότι.   (f) ἰδεάν.
(g) ἀκρότατον.   (h) ἐσχηκέναι.   (i) ἰΦ αυτ˜.

"True, O Father!"

"What, then, would anyone call the Sun, alone beyond all other things not changed, but abiding of itself, Truth? Wherefore, also, because it alone hath been entrusted (a) with the creation of all things in the world, ruling all things, and making all things, which I both reverence and also salute (b) the truth of it,[1] and after The One and First, I acknowledge this creator.

"What, then, may be the first Truth, O Father?"

"One and only, O Tatius! Him not from matter, Him not in body, the colourless (c), the very figureless (d), the irreversible, the [2] unalterable, the ever-being. But the falsehood, O Child! is corrupted. For corruption hath laid hold of all things that are upon earth, and encompasses them (e) and the providence of the True will encompass. For apart from corruption (f) neither can generation be sustained, since upon all generation corruption follows, that it may again be generate; for it is necessity that things generate be generated from those corrupted; but it is necessity that things generate be corrupted, that the generation of the things being do not stop. Acknowledge this First Creator for the generation of the Entities. Those things, then, generated from corruption, would be (g) falsehoods, because sometimes, indeed, becoming other things, then other things; for to become the self-same things is impossible; but that not itself (h) how can it be true? One ought, then, to call such things phantasies,[3] O Child! If we rightly designate

(a) πεπίστευται.	(b) προσκυνῶ.	(c) ἀχρώματον.
(d) ἀσχημάτιστον	(e) ἐμπεριέχει.	(f) φθορᾶς.
(g) εἴη.	(h) αὐτό.	

[1] This is a quotation from Aristotle, Plut., 770: "καὶ προσκυνῶ γε πρῶτα μὲν τὸν ἥλιον."

[2] "The Father of Light, with Whom there can be no variation, neither shadow that is cast by turning" (James i. 17). See Poemandres iv. 2, and note.

[3] Plato writes thus in "Sophistes," 263:—"Thought (διάνοιά), opinion (δόξα), and phantasy (φαντασία) are all generate in the souls. Is not thought and speech the same, except that one within the soul

the Man, phantasy of manhood; and the child, phantasy of a child; and the youth, phantasy of a youth; and the adult (*a*), phantasy of an adult; and the old man, phantasy of an old man. For neither the man is a man, nor the child a child, nor the youth a youth, nor the adult an adult, nor the old man an old man, for being transmuted, both the things previous and those existing are falsified. But these things, understand thus, O Son! as also of the falsehoods of these energies from above, dependent (*b*) from the Truth itself. But this being thus, I say the falsehood to be an operation (*c*) of the Truth."

II.—OF DEATH.

FROM ASCLEPIUS (*Meineke*, iv. 106; *Florilegium*, 120).

We must now speak of Death, for the Death frightens the many as a very great evil through ignorance of the fact. For death becomes dissolution of a defunct body; and also the number of the harmonies (*d*) of the body being completed. For the harmonization (*d*) of the body is number. But the body dies when it can no longer support the man. And death is this, the dissolution of body and disappearance of bodily sense.[1]

(*a*) ἄνδρα.
(*b*) ἠρτημένων.
(*c*) ἐνέργημα.
(*d*) ἁρμῶν ἁρμογή.

is a discourse with itself without voice, and that streaming from it through the mouth is called speech? But in words again there is affirmation and denial. When, then, this happens in the soul, through thought in silence, what can you call it but opinion? But when opinion, not by itself, but along with sense, is present with anyone as a passion, what can we call it but phantasy? Since, then, speech is true and false, and that the thought of these is a discourse of the soul with itself, but opinion the result of thought, and that what we call phantasy is the mixture of sense with opinion, and these being related to words, some and sometimes these are false."

[1] Here, as elsewhere, Hermes enunciates the Pythagorean axiom that definite number is of the essence of all things.

The subject of what death consists in, and that it is a destruction

III.—OF GOD.

FROM THE THINGS TO TAT (*Florilegium*, 78; *Meineke*, iii. 104).

To understand God is difficult, to declare Him (*a*) impossible. For body to signify (*b*) the incorporeal is impossible, and the perfect to be comprehended by the imperfect is not possible,[1] and for the eternal to be conversant with (*c*) the short-lived very difficult. For this ever is, but that passes away, and this indeed is Truth, but that is overshadowed by phantasy. For the weaker from the stronger and the less from the superior are as far distant (*d*) as the mortal from the Divine, and the intermediate distance of these dims the sight of the Beautiful. For the bodies, indeed, are seen by eyes, by tongue things visible are related, but those incorporeal and invisible and figureless and not composed of matter, it is impossible also to be comprehended by our senses. I apprehend mentally—I apprehend mentally (*e*), O Tat! what it is not possible to express (*f*) in speech, that is— The God![2]

(*a*) Φράσαί δε.   (*b*) σημῆναι.   (*c*) συγγενέσθαι.
(*d*) διέστηκε.   (*e*) εννοοῦμαι.   (*f*) ἐξειπεῖν.

of the harmonies of the body only, is discussed by Plato in the Phædon, 91 *et seq.* (Hermann's Edition, I., 122-139). His conclusion is this: "Death, then, coming upon the man, the mortal of him, as it seems, dies, but the immortal goes away, departing safe and indestructible, displacing itself from the death."

He had said, Phædon, 67: "Is not this called death—loosing and separation of soul from body? But ever especially and only, those philosophising rightly desire this loosing, and this is the very carefulness of the philosophers—this loosing and separation of soul and body."

See as to this subject Poemandres, ch. viii., i. 2; ch. x. 13, and xi. 15.

[1] This passage is quoted (nearly *verbatim*) by Lactantius, Epitome, ch. iv. *ad finem*, and previously Divin. Instit., lib. II., ch. ix., and by Cyrill. Alex. Contr. Jul., 33c. (*post*, Part III.).

[2] Plato, Timæus, 28, wrote: "The Maker then and Father of this

IV.

From Stobæus, Physica, 55; *Meineke,* i. 14:—"Hermes being asked what God is, said, 'The Creator of the Whole of things, most wise Mind, and Eternal.'"

From Stobæus, Physica, 134; *Meineke,* i. 33. (*It is not stated from what work of Hermes*).

FOR some very great Demon, O Child! hath been ordained (*a*), revolved (*b*) in the midst of the Universe, beholding all things that are generate on earth by the Men. For just as over the Divine order The Providence (*c*) and Necessity are ordained, in the same manner also over the Men is ordained Justice, energizing these things for them (*d*). For this indeed rules the order of the Entities as Divine, and not willing to sin nor being able; for it is impossible for the Divine to have been led astray (*e*), from which also succeeds (*f*), the being impeccable. But the Justice is ordained avenger of those sinning upon Earth. For the race of men, since mortal and consisting of evil matter, . . . and especially to them occurs the lapsing (*g*), with whom Godseeing power (*h*) is not present; over these then, and especially, does the Justice prevail, and they are subjected to the Fate through the energies of the generation; but to Justice through the sins in the life.[1]

(*a*) τέτακται. (*b*) εἰλουμένη. (*c*) ἡ πρόνοια.
(*d*) ἐκείνοις, aliter. ἐκείναις. (*e*) πλανηθῆναι. (*f*) συμβαίνει.
(*g*) τὸ ὀλισθάνειν. (*h*) θεοπτική.

Universe it is both a business to find, and having found, to all it is impossible to declare." This passage of Hermes is quoted by Justin Martyr (*post*, Part III.).

"One God Who can neither be defined by any words, nor conceived by the Mind" (Shepherd of Hermas, Lib. ii., Mandatum, i.).

[1] See the similar sentiments of Plato in his "Laws," 716 and 905; and Hermann, v. 118, 342.

V.

HERMES TO THE SON (*Stobæus, Physica*, 162; *Meineke*, i. 42; *Patrit.*, p. 38).

RIGHTLY hast thou spoken to me all things, O Father! but further remind me what things are those according to Providence and what according to Necessity, likewise also according to Fate.[1]

I said that there were in us, O Tat! three species of incorporeals, and the one indeed is something Intelligible. This then indeed is colourless, figureless (*a*), incorporeal, out of the first and intelligible Essence. But there are also in us, opposite to this, configurations (*b*) which that receives (*c*). That therefore moved by the Intelligible Essence for any reason (*d*), and received, immediately is changed into another species of motion, and this is image of the intelligence (*e*) of the Creator, . . . but third species of incorporeals is that which is occurrent (*f*) about the bodies; place, time, motion, figure (*g*), appearance, magnitude, form; and of these there are two differences. For some of them are properly qualities (*h*), but others of the body; those indeed properly qualities, are the figure, the colour, the form (*i*), the place, the time, the motion; but those proper of the body are the figured figure, and the coloured colour, and there are also the shaped out shape (*k*), and the appearance, and the magnitude; these are nonparticipate with those. The In-

(*a*) ἀσχημάτιστον. (*b*) σχηματότητες. (*c*) ὑποδέχεται.
(*d*) πρός τίνα λόγον. (*e*) εἴδωλον τοῦ νοήματος. (*f*) συμβεβηκός.
(*g*) σχῆμα. (*h*) ἰδίως ποιά. (*i*) εἶδος.
(*k*) μεμορφωμένη μορφή.

[1] Plato sometimes indeed speaks of the Matter, sometimes of the bearing (σχέσιν) of the Maker towards the Matter; and some things indeed he refers to Providence and some to Necessity. He says then in the Timæus: "Being mingled then the genesis of this the World was generated, by the conjunction (συστάσεως) of Necessity and Mind, but Mind ruling over Necessity." (See Stobæus, Physica, 160; Meineke i. 42).

telligible Essence then, being with The God (*a*), has free power (*b*) of itself, and of saving other saving itself, since the same Essence is not under Necessity; but having been abandoned by The God, it chooses the corporeal nature, and the choice of it according to Providence becomes that of the World. But the irrational Whole (*c*) is moved according to some reason, and the reason indeed according to Providence, but the irrational according to Necessity, and the things having occurred about the body according to Fate. And this is the relation (*d*) of things according to Providence and Necessity and according to Fate.

VI.

CONCERNING THE ECONOMY OF THE UNIVERSE OF HERMES FROM THOSE TO AMMON.

(*Stobæus, Physica*, 183; *Meineke*, i. 47; *Patrit.*, p. 38).

BUT that governing throughout the whole World is Providence (*e*), but that keeping together and encompassing it is Necessity, but Fate compelling (*f*) leads and brings about all things (for the nature of it is the compelling) cause of generation and destruction of life. The World then first has the Providence (for first it happens upon it) (*g*); but the Providence was expanded (*h*) in the heaven. Wherefore also Gods are turned around it and are moved having motion unwearied and ceaseless, and Fate, wherefore also Necessity. And the Providence indeed provides, but Fate is the cause of the disposition of the Stars. This is inevitable law, according to which all things are ordained.[1]

(*a*) πρὸς τῷ θεῷ. (*b*) ἐξουσίαν. (*c*) τὸ ἄλογον πᾶν.
(*d*) ὁ λόγος, discourse. (*e*) πρόνοιά. (*f*) καταναγκάζουσα.
(*g*) πρῶτος γὰρ αὐτῆς τυγχάνει. (*h*) ἐξήπλωται.

[1] See Poemandres, i. 9, and notes 4 and 5 there.

VII.

OF HERMES FROM THOSE TO AMMON (*Stobæus, Physica*, 188; *Meineke*, i. 48; *Patrit.*, 38).

But all things are generated by Nature and by Fate, and there is not a place destitute of Providence. But Providence is the self-sufficient Reason of The God above in heaven. But two are the spontaneous (*a*) Powers of this, Necessity and Fate. But the Fate subserves (*b*) to Providence and Necessity, but to the Fate subserve the Stars. For neither can any one fly from Fate, nor guard himself from the force (*c*) of these; for the constellations are the armour of Fate; for according to this all things are consummate (*d*) in the Nature and with the Men."[1]

VIII.

OF HERMES FROM THE THINGS TO TAT.
(*Stobæus, Physica*, 249, 250; *Meineke*, i. 64; *Patrit.*, 38).

So also to discover about the three Times; for neither are they by themselves (*e*), nor are they united (*f*), and again they are united and are of themselves. For if thou supposest the present (*g*) to be apart from the past, it is impossible to be present if it do not also become past; for out of that departing becomes the present, and from the present comes the future. But if one must examine further, we will reason thus; that the past time departs that it should no longer be, but the future does not exist (*h*) in that it is not yet present, but that neither is the present

(*a*) αυτοφυῖις. (*b*) ὑπηρετεῖ. (*c*) δεινότητος.
(*d*) ἀποτελοῦσι. (*e*) καθ' ἑαυτούς. (*f*) συνήνωνται.
(*g*) τὸν ἐνεστῶτα. (*h*) ὑπάρχειν.

[1] See Poemandres, i. 9, and iii. 3, and notes there. Plato's explanation of the operation of the Fates, Lachesis, Clotho, and Atropos, will be found in his "Politica."

together with us in the abiding (*a*). For Time which hath not stopped (*b*), having course, not even a point (*c*), how is it said to be present, which is not able even to stop? And again the past conjoining with the present and the present with the future becomes one; for they are not apart from themselves in the identity and the unity (*d*) and the continuity. Thus the Time being one and the same, becomes both continuous and disjoined.[1]

(*a*) συμπαρεῖναι ἐν τῷ μένειν.   (*b*) ἕστηκε.
(*c*) ῥοπὴν οὐδὲ κέντρου.   (*d*) ἑνότητι.

[1] Plato wrote thus (Timæus, 37): "When the Father having generated it had made that moving and living, The created Glory of the eternal Gods, He was delighted and determined to conform His work to the pattern (παραδείγμα) still more, and as this was eternal He sought to complete the Universe eternal as far as might be. Now the nature of the Intelligible Being is everlasting; but to attach eternity altogether to the generate (γεννητῷ) was impossible; wherefore He resolved to have a certain moveable image of eternity, and fitting it to heaven, eternity remaining in One, He makes along with it an everlasting likeness proceeding according to number, which being we have named it Time. For days and nights and months and years not being before heaven was generated, then along with that existing, He contrives the generation of these. These all are parts of Time, and the 'was' and 'shall be' generated forms of Time, referring which to the Eternal Essence, we are latently erroneous; for we say how it 'was,' 'is,' and 'shall be,' but to This that '*It is*' alone appertains, according to the true expression, but the 'was,' and the 'shall be,' should properly be affirmed of the generation proceeding in Time; for it is motion. But as to That always abiding at the same immoveably, it belongs neither to become older nor younger through time, nor ever to be generated, or now have been generated; nor again shall be, nor is it at all connected with such generation as is of things carried on in Sense. Moreover, when we say that what has become has become, and what is becoming is becoming, and that what will become will become, and that what is not is not, of none of these do we speak accurately." The reader will be reminded of (Exod. iii. 14), "And God said unto Moses, I am that I am" ("'Ἐγώ εἰμι Ὁ ὤν," Sept.).

IX.

OF HERMES FROM THE THINGS TO TAT.
(*Stobæus*, 319, *ibid.*, i. ch. 10; *Meineke*, i. 84; *Patrit.*, 51).

For the Matter also, O Child! hath been generated and was. For Matter is receptacle (a) of generation, but generation mode of energy of The unbegotten and pre-existing God. Receiving then the seed of the generation, it was generated and became variable and received Ideas being made into shapes (b). For there presided over it, being varied, that (energy) fabricating the ideas of the variation (c). The nongeneration (d) of the matter then was shapelessness, but the generation the being energized.[1]

X.

OF HERMES FROM THAT TO TAT.
(*Stobæus*, *Physica*, 699; *Meineke*, i. 190; *Patrit.*, p. 4).

Asclepius.—I, O Child! both because of the love of Men and of the piety towards The God, first write this. For there can be no piety more righteous than to understand the Entities, and to proffer thanks to the Maker on account of these, which I will never cease performing.

(a) ἀγγεῖον.   (b) μορφοποιουμένη.
(c) τροπῆς.   (d) ἀγεννησία.

[1] Stobæus (*ibid.*) remarks that Plato (Timæus, 30) affirmed The Matter to be bodylike, shapeless, formless, figureless, without quality as to its own nature; but having received the Forms it became as it were nurse, receptacle (ἐκμαγεῖον) and mother of them. Plato asserts that The Matter simply, as to its entirety, does not change its state (ἐξίσταται), but receives all things entering it, but has no original shape whatever. "Three kinds are to be distinguished, the thing generated, that in which it is generated, and that whence, being assimilated, the thing generated is produced." "We may fittingly compare the thing receiving to a mother, that from whence to a father, and the nature between these to offspring."

Tat.—What then can any one doing, O Father! if there is nothing truthful here, pass through the life rightly (*a*).

Asclepius.—Be pious, O Child! The pious man will philosophize pre-eminently (*b*); for apart from philosophy it is impossible to be pre-eminently pious; but he having learnt what they are, and how they have been arranged, and by whom, and on account of whom, will render thanks for all things to the Creator as to a good father, and useful nurse and faithful guardian; and he proffering thanks will be pious; but the pious man will know both where is The Truth and what that is; and having learnt he will be still more pious. But by no means, O Child! can Soul being in body, having elevated itself to the comprehension (*c*) of that being good and true, fall away (*d*) to the opposite; for Soul having learnt the Forefather of itself exercises vehement (*e*) love, and oblivion of all the evil things, and cannot any more apostatize from The Good. This, O Child! let this be end of Piety, attaining to which thou wilt both live rightly, and shalt die happily, the Soul of thine not being ignorant whither it behoves that she should soar up. For this is the only way, O Child! that to Truth, which also [1] our forefathers journeyed, and having journeyed attained The Good. This way is venerable and smooth, but difficult for Soul to journey being in body. For first it behoveth her to war with herself, and to make a great division, and to be prevailed over (*f*) by the one portion. For the resistance (*g*) becomes of one against two; of the one flying, of the others dragging downwards, and there comes to pass much strife and fighting of these with each other; of the one desiring to fly, of the others hastening to retain. But the victory of both is not alike; for the one hastens to the Good, the others dwell with the evils; and the one desires to be freed; but the others love

(*a*) καλῶς. (*b*) ἄκρως. (*c*) κατάληψιν. (*d*) ὀλισθῆσαι.
(*e*) δεινόν. (*f*) πλεονεκτηθῆναι. (*g*) ἡ στάσις.

[1] "Stand ye in the ways, and see, and ask for the old paths, where is the good way, and walk therein, and ye shall find rest for your souls" (Jer. vi. 16).

the servitude,[1] and should indeed the two portions be conquered, they remain deserted of themselves (a) and of their ruler; but if the one be vanquished it is led and carried off by the two, being punished by the mode of living here (b). This, O Child! is the guide of the way thither; for it behoveth thee, O Child! first to anoint the body before the end, and to conquer in the life of striving (c), and having conquered thus, to return.[2] But now, O Child! I will go through under heads, the Entities; for thou wilt understand the things spoken having remembered those which thou hast heard. All the Entities are moved, that not being only is immoveable. Every body changeable, not every body dissoluble. Some of the bodies are dissoluble. Not every animal mortal, not every animal immortal. The dissoluble is corruptible, that abiding immutable, the immutable eternal. That ever generate ever also is corrupted; but that once for all generate is never corrupted, nor becomes anything else. First The God, second the World, third the Man; The World because of the Man, but the Man because of The God. Of the Soul, the sensible (d) indeed is mortal, but the rational immortal.

(a) This passage is corrupt.　　(b) τῇ ἐνθάδε διαίτῃ.
(c) ἐναγώνιον βίον.　　(d) τὸ αἰσθητόν.

[1] The latter portion of the seventh chapter of the Epistle to the Romans is much in point, ending ver. 23: "But I see a different law in my members, warring against the law of my mind, and bringing me into captivity under the law of sin which is in my members," &c.

[2] In the Phædon (65), Socrates and Simmias agree that the philosopher must disengage his soul entirely from the communion with the body, differently from the many, who think pleasure only worth living for; the genuine philosopher must stand apart from all these. (66) Whence come wars and fightings, but from the body and its lusts? Wars are necessitated by love of money for the sake of the service of the body; money must be acquired for the body to the neglect of philosophy. (67) The purification of the soul, is it not this: the separating the soul as much as can be from the body, and to place itself altogether by itself, apart from the connection and conjunction of the body, and to dwell as far as possible at present and in future alone by itself, loosed as it were from the chains of the body?

Every Essence immortal, every Essence mutable. Every Entity double; None of the Entities is stable (*a*). Not all things are moved by Soul, but Soul moves every Entity. Everything passive (*b*) has sense, everything sensible is subject to passion (*c*). Everything grieved and is pleased a mortal animal; not everything pleased is grieved [but is](*d*) an eternal animal. Not every body is subject to disease (*e*); every body subject to disease is dissoluble. The Mind in The God; the reasoning(*f*) in the Man; the reasoning in the Mind, the Mind impassible. Nothing in body true, in incorporeal the whole without falsity. Everything generate mutable, not everything generate corruptible. Nothing good upon the earth, nothing evil in the Heaven. The God good, the Man evil. The Good voluntary, the evil involuntary. The Gods choose things good as good. The good rule (*g*) of what is great is good rule; the good rule the law. Time divine, human law. Evil is aliment of World, Time corruption of Man. Everything in Heaven unchangeable, everything upon earth changeable. Nothing in Heaven servile, nothing upon earth free. Nothing unknowable in Heaven, nothing known (*h*) upon the earth. Things upon earth are not in common (*i*) with those in Heaven. All things in Heaven blameless, all things upon earth subjects of blame. The immortal is not mortal, the mortal not immortal. That sown is not always generated, but that generated always also sown. Two are the times of dissoluble body, that from the sowing up to the birth, and that from the birth up to the death. Of the eternal Body time is from the birth only. The dissoluble bodies are increased and diminished. The dissoluble matter is changed about to the opposites, corruption and generation; but the Eternal either into itself or into the like. Generation of Man is beginning of corruption, corruption of Man of generation. That

---

(*a*) ἔστηκεν.   (*b*) τὸ πάσχον.   (*c*) τὸ αἰσθόμενον πάσχει.
(*d*) The construction doubtful.   (*e*) νοσεῖ.
(*f*) λογισμός.   (*g*) εὐνομια. The text is here deficient.
(*h*) γνώριμον.   (*i*) οὐ κοινωνεῖ.

EXCERPTS BY STOBÆUS.

being departing (a) [is also succeeding (b), the succeeding] is also departing. Of the Entities some indeed are in bodies, some in ideas (c), but some energies; but body is in ideas,[1] but idea and energy in body. The immortal partakes not of the mortal, but the mortal does partake of the immortal. The mortal indeed comes not into immortal body, but the immortal becomes present in mortal. The energies are not upward tending (d), but downward tending. Things upon earth profit nothing those in Heaven, those in Heaven profit all those upon earth. The Heaven is receptive of eternal bodies, the earth is receptive of corruptible bodies. The earth irrational, the Heaven rational. Things in Heaven lie underneath (e), things upon earth lie on the earth. The Heaven is first of elements. The earth last of elements. Divine Providence order, Necessity subservient to Providence.[2] Fortune,[3] course of the disorderly (f), effigy of energy, lying opinion. What is God? Immutable Good. What Man? Immutable Evil.

Having remembered these heads, thou wilt also be immediately reminded of what things I went through to thee in fuller words; for these are the summaries of those. But abstain from these conversations (g) with the many, for to grudge thee I do not wish, but rather that thou wilt appear to be ridiculous to many. For the like is accepted with the like, but the unlike is by no means friendly with the unlike. For these the words have altogether the listeners few, or speedily they will have not even few. They have also something peculiar in themselves; they rather stimulate those evil unto the evil. Wherefore one

(a) ἀπογιγνόμενον.   (b) ἐπιγίγνεται. The text incomplete.
(c) ἰδέαις.   (d) ἀνωφερεῖς.   (e) ὑπόκειται.
(f) τύχη φορᾷ ἀτάκτου.   (g) παραιτοῦ ὁμιλίας.

[1] The word ἰδέα seems here to signify shape or model.

[2] See Poemandres, x. 20, and note.

[3] Plato's definition of Fortune: "Cause in things unpreferred, according to accident, and consequence and chancing and variable habitude of choice in relation to the purpose respecting the end" (Stobæus, Physica, 204; Meineke, i. 53).

ought to guard oneself against the many understanding not the virtue of the things spoken.

Tat.—How mayest thou speak, O Father!

Asclepius.—Thus, O Child! every the animal of the men is rather propense (*a*) to the evil, and becomes (*b*) nurtured along with this; wherefore also he is pleased with it. But this the animal, if he have learnt that the World is generated and all things are generate according to Providence and by Necessity, Fate ruling over all things, will not be by much worse than himself,[1] having despised indeed the Universe as generated, and referring the causes of the evil to the Fate, he will never abstain from every evil work. Wherefore one should be on guard as to them, in order that they being in ignorance may be less evil, though fear of the obscure (*c*).

XI.

OF HERMES FROM THE THINGS TO AMMON.[2]
(Stobæus, ibid. i. 720; *Meineke,* i. 196; *Patrit.,* 40).

THE Soul then is incorporeal Essence, and though being in body, does not depart from its proper essentiality. For it happens being ever moveable according to Essence, and according to Intelligence self-moveable (*d*); not moved in something nor towards something, nor because of something; for it is prior (*e*) in the Power; but the prior has no need of the latter ones. That in something then is the place, and time, and nature; that towards something is harmony, and form, and figure (*f*), but that because of which, the Body; for because of Body both Time, and Place, and Nature; but these have communion with each

(*a*) ἐπιρρεπέστερον. (*b*) σύντροφον γίγνεται. (*c*) ἀδηλού.
(*d*) αὐτοκίνητος. (*e*) προτερεῖ. (*f*) εἶδος καὶ σχῆμα.

[1] Will only follow his own evil nature.

[2] This is Ammon, the contemporary of our Hermes, not Ammonius Saccas.

other according to cognate familiarity (a). Since then the body required place (for it were impracticable that Body be subsistent without place) and is changed by nature; it is impossible that there be change without time and the motion according to nature, nor that there be such a subsistence of body without Harmony. Because then of Body is the place; for receiving the changes of the body, it does not suffer the thing changed to be destroyed. But changed from other it falls apart to other, and is deprived of the condition (b) indeed, but not of the being Body; but being changed to other it has the condition of the other; for the body that was body continues Body, but the quality of disposition (c) does not continue; the Body then according to disposition is changed. Incorporeal then the place, the time, and the natural motion. But each of these possesses its peculiar property; but property of the Place is receptivity (d), of Time interval and number, of Nature motion, of Harmony friendship, of Body change; but property of Soul the Intelligence according to Essence.

XII.

Of Hermes from the things to Tat.
(*Stobæus, Physica*, 726; *Meineke*, i. 198).

Tat.—Rightly hast thou explained these things, O Father! but further teach me these. For thou saidest somewhere that the Science and the Art are the energy of the rational (e); but now thou sayest the irrational animals are and are called irrational through deprivation of the rational; it is plain there is necessity according to this the account, that the irrational animals do not partake of science (f), neither of art, through the being deprived of the rational.

(a) συγγενικὴν οἰκειότητα.   (b) ἕξεως.   (c) ποιὰ διάθεσις.
(d) παραδοχή.   (e) τοῦ λογικοῦ.   (f) ἐπιστήμης.

Asclepius.—For there is necessity, O Child!

Tat.—How then do we see, O Father! some of the irrational using science and art; such as the ants treasuring up the food for the winter, and the aerial animals also putting together nests for themselves, and the quadrupeds cognizant of their own folds?

Asclepius.—These things they do, O Child! neither by science nor by art, but by Nature. For the science and the art are things teachable (*a*), but of these irrationals none is taught anything. For things generate by nature are generate by a common (*b*) energy, but those by science and art belong to knowing ones, not to all; but what is generate in all is energized by Nature. Thus the Men look upwards, but not all men are musical, nor all archers, nor hunters, nor all the rest; but some of them have learnt something, science and art energizing. In the same way, if some of the ants had done this but some not, fairly thou hadst said, they do this very thing by science, and by art collect the food; but if all are led alike by the Nature to this even unwilling, it is plain that they do this neither by science nor by art. For Energies, O Tat! themselves being incorporeal, are in bodies and energize through the bodies. Wherefore, O Tat! in that they are (*c*) incorporeal (and thou sayest them to be immortal), and in that they cannot energize apart from bodies, I say that they are always in Body. For things generate for something or because of something, having fallen under (*d*) Providence or Necessity, it is impossible ever to remain inert of the proper energy. For the Entity always will be; for this is of it both body and life. To this reason follows there being also always the bodies. Wherefore also I say the very embodiment (*e*) to be eternal energy. For if bodies upon earth are dissoluble, but bodies there must be, and these places and organs of the Energies, and the Energies are immortal (but the immortal ever is); Energy, and the making of bodies therefore (*f*) ever is. But they follow upon

(*a*) διδακτικά. (*b*) καθολική. (*c*) καθότι.
(*d*) ὑποπεπτηκότα. (*e*) σώματωσιν. (*f*) εἴγε.

EXCERPTS FROM STOBÆUS.

the Soul, not simply generate along with it. But some of them energize along with the generating the Man, being together with (a) the Soul as to things irrational; but the purer energies according to change of the age energize along with the rational part of the Soul. But the Energies themselves are dependent (b) from the bodies. And from the Divine bodies, these the bodymaking come into things mortal; and each of them energizes either about the Body or the Soul. And they are congenerate (c) with the Soul itself apart from body. Always are there energies, but not always is the Soul in mortal body, for it is able to be apart from the body; but the Energies cannot be apart from the bodies. This is a sacred word, O Child! Body indeed cannot subsist apart from Soul, but the To Be (d) can.

Tat.—How sayst thou this, O Father!

Hermes.—Understand thus, O Son! The Soul having been separated from the body, the Body itself remains; but this the body during the time of the remaining (e) is energized, being dissolved, and becoming formless (f); but the body is not able to suffer these things apart from Energy. There remains then with the Body the energy itself of a separated Soul. This then is the difference of immortal body and of mortal, that the immortal indeed consisted of one matter, the other not, and the one makes, the other is passive (g); for everything that is energizing rules, but that energized is ruled, and the ruling indeed being ordinative (h) and free, leads, but the servile is led. The Energies then not only energize the Bodies with Souls, but the bodies without souls; woods, stones, and the others like, both increasing and making fruitful, and cooking, and corrupting, and liquefying, and putrefying, and breaking up, and energizing the like, such as bodies without Souls are capable to suffer. For Energy is called, O Child! that very same thing whatever ever is the thing generate; for ever

(a) ὁμοῦ.   (b) ἠρτημέναι.   (c) συγγίγνονται.
(d) τὸ εἶναι.   (e) τῆς ἐπιμονῆς.   (f) ἀειδὲς.
(g) πάσχει.   (h) ἐπιτακτικόν.

also must there be generate many things; but rather all things. For never ever fails (*a*) the World of some one of the Entities, but always borne onward it brings forth (*b*) in itself the Entities never ever abandoned, by the corruption of it (*c*). Let every energy then be thought of as always being immortal, which may be in any body whatsover. But of the Energies some are of the divine Bodies, but some of the corruptible, and some indeed are general, but some special (*d*), and some indeed of the kinds, and some of the parts of each one. Divine indeed then are those energizing in the eternal Bodies, and these are also perfect as in perfect bodies: but partial those, in one of each kind of the animals, but special somewhat those in each of the Entities. This the discourse then, O Child! concludes, that all things are full of Energies. For if it be necessity that the energies be in bodies, but many bodies in World, more I say are the Energies than the Bodies. For in one body often is one, and second, and third, apart from those general following thereon (*e*). For I call general Energies those really corporeal, generate through the senses and the motions; for apart from these the energies, it is not possible that the body subsist. But there are other special Energies in the souls of men, through Arts, Sciences, and studies and energizings. For the Senses follow along with the Energies, or rather the senses are effects (*f*) of the energies. Understand then, O Child! the difference of Energy and Sense; for Energy is sent from above; but the Sense being in the body, and from this having the Essence, having received the Energy makes it manifest, just as if having made it corporeal (*g*). Wherefore I say the Senses are both corporeal and mortal, subsisting so long as the body. For also the senses are generated with the body, and die with it; but the immortal Bodies themselves indeed have not immortal sense, as if consisting of such sort of

(*a*) χηρευέι.
(*b*) κυίσκει.
(*c*) ἀπολειφθησόμενα αὐτοῦ τῆς φθορᾶς. The passage is corrupt.
(*d*) εἰδικαί.
(*e*) τῶν παρεπομένων καθολικῶν.
(*f*) ἀποτελέσματα.
(*g*) σωματοποιήσασα.

essence; for the sense is wholly of nought else than of the evil or of the good accruing to (*a*) the body, or of that again quitting it; but in the eternal Bodies there is neither accruer nor departure; wherefore sense in these is not generated.

Tat.—In every body then is sense sensational (*b*)?

Asclepius.—In every, O Child! and energies energize in all.

Tat.—Also in the soulless, O Father?

Asclepius.—Also in the soulless, O Child! But there are differences of the senses; for those of the rational are generate with Reason, but those of the irrational are corporeal only, and those of the soulless are senses indeed, but generated passive according to increase only and according to diminution. But the passion and Sense are dependent from one head (*c*), but are brought together (*d*) into the same, and by the energies. But of the animals with souls there are two other energies, which follow upon the senses and the passions: Grief and Joy; and apart from these it is impossible for an animal with soul, and especially a rational, to have sense. Wherefore also I say that these are ideas of the passions, ideas ruling rather over the rational animals. The Energies then indeed energize, but the Senses make manifest the energies. But these being corporeal are moved by the irrational parts of the Soul, wherefore also I say that both are evil imbued (*e*); for both the rejoicing, occasioning the sensation with pleasure, forthwith happens to be cause of many evils to him having experienced it (*f*), and the grief occasions stronger sorrows and pains; wherefore both as it seems would be evil imbued.

Tat.—Would the sense of body and of soul be the same, O Father?

Asclepius.—How understandest thou, O Youth! Sense of Soul?

Tat.—Is not indeed Soul incorporeal? but the sense may be body, O Father! the sense which happens being in body.

(*a*) προσγενομένου.   (*b*) αἰσθάνεται.   (*c*) κορυφῆς ἤρτηνται.
(*d*) συνάγονται.   (*e*) κακωτικὰς.   (*f*) τῷ παθόντι.

Asclepius.—If we place it in body, O Child! we declare it like the soul or the energies. For these being incorporeal we say are in bodies. But the Sense is neither energy nor Soul nor anything other of body beside the aforesaid; it would not then be incorporeal; but if it is not incorporeal, it would be body; for of the Entities must some be bodies, but some incorporeal.

XIII.

OF HERMES FROM THOSE TO AMMON.
(*Stobæus, Physica*, 741; *Meineke*, i. 203; *Patrit.*, p. 40).

THAT moved then is moved according to the energy of the motion, that moving the Universe. For the Nature of the Universe affords motion to the Universe, one indeed that according to its power, but other that according to energy. And this indeed permeates (*a*) through the entire World, and holds it together within, but that pertains to (*b*) and encompasses it without, and they proceed (*c*) through all things in common. And the Nature of all things producing things generate affords produce (*d*) to those produced, sowing indeed the seeds of itself and having generations through moveable matter. But the Matter being moved is warmed, and becomes fire and water, the one potent and strong, but the other passive. But the fire opposing the water, dried up somewhat of the water (*e*), and the earth was generated sustained (*f*) upon the water.[1] But being dried up around vapour (*g*) was generated from the three,[2] the water, the earth, and the fire, and air was generated. These things came together (*h*) according to the reason of the Harmony, hot with cold, dry with moist, and from the concurrence (*i*) was generated Spirit and seed, analogous

(*a*) διήκει. (*b*) παρήκει. (*c*) πεφοιτήκασι.
(*d*) φυήν. (*e*) ἐξήρανε τοῦ ὕδατος. (*f*) ὀχουμένη.
(*g*) ἀτμός. (*h*) συνῆλθε. (*i*) συμπνοίας.

[1] See Poemandres, ch. i. 5, 11, and ch. iii. 2.   [2] See Gen. ii. 6.

to the encompassing Spirit. This falling into the matrix is not quiescent (*a*) in the seed; and not being quiescent changes the seed, and being changed it possesses increase and magnitude. But upon the magnitude an image of figure is impressed (*b*) and it is figured; and the form is carried (*c*) upon the figure, through which that made into image is made into image (*d*). Since however the Spirit had not in the womb the vital motion but the fermenting (*e*), Harmony harmonized this also, being receptacle of the intellectual life. But this is simple and unchangeable, by no means ever desisting from this immutability. But that in the womb is brought forth (*f*) in numbers and delivered, and breaks (*g*) into the outer air, and being very near the Soul is associated with it, not according to the congenerate association (*h*), but according to that fated; for there is no love in it to be together with body. Through this according to Fate, it affords to that generated intellectual motion, and the intelligent Essence of its life; for it creeps into it along with the spirit, and moves it vitally.

XIV.

OF HERMES FROM THOSE TO AMMON TO TAT.
(Stobæus, Physica, 745; Meineke, i. 204).

AND the Lord indeed and Creator of all the eternal Bodies, O Tat! having once made hath not made any further, nor does make. For having delivered up these things to themselves and united them to each other He let them go to be borne (*i*) on, wanting in nothing as eternal. If they want anything, they will want of one another, but of no kind of importation (*k*) of that from

(*a*) ἠρεμεῖ. (*b*) ἐπισπᾶται. (*c*) ὀχεῖται τὸ εἶδος.
(*d*) εἰδωλοποιεῖται. (*e*) βραστικήν. (*f*) λοχεύει.
(*g*) ἄγει. (*h*) συγγενικὴν οἰκειότητα. (*i*) ἀφῆκε φέρεσθαι.
(*k*) ἐπιφορᾶς.

without, as being immortal. For it behoved that the Bodies generated by Him to have such sort also the Nature. But He our Creator being in body hath made us and makes, and ever will make bodies dissoluble and mortal. For it was not lawful for Him to imitate the Creator of Himself, besides it also being impossible. For He indeed made out of the first Essence being incorporeal; but He out of that embodiment (*a*) made us. Justly then according to the right reason, these the bodies indeed, as having been generated from an incorporeal Essence, are immortal; but ours are dissoluble and mortal (the material of us being composed out of bodies), because of being weak and requiring much succour. For how ever even haply had the connection of our bodies kept up, if it had not some nourishment superinduced thereon from the like elements, and refreshing us (*b*) each day by day? For both of earth and of water and of fire and of air there is an influx generated upon us, which renovating our bodies keeps together the tabernacle. So also for the motions we are rather weak, bearing motions not even one day. For be well assured, O Child! that unless in the nights the bodies of us reposed, we should not bear up for one day. Whence the Creator being good having foreprovided (*c*) all things made the Sleep for the preservation of the Animal, the greatest soother of the fatigue of the motion, and ordained an equality to each time, or rather a longer for the repose. But understand, O Child! the very great energy of the sleep, opposite to that of the Soul, but not less than that. For as the Soul is energy of motion, the same way the bodies also cannot live apart from the sleep; for it is relaxation and liberation of the compacted members, and it energizes within, making into body the superinduced (*d*) matter, distributing to each that congenial (*e*) to it; the water indeed to the blood, but the earth to the bones and marrows, the air to the nerves and veins, but the fire to the vision. Where-

(*a*) γείναμένης σωματώσεως.   (*b*) ὑπεσωμάτου.   (*c*) προυπιστάμενος.
(*d*) ἐπεισελθοῦσαν.   (*e*) τὸ οἰκεῖον.

fore also the body is supremely delighted with the sleep, energizing this the pleasure.

XV.

OF HERMES (*Stobæus, Physica*, 750; *Meineke*, i. 206; *Patrit.*, 516).

THERE is then that pre-existent (*a*) beside all the Entities and those really Entities (*b*). For there is that pre-existent through which is the Essentiality (*c*), that predicated of the entire Whole (*d*): common with the intelligibles of things really Entities and of the Entities as considered by themselves (*e*). But the contraries to these, in another way again, themselves are by themselves. But Nature is sensible Essence, having in itself all sensible things. But in the midst of these are intellectual (*f*) and sensible Gods. The things intellectual are those having part with the intelligible (*g*) [Gods], but things of opinion (*h*) those having communion with the sensible Gods. But these are (*i*) images of intelligences; like as Sun is image of The Creator God in Heaven. For as He created the Whole (*k*), so the Sun creates the animals and generates plants and presides over the winds.[1]

The next extract in Stobæus (754) is entitled "Hermes from the Aphrodite" (*Meineke*, i. 207); but the very title and the contents prove that he was not the author of it.

(*a*) τὸ πρὸ ὄν.   (*b*) ὄντως ὄντων.   (*c*) οὐσιότης.
(*d*) ἡ καθόλου.   (*e*) καθ᾽ ἑαυτὰ νοουμένων.   (*f*) νοηματικοί.
(*g*) νοητῶν.   (*h*) τὰ δυξαστά.   (*i*) εἰκόνες νοημάτων.
(*k*) τὸ ὅλον.

[1] This Excerpt is obscure and probably imperfect. It is not mentioned in the editions of Stobæus from what work of Hermes it is extracted.

XVI.

OF HERMES (*Stobæus, Physica*, 800;[1] *Meincke*, i. 227; *Patrit.*, 41 and 40b).

SOUL then is an eternal intelligent Essence having understanding after its own mode.

Ibid.—The Soul then is incorporeal Essence; for if it has body it will be no longer conservative of itself. For every body has need of the To Be (*a*) and has need also of life, that situate in order. For universally upon that having generation change also must follow. For the generate is generate in magnitude, for generate has increase; but universally upon that increased follows after diminution; upon diminution corruption. Having received the form of life it lives and has community of the To Be with the Soul. But the cause of the To Be to another itself first is Being (*b*). But the To Be now I call generation in Reason (*c*) and partaking of intelligent life (*d*); but the Soul affords intelligent life. But it is named Animal indeed because of the life, but rational because of the intelligent, mortal because of the body. Soul therefore is incorporeal, having the power without degeneration. For how is it fitting (*e*) to speak of the intelligent animal, there not being Essence of that also affording life? Neither is it fitting to say Rational, there not being the thoughtful (*f*) Essence, that affording also intelligent life. But in all the intelligence does not follow on (*g*) because of the constitution of the body as regards (*h*) the Harmony. For if in the constitution the warm is superabundant it becomes light and ardent, but if the cold, it becomes heavy and slow; for nature adapts (*i*) the constitution of the

(*a*) δεῖται τοῦ εἶναι.   (*b*) αὕτη πρώτη ὄν ἐστι.   (*c*) τὸ ἐν λόγῳ.
(*d*) ζωῆς νοερᾶς.   (*e*) οἷόν τε.   (*f*) διανοητικῆς.
(*g*) ἀφικνεῖται.   (*h*) πρός.   (*i*) ἁρμόζει.

[1] In this and the three following Excerpts, Stobæus does not state from what works of Hermes they are extracted.

body to the Harmony. But of the Harmony there are three forms, that according to the warm, and that according to the cold, and that according to the mean. But it adapts according to the prevailing Star (a) of the combination (b) of the Stars. But Soul having received it as is fated, to that affords life by the operation of the Nature. The Nature then assimilates the Harmony of the Body to the combination of the Stars, and unites the commixture (c) to the Harmony of the Constellations, so as to have sympathy towards each other. For the end of the Harmony of the Stars is the engendering sympathy according to their Fate.

XVII.

OF THE SAME (*Stobæus, Physica*, 803; *Meineke*, i. 228; *Patrit.*, 41).

THE Soul then, O Ammon! is Essence having finality in itself (d), in origin having received life, that according to Fate, and has drawn to itself Reason like to the Matter, having Vehemence (e) and Desire. And the Vehemence indeed exists as Matter; this if it shall habituate itself (f) to the intelligence of the Soul becomes Courage, and is not led away by cowardice. But the Desire is accordingly. It, if it shall habituate itself to the rationality (g) of the Soul, becomes Modesty, and is not moved by pleasure. For the rationality completes that deficient in the Desire. But when both shall mentally agree and shall practise an equal habitude (h), and both be holden (i) by the rationality of the Soul, Justice is generated. For the equal habitude of these takes away the excess of the Vehemence, and equalizes that defective in the Desire. Origin of these

(a) ἀστέρα.   (b) συγκράσεως.   (c) τὰ πολυμιγῆ.
(d) αὐτοτελής.   (e) θυμός.   (f) ἕξιν ποιήσῃ.
(g) λογισμόν.   (h) ἴσην ἕξιν.   (i) ἔχηται.

is the thinking (a) Essence, being itself according to the same in its own comprehending (b) Reason, having power over its own Reason. But the Essence leads and governs as ruler; but the Reason of it as the comprehending counsellor. The Reason then of the Essence is knowledge of the ratiocinations, those affording a resemblance of rationality to the irrational; obscure indeed as regards rationality, but rationality as regards the irrational, just as Echo is to Sound, and the shine of the Moon to the Sun. Vehemence and Desire are arranged after a certain ratio (c) and attract one another, and establish in themselves reciprocal mental action (d).

XVIII.

OF THE SAME (*Stobæus, Physica*, 806; *Meineke*, i. 229; *Patrit.*, p. 41. *It is not said from what work of Hermes this is taken*).

EVERY Soul is immortal and ever moveable. For we have said in the generalities (e) that motions, some indeed are from the Energies and some from the Bodies. We said too that the Soul was generated from a certain Essence, not of matter, being a thing incorporeal, and being itself of a thing incorporeal. For every generate thing of necessity must be generated from somewhat. Upon the generation of as many then as corruption follows, upon these of necessity two motions follow: that of the Soul by which it is moved and that of the Body by which it is increased, decays and moreover also being decomposed is decomposed (f). This I define is the motion of corruptible bodies. But the Soul is ever moveable, because it always itself is moved and energizes motion in others. According to this reason then, every Soul is immortal and ever move-

(a) διανοητική.
(b) περινοητικῷ.
(c) λογισμόν.
(d) κυκλικὴν διάνοιαν.
(e) γενικοῖς.
(f) ἀναλυθέντος ἀναλύεται.

able, having motion, the energy of self. Ideas of Souls are Divine, human, irrational. The Divine then indeed is of the Divine body in which is the Energy of Self, for indeed it is moved in Self, and moves itself, for when it hath departed from mortal animals, having been separated from the irrational parts of itself, going forth into the Divine body as ever moveable, in itself it is moved, carried round along with (*a*) the Universe. But the human has indeed also somewhat of the Divine, but with it are also conjoined (*b*) the irrationals, both the Desire and the Vehemence (*c*); and these indeed are immortal, because they also happen to be Energies, but the Energies of mortal bodies. Wherefore indeed from the Divine part of the Soul being in the Divine body, they happen to be afar off; but when this has entered into a mortal body, these also walk in (*d*), and by the presence of them is generated ever Human Soul. But that of the irrationals is constituted of Vehemence also Desire. Wherefore also these the animals were called irrational, through deprivation of the Reason of the Soul. But Fourth (Idea) understand that of the inanimate, which being without the bodies, energizes moving them. But this would be moved in the Divine Body, and as it were in (*e*) passing moving them.

XIX.

OF THE SAME (*Ibid. ibid.*, 809; *Meineke*, i. 230).

SOUL is then eternal intelligent Essence, having as intellect (*f*) its own Reason. But thinking with it it acquires (*g*) thought of the Harmony. But separated from the physical body it abides self according to self; it being of itself in the intelligible World (*h*). But it rules over its own Reason

(*a*) συμπεριφερομένη. (*b*) συνῆπται. (*c*) ἥ ἐποθυμία καὶ ὁ θυμός.
(*d*) ἐπιφοιτᾶ. (*e*) κατὰ πάροδον. (*f*) νόημα.
(*g*) συννοοῦσα δὲ ἐπισπᾶται. (*h*) νοητῷ κόσμῳ.

bringing like motion, by name Life, through its own intelligence (a) to him that comes into life. For this is proper to Soul, the affording to others like to its own property. There are thus two lives and two motions; one indeed that according to Essence, but the other that according to nature of Body. And the one indeed more general, the other more partial. But that according to Essence is self determinate (b), but the other of Necessity; for everything moved is subordinated to the Necessity of the mover. But the moving motion is associated (c) with the love of the intelligent Essence. For the Soul would be incorporeal Essence, nonpartaker of the physical body; for if it has body it has neither Reason nor Understanding. For every body is unintelligent (d); but having received of Essence, it came (e) to be a breathing animal—and the Spirit [or breath] (f) indeed is of the body, but the Reason is contemplative of the beauty of the Essence. But the sentient Spirit is judicial (g) of the things appearing. It hath been divided into the organic senses, and some portion of it is spiritual vision, and Spirit hearing and smelling and tasting and touching. This the Spirit educated (h) by thought judges the Sensible; but if not it fancies only, for it is of Body and receptive of all things. But the Reason of the Essence is the being wise (i). But there co-exists with the Reason the Knowledge of things honourable, but with the Spirit the Opinion (k). For this indeed has the energy from the circumambient World, the other from Itself.

[*Stobæus, Physica*, 928, makes a long Extract purporting to be from "Hermes Trismegistus," from the Sacred Book that called "Virgin of World" (*Patrit.*, p. 276; *Meineke*, i. 281), but it is alien from the genuine writings of our Hermes, being a dialogue between Isis and Horus, and

(a) νοήματι.   (b) αὐτεξούσιος.   (c) ᾠκείωται.
(d) ἀνόητον.   (e) ἔσχε.   (f) πνεῦμα.   (g) κριτικόν.
(h) ἀναγόμενον.   (i) τὸ φρονοῦν.   (k) ἡ δόξα.

with Ζεὺς, Κρόνος, and ῝Ηλιος—Greek and Egyptian Deities —to whom no allusion is made in the other writings of our author, which are also manifestly inconsistent with any belief in the existence of such beings.]

XX.

Of Hermes (*Stobæus, Ethica, Lib. ii., 358; Meineke, Vol. ii., p. 100. It is not stated from what work of Hermes this is taken*).

There is then Essence and Reason and Understanding and Thought. Both Opinion and Sense are referred to (*a*) the Thought, but the Reason goes to the Essence, but the Understanding goes by itself. But the Understanding is interwoven (*b*) with the Thought; but permeating one another (*c*) they become one Form [or Idea], and that is that of the Soul. But Opinion and Sense are referred to the Thought of the same; but these do not remain at the same; whence they both exceed and fall short and differ with Itself (*d*). Worse indeed it becomes when drawn away from the Thought; but when it accompanies and is obedient, it holds communion with the intellectual Reason through the Sciences. But we have the choosing. For the choosing the superior is with us, and likewise the worse at our will.[1] For choice being made of the evils brings us near to the corporeal nature; through this Fate tyrannizes over the chooser (*e*). When then the corporeal Essence in us, the intellectual Reason, is self-determinate (*f*), and this [Essence] holds on always according to this and in such wise, through this Fate

(*a*) φέρεται.
(*b*) ἐπιπλέκεται.
(*c*) ἐλθόντα δὲ ἀλλήλων.
(*d*) ἑαυτῷ (i.e., νοήματι).
(*e*) δυναστεύει τῷ ἑλομένῳ.
(*f*) αὐτεξούσιος.

[1] See Poemandres, *ante*, ch. iv. 6.

does not touch this man,[1] but having taken for aid (a) the first from the First God, it passes beyond thoughtful Reason (b) and the entire Reason which Nature hath ordained for those generate. With these Soul having had communion has communion with the Fates of these, being not partaker of the nature of the fated.

XXI.

[IT is questionable whether the following Excerpt, or any and what part of it, has Hermes for its author. The larger portion of it is not in Patricius nor in the earlier editions of Stobæus. There is no allusion to the "Decans" or "Tanæ" in his other works, and it has the air of a supplement composed by some subsequent writer, possibly an Alexandrian Jew. Although the words of Hermes are cited, and some passages of Poemandres referred to, yet the style is different, and there are therein many words not found in his genuine writings, as well as variant dicta, such as that the Stars generate demons to be their servants. The astronomical portion is very curious, and is not inconsistent with the theory propounded by Hermes. The account of the celestial Demons or Angels seems to be a compound of Jewish traditions combined with classical notions on the subject. The last part of the dialogue is more like the theology of Hermes, except that the author speaks of the potency of the Name of God, whereas he had frequently maintained that God had no name].

(a) παραθεῖσα.   (b) διανοητικὸν λόγον προΐησι.

[1] See Lactantius (Divin. Instit., lib. ii. ch. 16, *post*), where this passage is quoted.

Plato in Menon (99): "Opinions, although true, last but a short time, and are worth little; but when one finds them through reasoning to be causes, they become sciences and are permanent." In Politicus (309): "The true opinion about things beautiful and just and good and the contrary to these, with firmness, when it is generated in Souls, is the generating Divine Nature in a Godlike (δαιμονίῳ) race."

OF HERMES FROM THAT TO TAT.
(*Stobæus, Physica,* 469; *Meineke,* i. 129).

Asclepius.—Since in the former general discourse thou promisedst[1] to inform me concerning the thirty-six Decans, now inform me concerning them and the energy of these.

Hermes.—There is no grudging, O Tat! and this should be the most principal and most elevated discourse of all; but do you understand accordingly. We spake to thee concerning the Zodiacal Circle, and of that also bearer of animals (*a*), and of the five planets and Sun and Moon, and of the circle of each of these.

Asclepius.—For Thou spakedst thus, O Trismegistus!

Hermes.—Thus I wish thee having remembered those, to understand also concerning the thirty-six Decans, that the discourse also concerning these may be well known to thee.

Asclepius.—I remember, O Father!

Hermes.—We affirmed somewhere, O Child! Body to be comprehensive (*b*) of all these things; apprehend then also mentally of it, as a circularly formed figure; for thus also exists the Universe.

Asclepius.—Such sort of figure I understand thus as thou sayest, O Father!

Hermes.—Under the circle then of this the Body have been ordered the thirty-six Decans middle between the circle of the Universe and of the Zodiac, setting bounds between (*c*) both the circles, and as it were easing (*d*) that

(*a*) ζωοφόρου.   (*b*) περιεκτικόν.   (*c*) διορίζοντας.   (*d*) κουφίζοντας.

[1] No such promise is to be found in any of the genuine works of Hermes which have as yet come to light, but the following is found in the "Asclepius," ch. viii.: "The Ousiarque of Heaven or of all that is comprised under that name is Zeus, for it is by Heaven that Zeus gives life to all things. The Ousiarque of the Sun is the light, for it is from the disk of the Sun that we receive the benefit of the light. The thirty-six Horoscopes of the fixed constellations have for Ousiarque or Prince him whom they name Pantomorphos or Omniform, because he gives divers forms to divers species."

the Zodiac and defining it, carried along with the planets both to equalize its power with the progression (*a*) of the Universe in contrariwise to the Seven; and to hold back (*b*) the comprehending body; for it[1] would have been last in the course, it by itself in the effect (*c*). But to accelerate the Seven other circles because of their being moved with a slower motion than the circle of the Universe.[2] For necessity is there that they should be moved as that of the Universe.

Let us understand then of them that they are stationed around (*d*) the Seven and the circle of the Universe, or rather of all things that are in the World, as if it were guardians; keeping together all things, and maintaining the good order of all of them.

Asclepius.—For so I understand, O Father! from what thou sayest.

Hermes.—But understand further, O Tat! that they are also unaffected (*e*) by those things which the other stars suffer. For neither kept back in their course do they stop, nor hindered do they retreat, nor are they enveloped with the light of the Sun which the other stars experience, but being free up above all things as watchful guardians and overseers of the Universe they encompass the Universe in the day and night.

Asclepius.—Whether then also do these, O Father! possess energy as to us?

Hermes.—The very greatest, O Child! For if they energize upon those, how not also upon us, both as to each one and in common. . . . Thus, O Child! of all the things happening universally (*f*), in the energy is from these; such as (understand what I say) revolutions of kingdoms,

(*a*) ἰσοδυναμεῖν τῇ φορᾷ.   (*b*) ἐπέχειν.   (*c*) ἐν τῷ πάσχειν.
(*d*) περιίστασθαι.   (*e*) ἀπαθεῖς.   (*f*) καθολικῶς.

[1] *i.e.*, The Zodiac.
[2] See as to this Poemandres, ch. ii. 6. As explained there and elsewhere, Plato as well as Hermes believed the Κόσμος to be in the Form of a Sphere, and that the outer Periphery controlled the motions of the planetary circles.

rebellions of cities, famines, pestilences, tides of the ocean, earthquakes. None of these things, O Child! happens apart from the energy of those. But further in addition to these things understand: for if they preside (*a*) over them and we are also under the Seven, understandest thou not that a certain energy of them attains (*b*) even to us as their sons or by their means?[1]

Asclepius.—What may be the form of the body to them, O Father?

Hermes.—These then the Many call Demons; but that of the demons is not any peculiar race, nor having different bodies out of some peculiar matter, not being moved by Soul as we are; but they are energies of these thirty-six Gods. Further, in addition to these things understand, O Tat! the energizing (*c*) of these, that also they sow upon the Earth what they call Tanæ, some indeed salutary but others destructive. Moreover also Stars borne onward in heaven they generate for themselves subministers (*d*), and have servants and soldiers. But these, mingled with them, are borne onward, raised aloft in the ether, filling up the space of that, so that there should be no space on high void of stars;[2] arranging together (*e*) the Universe having a proper Energy subordinate as to the Energy of the thirty-six. From whom also about the countries destructions are generated of the other living animals, and the multitude of the live creatures devastating the fruits. But above these is that called Bear (*f*) in the midst of the Zodiac, composed of seven Stars, having another in opposition (*g*) overhead. The Energy of this indeed is as if an axle, by no means indeed either setting or rising, but remaining in

(*a*) ἐπιστατοῦσιν.   (*b*) φθάνειν.   (*c*) ἐνέργημα.
(*d*) ὑπολειτουργούς.   (*e*) συγκοσμοῦντες.   (*f*) Ἄρκτος.
(*g*) ἀντίζυγον.

[1] See as to the power and influence of the Stars and their Angels, Poemandres, iii. 3, and notes there.

[2] This will be in anticipation of the modern theories, that the fixed Stars are Suns with attendant satellites or luminaries, that the shape of the heavens is spherical, and that celestial space is replete with stellar matter.

the same place and turned about itself but energizing the revolution of the Zodiacal circle (*a*), delivering over this the Universe from the night indeed to day, and from the day to night. But after this there is another Chorus of Stars which we have not thought worthy of appellations, but those hereafter having imitated us, will themselves too apply to these appellations. But below the Moon are other stars perishable, while subsisting for little time, exhaled from the earth itself, into the air above earth; which also we see dissolved, having the nature like to the useless of the animals upon earth, and are generate for nothing else than that only they perish; such as the race of the flies, the fleas, the worms, and the others the like. For verily these, O Tat! are neither useful to us nor to the world: on the contrary are hurtful, being troublesome, being appendices(*b*) of the Nature, and having the generation by way of the superfluous (*c*); the same way also the stars exhaled from the Earth do not indeed assume the place above, for they are unable as issuing from beneath. But having the weight great, drawn downwards by their own matter, they are quickly dissipated, and being dissolved fall again to earth, having energized nothing except only having disturbed the air above Earth. But there is another kind, O Tat! that of those called comets, appearing occasionally(*d*), and again after a short time becoming invisible, neither rising nor setting nor being dissolved; which become conspicuous messengers and heralds of universal events about to be in future; but these have their place beneath the circle of the Sun. When then anything is about to happen in the world, these appear; but having appeared a few days again having gone under the circle of the Sun, they remain invisible, having appeared in the West, others in the North, others again in the East (*e*), and others in the South. But we denominated them Prophets. This is the nature of Stars. But (*f*) Stars have difference with Constellations (*g*); for Stars are those suspended aloft in the

(*a*) ζωοφόρου.   (*b*) παρακολουθήματα.   (*c*) κατὰ τὸ περισσὸν.
(*d*) κατὰ καιρὸν.   (*e*) τῷ λιβί.   (*f*) ἀστέρες.   (*g*) ἄστρων.

heaven, but Constellations are those enclosed (a) in the body of the Heaven, and carried along with the Heaven, of which we have mentioned the twelve of the Zodiac. He who is not ignorant of these things is able accurately to understand The God, and if one ought to speak also with boldness, becoming eyewitness also to behold Him (b), and having beheld to become blessed.

Asclepius.—Blessed how truly, O Father! he having beheld Him!

Hermes.—But it is impossible, O Child! that one in body should have this happiness. But it behoves each first to exercise the Soul of his here, in order that becoming there where it is permitted to behold, it may not have mistaken the way. But so many men as are body lovers, these can never ever behold the Vision of The Beautiful and Good. For what sort of beauty, O Child! is that which has neither figure nor colour nor body?

Asclepius.—Could there be anything, O Father, apart from these beautiful?

Hermes.—The God alone, O Child! but rather that being something greater, The Name of The God.

(a) ἐγκείμενα.   (b) αὐτόπτην θεάσασθαι.

END OF PART II.

HERMES TRISMEGISTUS.

PART III.

NOTICES OF HERMES IN THE FATHERS.

I.

JUSTIN MARTYR (born circa A.D. 100; martyr. A.D. 165).
"Παραινετικὸς πρὸς ῾Ελληνας," "Paraenetica ad Graecos" Opera Edit. Colon. 1636, p. 37, *ad fin.*

"BUT if any one should think it worth (*a*) while to have learnt from the most ancient philosophers named among them, as to the discourse concerning The God, let him hear both Acmon[1] and Hermes; Acmon indeed in his discourses concerning Him calling Him 'The altogether hidden God,' and Hermes wisely and openly saying, 'To understand The God indeed is difficult, but to express [or declare] Him impossible.' To whom then it is possible to understand it is altogether therefore becoming to know."[2]

(*a*) οἴοιτο.

[1] This Acmon was probably the Greek philosopher who lived just previously to the Emperor Hadrian (A.D. 76-138), and was master of Plutarch, and taught at Delphi in the 12th year of Nero's reign (A.D. 66). He professed Syncretism, and endeavoured to reconcile Aristotle with Platonism (Plutarch, "De adulatoribus," Fabricius Bibliotheca Graeca, v. 153). He has been confounded wrongfully with Ammonius Saccas, the master of Plotinus and the reputed founder of Neoplatonism, who died at Alexandria A.D. 241. A reference, however, may be intended to the Egyptian Ammon.

[2] See "Poemandres," ch. v., sec. 10, and more particularly the

Ibid., *Apologia*, i., secs. 21, 22.

"When we say that The Word, Who is the First begotten of God, was born, &c., we introduce nothing different from what you say of those whom you call sons of Jupiter. For you are aware how many sons the writers of repute among you assign to him. Hermes the interpreting Word and teacher of all." "If we affirm that The Word Who is of God was begotten of God even in a peculiar manner, and beyond the ordinary generation as I have already said, let this be common to you who affirm Hermes to be the Messenger Word from God."—*Translated Library of the Fathers*, Oxford, 1861.

Ibid., *Apologia*, ii., sec. 6.

"But proper name for The Father of all things Who is unbegotten there is none. For who ever is called by a name, has the person older than himself who gives him the name. But these terms 'Father,' 'God,' and 'Creator,' and 'Lord' and 'Master,' are not names, but terms of address derived from His benefits and His works."[1]—*Translated Library of the Fathers*, Oxford, 1861.

II.

TERTULLIAN (born, according to Tillemont, A.D. 136; according to others 160; died very old, A.D. 216-1). *Contra Valentinianos*, ch. xv.

"Now the Pythagoreans may learn, the Stoics may know, Plato himself, whence Matter, which they will have to be unborn, derived both its origin and substance for all this pile of the World, which not even the renowned Mer-

extract from "The things to Tat," Stobæus, Florilegium, 78; Meineke, iii. 134. Quoted also by Lactantius. See *post*.

[1] Quoted also by Lactantius (Divin. Instit., i., vi.). See a nearly identical passage in Poemandres, ch. v. sec. 10.

curius Trismegistus, Master of all physical philosophy thought out."

[The Author of the "Poemandres," however, distinctly states several times that "το παν" was created by The One God].

Ibid., De Anima, ch. xxxiii.

"Even if Souls have permanency enough to remain unchanged until the judgment, a point which Hermes Egyptius recognised when he said that the Soul after its separation from the body was not dissipated back into the Soul of the Universe, but retained permanently its distinct individuality. 'In order that it might render,' to use his own words, 'an account to The Father of those things which it has done in the body.'"

III.

CYPRIAN (born circa A.D. 200; martyred A.D. 258). Baluze Edit. Paris, 1726. *De Idolorum Vanitate*, p. 220.

"HERMES TRISMEGISTUS unum Deum loquitur eumque incomprehensibilem atque inestimabilem confitetur." "Hermes Trismegistus speaks of One God, and confesses Him to be incomprehensible and inestimable."

IV.

EUSEBIUS PAMPHILI (born circa 264), *Hist. Lib.*, v. ch. 8, has a clear quotation from the "Poemandres" of Hermes (whom, however, he probably confounds with the Shepherd Hermas)—" οὐ μονον δε ᾔδεν, ἀλλὰ καὶ ἀποδέχεται (ὁ Εἰρηναῖος) την τοῦ Ποιμένος γραφὴν λέγων, Καλῶς οὖν εἶπεν ἡ γραφὴ ἡ λέγουσα Πρῶτον πάντων πίστευσον ὅτι εἷς ἐστιν ὁ Θεὸς, ὁ τὰ πάντα κτίσας καὶ καταρτίσας, καὶ τὰ ἐξῆς."

"Irenæus not only knew but approves the writing of the Shepherd, saying, 'Well then spake the Scripture saying first of all things believe that The God is One, He having created and arranged the Universe, and the rest.'"

V.

CLEMENS ALEXANDRINUS (born circa 150), (*Stromata*, Lib. i., ch. 21, Lib. vi., ch. 4, p. 379. Oxford Edition). He mentions Hermes of Thebes and Esculapius of Memphis, "e vate Deus." *Ibid.*, Lib. vi., ch. iv., p. 737.

CLEMENS gives a long description of the various works attributed to this Egyptian Hermes, Forty-two in number. Four of Astrology, others of Astronomy, Geology, and Hieroglyphics, and thirty-six containing all Egyptian philosophy at great length, including Hymns to God, religious ceremonies, and sacerdotal discipline. As no particular reference is there made to any of the treatises in this volume, it is unnecessary to go into further details concerning those mentioned by Clemens.

VI.

FIRMIANUS LACTANTIUS (died A.D. 325). Edition of Le Brun and Dufresnoy, Paris, 1747. *Divine Institutes*, i. ch. vi.

AFTER recounting shortly the history of the legendary Hermes (whom he uncritically confounds with our Author), he subsequently quotes our Hermes, and proceeds thus:—

"Hermes" (or the fifth Mercury), "although he was a man, yet he was of great antiquity, and most fully imbued with every kind of learning, so that the knowledge of many subjects and arts acquired for him the name of Trismegistus. He wrote books, and those in great numbers, relating to the knowledge of divine things, in which he asserts the Majesty of The Supreme and Only God, and makes mention of Him by the same names which we use, 'God and Father.' And that no one might inquire His name, he said that He was without name, and that on account of His very Unity He does not require the peculiarity of a name. These are his own words:[1] The 'God is One, but He who is only One does not need a name; for He Who is Self Existent is without a name.'"

Ibid. i. ch. 11.

"Therefore it appears that Saturn was not born from heaven, which is impossible, but from that man who bore the name of Uranus. And Trismegistus asserts the truth of this; for when he said that very few existed in whom there was perfect learning, he mentioned by name among these his forefathers Uranus, Saturn, and Mercury."[2]

Ibid. ii. ch. 9.

"For that the world was made by Divine Providence, not to mention Trismegistus, who proclaims this."

Ibid. and Epitome, ch. 4, *ad fin.*

"His (God's) works are seen by the eyes, but how He made them is not even seen by the Mind; because, as Hermes says, Mortal cannot draw nigh to (that is approach nearer and follow up with the understanding) the immortal; the temporal to the eternal, the corruptible to the incorruptible." "And on this account the earthly animal is as yet incapable of perceiving heavenly things, because it is shut in and held as it were in custody by the body."[3]

---

[1] *Vide* Poemandres, ch. v. 10; Parthey's Edit., p. 47, and note there; ch. xi. 7-12, *ibid.* 92. Asclepius I. It may be here observed that when Lactantius quotes the genine Hermes, he always transcribes the original Greek.

[2] Poemandres, ch. x.; Parthey's Edit., 70.

[3] Hermes, from "The things to Tat," extracted by Stobæus, Florilegium, ch. 80; Meineke, iii. 104.

Ibid., Divin. Instit., ii. ch. 11.

"But the making of the true and living Man from clay is the work of God. And this also is related by Hermes, who not only says that Man was made by God after the image of God, but he even tried to explain in how skilful a manner he formed each limb in the human body, since there is none of them which is not available for the necessity of use as well as for beauty."[1]

Ibid. ch. 13.

"Empedocles and Lucretius and Varro among the Romans determined that there were four Elements, that is Fire, Air, Water, and Earth, perhaps following Trismegistus, who said that 'our bodies were composed of these four Elements by God, for' (he said) 'they contained in themselves something of fire, something of air, something of water, and something of earth; and yet that they were neither fire, nor air, nor water, nor earth.'"[2]

Ibid. ch. 15.

"Thus there came to be two kinds of demons, one of heaven the other of earth. The latter are the wicked Spirits, the authors of all the evils which are done, and the same Devil is their prince, whence Trismegistus calls him the ruler (*a*) of the demons."[3]

Ibid. ch. xvi.

"In short, Hermes affirms that those who have known God are not only safe from the attacks of demons, but that they are not even bound by Fate. 'The only pro-

(*a*) Δαιμονιάρχον.

[1] Poemandres, ch. i. *passim*, ch. v.; Parthey, 44, ch. xiii.; *ibid.* 116.
[2] Poemandres, ch. ii. 11, and note there. See also the extract from Hermes, "Of the things to Ammon to Tat," Stobæus, Physica; Meineke, Edit. i. 204, and more expressly the extract in the Florilegium, xi.; Meineke, i. 248.
[3] See Poemandres, ch. ix. 3.

tection,' he says, 'is piety; for over a pious man neither evil demon nor fate has any power; for God rescues the pious man from all evil; for the one and the only good thing among men is piety.' And what piety is he testifies in another place in these words: 'For piety is the knowledge of God' (Θεοῦ γνῶσις). Asclepius also, his disciple, more fully expressed the same sentiment in that finished discourse which he wrote to the king.[1] Each of them, in truth, affirms that the demons are the enemies and harassers of men, and on this account Trismegistus calls them wicked angels, so far was he from being ignorant that from heavenly beings they were corrupted and began to be earthly."[2]

Ibid. iv.

"Assuredly He is The very Son of God Who by that wise King Solomon full of Divine inspiration spoke these things which we have added: 'God founded me in the beginning of His ways, &c. (quoting Proverbs viii. 22, 31, from the Septuagint). But on this account Trismegistus spoke of Him as "the Artificer of God."[3]

Ibid. iv. ch. 8.

"But Hermes also was of the same opinion when He says that He was 'His own Father' and 'His own mother'" (Αὐτοπάτορα Αὐτομήτορα).[4]

Ibid. ch. 9.

"For the Greeks speak of Him as The Logos, more befittingly than we do, as the Word or Speech; for Logos signifies both Speech and Reason, inasmuch as He is both the Voice and the Wisdom of God. . . . For Trismegistus

---

[1] It is plain then that the "*Ὅροι, or 'Definitions of,' Asclepius to King Ammon" were written by him, not by our Hermes.

[2] Poemandres, ch. ix. 3, 4; Parthey, 61, 62; ibid. ch. xii. 9; ibid. 104. Extracts from Hermes in Stobæus, "Ethica, 358; Meineke, ii. p. 100."

[3] See Poemandres, i. 10; Parthey, 5.

[4] (q) Poemandres, i. 8; Parthey, 4.

who I know not how investigated almost all Truth, often described the Excellency and Majesty of The Word, as the instance before mentioned declares, in which he acknowledges that there is an ineffable and sacred Speech, the relation of which exceeds the measure of man's ability." [1]

Ibid., Divin. Instit., Lib. iv. ch. 6.

"But that there is a Son of The Most High God Who is possessed of the greatest power, is shown not only by the unanimous utterances of the prophets, but also by the declaration of Trismegistus, and the predictions of the Sibyls. Hermes in the book which is entitled 'The Perfect Word' made use of these words:—'The Lord and Creator of all things Whom we have thought right to call God, since He made the Second God visible and sensible. But I use the term sensible, not because He Himself perceives (for the question is not whether He Himself perceives), but because He leads (a) to perception and intelligence. Since therefore He made Him First and alone and One only, He appeared to Him beautiful and most full of all good things, and He hallowed Him and altogether loved Him as His own Son.'" [2]

Ibid., Divin. Instit., v. ch. 65.

"But Piety is nothing else but 'the Knowledge of God,' as Trismegistus most truly defined it." [3]

(a) ὑποπέμπει.

[1] Poemandres, i. 3, 6-9; Parthey, 3, 5.

[2] This passage is found nearly verbatim in the Asclepius, ch. iv. Lactantius gives the original Greek, which is not extant elsewhere. But it is also to be found in the original Greek in Poemandres, ch. i. 6, 10, 12; Parthey's Edit., 3, 5, 6; whence it would seem that Asclepius copied from Poemandres. See also Poemandres, ch. xiii. 4; Parthey's Ed., 117. This is also cited by Lactantius in the Epitome of the Divin. Instit., ch. xlii.

[3] Poemandres, ix. 3, 4.

Ibid., Lib. vi. ch. 25.

"We ought therefore to hold forth and offer to God that alone for the receiving of which He Himself produced us. But how true this twofold kind of Sacrifice is, Trismegistus Hermes is a befitting witness, who agrees with us, that is with the Prophets whom we follow as much in facts as in words. He thus spoke concerning Justice: 'Adore and worship the Word, O Son! but the worship of God consists of one thing, not to be wicked.'[1] Also in that 'Perfect Discourse' when he heard Asclepius enquiring from his Son (Tat) whether it pleased him that incense and other odours for divine Sacrifice were offered to his father, exclaimed: 'Speak words of good omen, O Asclepius! for it is the greatest impiety to entertain any such thought concerning that being of pre-eminent goodness. For these things and things resembling these are not adapted to Him. For He is full of all things as many as exist, and He has need of nothing at all. But let us give thanks and adore Him, for His Sacrifice consists only of Blessing.'[2] And he spoke rightly."

Ibid., Lib. vii. ch. 4.

"But Hermes was not ignorant that Man was both made by God and after the image of God."[3]

Ibid. ch. 9.

"Man alone of all the animals is heavenly and Divine; whose body raised from the ground, elevated countenance and upright position, goes in quest of its origin, and despising as it were the lowliness of the Earth, reaches forth to that which is on high, because he perceives that the

---

[1] Poemandres, ch. xii. 23; Parthey, 113.

[2] In Asclepius, ch. xv. As before shown, this "Perfect Discourse" was not written by Hermes but by Asclepius, his disciple, subsequently. Here Lactantius quotes in Latin, not in Greek. See also Poemandres, ch. xiii. 19, 20.

[3] Poemandres, ch. i. 12; Parthey, 6.

highest good is to be sought by him in the highest place, and mindful of his condition in which God made him illustrious, looks towards his Maker. And Trismegistus most rightly called this looking, a contemplation of God which has no existence in the dumb animals."[1]

Ibid. ch. 13.

"Hermes describing the nature of Man, that he might show how he was made by God, introduced this statement: 'And the same out of two natures, the immortal and the mortal, made one Nature, that of Man; making the same partly immortal and partly mortal, and bringing this He placed it in the midst between that nature which was Divine and immortal, and that which was mortal and changeable, that seeing all things he may admire all things."[2]

Ibid., Divin. Instit., Lib. vii. ch. 18.

"This Hermes did not conceal; for in that book which is entitled 'The Perfect Discourse,' after an enumeration of the evils concerning which we have spoken, he added these things: 'But when these things thus come to pass, then He who is Lord and Father and God and the Creator of the First and One God, looking upon what is done, and opposing to the disorder His own will, that is Goodness, and recalling the wandering, and cleansing wickedness, partly inundating it with much water and partly burning it with most rapid fire, and sometimes pressing it with wars and pestilences, He brought His World to its ancient state and restored it.'"[3]

---

[1] Poemandres, ch. xii., xiii., xiv. *passim;* Parthey, 106, 111, *et seq.*

[2] Poemandres, ch. iv. 2, substantially. It is found also in the "Perfect Discourse," Asclepius, ch. iv.

[3] This passage is cited in the original Greek by Lactantius, which otherwise we do not possess. In the Latin translation ascribed to Apuleius, it varies much. It is found in the Epitome of Lactantius, ch. viii.; also in Asclepius, ch. ix., nearly verbatim, apparently copied from some former work of Hermes. As before stated, this last was

Lactantius, Epitome of Divin. Instit., ch. iv.
(In Latin).

"Hermes, who on account of his virtue, and his knowledge of many arts, deserved the name of Trismegistus, who preceded the philosophers in the antiquity of his doctrine, and who is reverenced by the Egyptians as a God, in asserting the majesty of The One God with infinite praises, calls Him Lord and Father, and says that He is without a name, because He does not stand in need of a proper name, inasmuch as He is alone, and that He has no parents, since He exists of Himself and by Himself. In writing to His Son He thus begins:—'To understand God is difficult, to describe Him in speech is impossible even for one to whom it is possible to understand Him; for the perfect cannot be comprehended by the imperfect, nor the visible by the invisible.'"[1]

VII.

ARNOBIUS (circa 305, about the abdication of Diocletian) writes thus (*Adversus Gentes*, Lib. ii. 13).

"You, you I address who zealously follow Mercury, Plato, and Pythagoras, and the rest of you who are of one mind and walk in union in the same paths of doctrine."

not written by Hermes but by this Asclepius; for the same chapter contains also a defence of Image worship, and a recognition of Jupiter as Supreme God, which is wholly inconsistent with what Hermes has previously inculcated.

[1] See the references, *ante*, p. 6. Also the Excerpts from Justin Martyr, *ante*, 1.

VIII.

Augustine of Hippo (born 354).

He relates without doubt ("City of God," viii. 23, 26) how the fifth Mercury and his friend Asclepius (or Æsculapius), grandson of the first, were men, and became Gods as Mercury and Æsculapius after the Greek fashion. To Hermes, who like Horus was represented by a bird with a hawk's head, was sacred the Ibis and the Moon. [In the same chapters Augustine quotes a Latin translation of the "Asclepius" at length—the Greek version as it seems not even then being extant—as advocating the worship of Images as Gods. It has been shown that this is not a work of the true Hermes, and consequently the observations of St Augustine thereon are not here extracted.]

IX.

Cyrillus Alexandrinus (*Patriarch of Alexandria*, 412), Lib. i., *Contra Julianum*, 30a.

"This Hermes then, him of Egypt, although being Initiator (*a*) and having presided at the fanes of the Idols, is always found mindful of the things of Moses, and if not altogether rightly and completely yet still in part. For he hath profited, and he hath made mention of him also in his own writings, which he having composed for Athenians (*b*), are called Hermaiea fifteen Books."

Lib. i., *Contra Julianum*, 31b.

The same Cyril writes thus:—

"The Trismegistus Hermes in this wise says: To understand (*c*) God is difficult, to declare (*d*) Him impossible

---

(*a*) τελεστής; "etsi Sacerdos esset," Latin translation.
(*b*) Ἀθήνῃσι.   (*c*) νοῆσαι.   (*d*) Φράσαι δὲ.

if even it were possible to understand Him, for the incorporeal to be signified by body impossible and the perfect to be comprehended (*a*) by the imperfect not possible, and the eternal to be conversant with the short-lived difficult; for this ever is, but that passes away, and this is true, but that is overshadowed by phantasy.[1] For as much as the strengthless and the stronger and the less from the superior, are distant, so much the Mortal from the Divine and immortal. If then there be any incorporeal eye, let it come forth from the body, and to the Vision of the Beautiful. Let it fly up and be lifted into air; not figure, not body, not ideas, seeking to contemplate, but that rather, The Maker of these; the quiet, the serene, the stable, the invariable, the Self, all things and Only, The One; the Same out of Itself, the same in Itself, the like to Itself, which neither is like to another, nor is unlike to Itself,[2] and again The Same."

Ibid. 33*c*.

"But the Trismegistus Hermes thus speaks concerning The God :—' For The Word of Him proceeding forth being altogether perfect and generative and Creator in a generative nature falling upon generative Water, made water pregnant.' "[3]

And the same again :—

"The[4] Pyramis" (he says) "lying under the Nature, and to the intelligible world. For it has resting upon it a Ruler and Creator, Word of The Lord of all, Who, after

(*a*) καταλαμβάνεσθαι.

[1] See Stobæus, Florileg., 80; Meineke, iii. 104; *ante*, Stobæus, vii., Part II.

[2] Extracted by Stobæus also substantially, Florilegium, xi. 23, *ad fin.* See 1, *ante*, Part II., and Meineke, i. 251.

[3] See Poemandres, i. 8, 14, 15; Suidas, Lexicon, *post*, x., who quotes this same passage.

[4] In the commencement of Poemandres, ch. i., Hermes had asserted that Fire or heat was the chief medium which the Creator had employed for the arrangement of Creation. Fire as Flame is in form a Cone or Pyramid, hence that appellation was given to the Pyramids, which are Cones. See Poemandres, i. 17.

Him First Power ingenerate, infinite, from Him having issued forth (a), rests upon and rules those things, having been created by Him. He is Forebegotten of the All-perfect, and perfect, and generative, own kindred Son."[1]

"And again the same, replying as if to some enquirer of the priests in Egypt, saying:—'For what then, O Megistus! was the good Demon[2] called by this name by The Lord of all?' He saith, 'And in those previous I said, but thou hast not understood, The nature of The same Intelligible Word. This is a generative nature, just as the generation of Him, either nature or mode, or call it what you wish to call it. This only understanding, that perfect He is in perfect, and from perfect; perfect things He effects, and creates and vivifies. Since then He has such kind of nature He has been well thus addressed.'"

"And the same in the first discourse of the Digressions to Tat,[3] he thus speaks concerning God:—'The Word of the Creator, O Child! is eternal, Self-moveable, unaugmentable, undiminishable, unchangeable, incorruptible and Only, always like to Himself, equable and even, stable, well-ordered, being One after the pre-acknowledged God;' and as I think he signifies by this The Father."

"Hermes says also in the third discourse of those to Asclepius:—'It is not attainable to impart such sort of Mysteries to uninitiated; but hear with the Mind. One only was intelligent Light before intelligible Light and Mind always is luminous with light, and nothing other was than Oneness of this always being in Itself, always within the Mind of its own Self, and with light and with Spirit encompasses all things.' And afterwards: 'Without this, not God, nor Angel nor Demon nor any other Essence, for He is Lord and Father of all things, and God and source of life and Power and Light and Mind, and all things are in Him and under Him.'

(a) προκύψασα.

[1] See Poemandres, i. 6, 9, 10; xiii. 3; xiv. 3.
[2] See as to the "Good Demon," Poemandres, xii. *passim*.
[3] See Poemandres, iv. and v., and elsewhere.

"For as to Mind out of Mind I opine he speaks of the Son, and so Light out of Light. He mentions also the Spirit as encompassing all things, and he says that neither Angel nor demon, nor verily any other nature or Essence, lies without the Divine Supremacy, therefore power; but under Him are all things and by It are determined."

"And again the same in the same third discourse of those to Asclepius, as if some one enquiring concerning The Divine Spirit he speaks thus:—'Unless there were some providence of the Lord of all things that I should reveal this discourse, neither had such kind of desire now taken hold of you that you should have made enquiry concerning this. But now hear the remainder of the discourse. Of this Spirit of which I have often previously spoken all things are in want. For supporting according to worth He vivifies all things and nourishes and is dependent (a) from the Holy Source, assisting with Spirit and ever originating (b) life to all, being the One generative (c). He knew It then both originating in its own subsistence (d) and all things vivifying and nourishing, and as dependent from a Holy Source of The God and Father; for it proceeds from Him according to Nature, and through The Son is made instrumental in Creation.'" (e)[1]

Cyrillus, ibid., Lib. ii. 52a.

"I will also add to these what formerly the Trismegistus Hermes wrote to his own Mind, for thus the book is named: 'Dost thou say then God is invisible,' &c."[2]

Cyrillus, ibid., 56b.

"I will mention the words of Hermes thrice greatest only which he uses in that dialogue which is to Asclepius:

(a) ἐξήρτηται. (b) ὑπάρχον. (c) γόνιμος.
(d) ἰδιοσυστάτως. (e) χορηγεῖται τῇ κτίσει.

[1] As Ménard has remarked (Preface, i.), this passage states the doctrine of the Trinity as held by the Greek Church, viz., The Holy Ghost proceeding from the Father through the Son. See Poemandres, ch. xiii. 4, 19, 21.

[2] See the passage, Poemandres, ch. xi. 22.

'And Osiris said,'" &c. This passage being part of the Asclepius, not the work of Hermes himself, is not here extracted.

Cyrillus, ibid. 57b.

"In the first Book of his Digressive discourse (a) to Tat: 'The Lord of all things immediately spoke to His Holy and Intelligent and Creative Word, "Let there be Sun;" and along with the speaking, the Fire having the uplifting (b) Nature, I say then the unmixed the most brilliant and more drastic and generative, by its own Spirit the Nature was attracted (c) and raised aloft from the water.' Again of this make mention, he among them Trismegistus Hermes; he introduced The God saying to the formations (d), 'On you, those from Me, I will impose Necessity; this, that commandment by my Word given to you; for this law ye have.'"[1]

Cyrillus, ibid. 63c.

"For Hermes by name thrice great, writes thus to Asclepius concerning the nature of the Universe:—'If then the beings are acknowledged to be two, that generate,' &c."[2]

Ibid. 64c.

"And again after other things in warmer words he comes speaking, having put a most plain example, and says:—'Besides indeed to the same limner it is allowed,' &c."[3]

Cyrillus, Lib. viii. p. 274c.

"Hermes thrice great hath said also somewhere of God The most excellent Artificer:(e)—'Moreover as perfect and wise, He hath imposed order and want of order; when the Intelligible indeed He placed first as older and superior, and

(a) διεξοδικῶ λόγῳ.   (b) ἀνωφεροῦσα.   (c) ἐπεσπάσατο.
(d) κτίσμασιν.   (e) ἀριστοτέχνου.

[1] This from Poemandres, i. and iii.
[2] This from Poemandres, xiv. 6, 7.
[3] This from Poemandres, xiv. 8.

should have the first place; but the Sensible as second, that they should be subject to those (*a*). That then, borne lower than the Intelligible and weighed down (*b*), has in itself a wise creative Word."

Cyrill. Contra. Julian., citing Hermes.

"If thou understandest that Only and Sole God, thou wilt find nothing impossible, for it is all Virtue. Think not that it may be in some one, say not that it is out of some one. It is without termination, it is the termination of all. Nothing contains It, for It contains all in Itself. What difference is there between the body and the incorporeal, the created and the uncreated, that which is subject to the Necessity, and that which is free, between the things terrestrial and the things celestial, the things corruptible and the things Eternal? Is it not that the one exists freely and that the others are subject to Necessity? That which is below is imperfect and corruptible."

Cyrill. Contra. Julian., Lib. v. 176*b*.

"The Egyptians also have to tell, numbering among themselves names of not few wise men, that they had many, who were of succession after Hermes. I speak of Hermes, him having sojourned third[1] in Egypt."

X.

SUIDAS (under Alexander Comnenus), *Lexicon. Voce Hermes.* [Edit. Godofredus Bernardy (after Gaisford) Halis et Brunsvigæ, 1853.]

"HERMES the Trismegistus. He was an Egyptian sage, and flourished before Pharaoh. He was called Trisme-

(*a*) ὑποστήκη.   (*b*) βρίθον.

[1] Pietschmann, in his dissertation on Hermes Trismegistus (Engelmann, Leipzig, 1875), attempts (pp. 51-54) to determine who these three Hermes were: one contemporary with Enoch and Seth; the

gistus because he spoke concerning a Trinity (*a*), saying that in Trinity there is One Godhead (*b*) thus: There was intelligent Light before intelligent Light, and there was always Mind luminous of Mind (*c*), and the Unity of This was nothing other,[1] and Spirit encompassing all things. Without This God is not nor angel[2] nor any other Essence. For of all things He is God and Father and Lord, and all things are under Him and in Him. For His Word going forth, being altogether perfect and generative (*d*) and creative (*e*) having fallen on Water also generative, rendered the Water pregnant (*f*).[3] And having said this he prayed, saying: 'I adjure thee, O Heaven-wise work of The great God. I adjure thee, Voice of Father Which He spoke first when He stablished the whole World. I adjure thee by that His Only begotten Word and The Father of Him embracing around all things.'"[4]

(*a*) περι τριάδος. (*b*) θειότητα. (*c*) νοὸς Φοτεινός.
(*d*) γόνιμος. (*e*) δημιουργικός. (*f*) ἔγκυον.

second a Chaldæan, contemporary with Sardanapalus, who had Pythagoras for his pupil; the third a physician, who was born in Memphis of uncertain age. It is clear, however, that none of these was the Hermes, the author of Poemandres.

[1] The Editor of Suidas remarks that Cyrillus Alexandrinus quotes this passage thus ("from Hermes in that to Tat to his own Mind," i. Contr. Julian., pp. 33 and 52):—"And the Unity of this was nothing other always, being in Himself, and with His own Mind and Light and Spirit He embraces around all things."

[2] See Poemandres, ii. 14. The word there however is "God," not angel.

[3] See the same passage quoted by Cyrillus Alexandrinus, Contra. Julian., 33*c*, *ante*, p. 150.

[4] Cyrill. Alex. and Justin Martyr in his Παραινετικὸς πρὸς Ἑλληνας attributes this last invocation, with a trifling variation, to Orpheus.

It is noteworthy that the last poem of Longfellow was a lyrical Ode in celebration of Hermes Trismegistus.

FINIS.

INDEX.

Administrators, Seven, of Fate, 5; Energy of, Creator has, 8, 9.

Air, feminine, 6, 9, 27; is Body, permeating all things, 20, 21; one of the Four Materials of Creation, 20, 21; how generated, 2, 122.

All in All, constituted of all Powers, 87.

Almighty, Dominus, Supreme, (Ἀυθέντης), 1, 15, 93.

Ambrosial water, 14.

Ammon, 127.

Animal, Animal Being; made existent by God, 26; energies and instincts of, 118; not arts or sciences, *ibid.*; has life rational in Soul, mortal in body, 126.

Antithesis and contrariety of all things, 59.

Apparent things delight, non-apparent difficult of belief.

Appetites of irrationals, 80; are their instincts, 118.

Archetypical Form, 3; Archetypical Light and Soul, 21.

Arts and Sciences, rays of Man, 66; Special Energies of the Rationals only, 117, 120; sent from above, and differ from Sense, *ibid.*, 122.

Ascent to Good of Soul, what, 13; through Harmony leaving Vices, *ibid.*

Asclepius, 16-19, 44, 54, 96.

Atheism, great disease of Soul, 78.

Avengers, irrational, of Matter, to be abandoned, 89; are twelve principal Vices, 90; of darkness are expelled by ten Virtues, 90.

Baptism of Men with Cup, 31; Baptized receive Mind, 32.

Bear, Constellation of, how energizing, 136.

Be, The To Be, 126.

Being in Essence, cause of, is common to generate and to Soul; Generation in Reason; Intelligent Life; Animal causing Life, rational, mortal, 126.

Beautiful and Good, Essence of is God; integral parts of, 44, 45, 73; Beautiful also Good, *ibid.*; inseparable from Him and in Him only, 50; Vision of, what, 137.

Beauty of Good, cannot be fully be seen here or in Body, in Divine Silence and repose only, 57, 137; God moves with all that is, 85; lover of Body and Evil cannot understand, 76.

Beginning (Ἀρχη, Μονάς), what is, 24; is out of nothing, 34; all things from One, *ibid.*, 61.

Belief in God, how attained, 55.

Birth, Body and Soul associated at by Fate, 123.

Body, Bodies, love of is death, 10, 11; constituted out of Moist Nature, 11; how dissolved [*see* Death], 13; World, a Body, 17; opposite of Incorporeal, 18; cannot move Soul, 19; without Soul moved by body with Soul, 20; given up to passion, cannot admire good, 43, 76; to be hated, 32; a hateful garment, bond of corruption, prevents men seeing Truth and good, 46,

47; Earthly, want order when dissolved; return to indissoluble and immortal, 53; all composite of Matter and Soul, *ibid.*, 71.

Body, Bodies, are moveable, 81; sensible, are dissoluble and mortal, 24, 92; when dissolved, it is dissolution of mixture only to become new, 82; of spiritual Power immortal and indissoluble, 92; require much help and succour, 124; properties and qualities of dissoluble and indissoluble, 107; are never true, 114; Ideas and Energies of, 115; has communion with Soul in Time, Place, and Nature, and how, 116-17; cannot exist apart from Soul, 119; how energized in dissolution, *ibid.;* Harmony of, its relation to Stars, 127; lovers of, cannot behold God, 137.

Bodies, heavenly, have one order, indissoluble, maintained by return of each to its place, 49, 92; Bodies, Eternal, alone true, 100; made once for all, 123.

Breath (Πνοή) gives qualities of life, 53.

Change, all men subject to, 79; things changeable and gendered not true, 103.

Chaos, description of, 2, 24.

Child of God, Typical Man in His Image, 6.

Children, anxiety to have [*see* Man]; how punished who have not, 23.

Choice between corporeal and incorporeal, mortal and Divine left to man, 33; cannot use both; of excellent deifies him, of worse destroys, *ibid.;* of good and evil is with each, 131; of evil subjects to fate; of good, fate touches not, *ibid.*

Circles of Planets and of Heaven, Seven, 16, 134; of Universe, 133-34; of Gods, 28; Zodiacal, 136.

Comets described, predict future events, 136.

Constellations appear and signs, 27; Gods in them, *ibid.;* are armour of fate, 109; what are, 137.

Contemplation of Heaven and works of God, Man created for, 28, 31; of image of God, guide to things above, 35, 37; detains and attracts, *ibid.*

Corporeal. *See* Body.

Corruption necessary to generation, 103.

Courage in Soul, what, 127.

Creation, mode of, 4, 5, 8, 24; of Universe good, 48; of all forms yet one Idea, 74; of eternal Bodies once for all, 123-4; of mortal and dissoluble continually, *ibid.;* of Man, 39.

Creator (Δημιουργός) who, is Mind, 4, 5; willed to create, 6; shewed forth from of God, 8; of Man, 39.

Cup (Κρατῆρ) is Divine, 31, 32; man to be baptized in it, *ibid.;* obtains knowledge, perfection, and immortality thereby, 32; unwilling then to remain on earth; hastens to One and Only, *ibid.*

Darkness in Abyss, 2, 24.

Death, cause of, love of body, 10; derived out of original Darkness, 11; what it is, not destruction, 47, 48; deprivation of sense only, 49, 50; is dissolution of union of body and soul, 73, 74; how carried on this, 13; of the mixture, 83; not change but oblivion, 84; dissolution of Harmonies of body, 104.

Decade of Virtues regenerates, expelling vices, 90, 91, 92; is intelligent regeneration, according to God, *ibid.;* is Soul generative, 92; is the Mind, *ibid.*

Decans, Thirty-six, 133; where stationed, and their office, 134; encompass Universe and influence earth, 135; generate

INDEX. 159

Tanæ as sub-ministers, *ibid.*; are under the Seven, *ibid.*

Demon, Demons, Avenging, punishes wicked, 71; evil in all the world, 51-52; inspire evil and evil thoughts, 51; separate from God, sow seeds of crime, *ibid.* Good who, 66, 77, 79; is Firstbegotten God, 80; Blessed God, 82.

Desires, excessive, are vices, 7; in Soul modified by Reason, 127; as energies, ratio of, 128; of immortal bodies; are far off the Divine part of the Soul, 129; of irrational, *ibid.*

Divine, men made, by attaining Knowledge, 14; after death, Souls are; how they enter Body, 129; Man's Soul has something of, *ibid.*; body what, *ibid.*

Divinity (Θειότης), how different from God; is generated by Him, 51.

Dreams apart from Sense, 51; how they affect men, *ibid.*; Body and Soul awakened in, *ibid.*

Earth, how produced from Fire, Water, &c., and Divine Bodies, 2, 6-24, 122; God willed to dedicate it to Himself and adorn it; region of Wickedness, 52; Time and Generation in, 68; support of World; nurse of animals, 71; not immoveable or inert, full of motion yet stable, 84; how arranged by God, 93, 94; Truth not of, 101; corrupt, 103; changeable, not in common with Heaven, nothing known on, all blameable, 114; contrast between and Heaven, 115; is last of Elements, *ibid.*; how first generated, 26, 122.

Elements, Four, of Universe, 4, 99; how generated, 122; Heaven first, of Earth last, 115.

Energy, Energies, of Soul, 47; of God's good things may make their qualities evil or good, 53; are rays of God throughout world and in man, 66; of God what, His will, 55, 69; of Mind and Soul, 68; all of are from God, 85; of Universe from Him, 86; of matter and bodies, *ibid.*; incorporeal in bodies, and common to brutes, and those different in each, 118; of irrationals, how operating, 118, 119-120; how connected with bodies, *ibid.*; bodies have many souls, 119-120; some divine, some corruptible, *ibid.*; all things full of; general and special; general account of, 120.

Engendered things imperfect, 35.

Entities (τὰ Ὄντα), Hermes wishes to know of, 1; constituted by Word of God, 15; none are void, 20; God cause of, beginning of, 21-24; none left beside by God that is not, 21-22; Nature of, *ibid.*; all good, 22; created at God's will, 30; God is not, but all from Him, 31; two in general, corporeal and incorporeal, mortal and Divine, 33; God has all in Himself, never deficient, 54; in World, diminution or increase, 84; if generate, must be by One other, 96; but Two, Generate and Maker, 97-8; these One by Union, *ibid.*; Generate are Four, 99; by First Creator only, 103; to understand is Piety, 111; Qualities of, summed up, 113; First God, Second World, Third Man, World because of Man, Man because of God, 113-14; all double, none stable, 114; moved by Soul, *ibid.*; some in Bodies, some in Ideas, some Ideas, 115; World always has, 120; Pre-existent Essentiality before all other Entities, 125; belongs to entire Universe, *ibid.*

Envy in Men without Mind, 31; God has not.

Essentiality, the Divine God, 18, 125; what are, 21.

Essence (Οὐσία), (*see* Soul); of God, to be pregnant of all things, 40; has no evil, is good only, 43; is the Beautiful and Good, 44, 68; has happiness and wisdom, 68; is His willing all things to be, 55; Soul, how transformed into, 58; First of World Order, of Time Generation, 68; Intelligible, not under Necessity or Fate, 108; immortal and mutable, 114; of God, Eternity, 68; First what, 124; relation of, with Reason, 128.

Eternal, different from everlasting, 48.

Eternity ('O Aἰών), made by God in and around Him, 68; its energy, permanence, and immortality, *ibid.*, 69; World moved in, and work of, Powers of God, 67, 68; incorruptible, 69; keeps together World and Universe; makes matter immortal; what it has in it, *ibid.*

Evil, man, not God, cause of, 33; more apparent than good, and delights men, 34; not of God, but separate, 43; mixed with good on earth, *ibid.*; thought to be good by ignorant, 45; compared to dirt and incrustations on creation, 98; involuntary, 114; is aliment of the World, *ibid.*

Existence, Subsistence ("Ὕπαρξις), God is, The, 21, 22, 55, 56.

Eyes of man cannot behold God, or Good and Beautiful, 44; of body cannot consider Truth, 88.

Falsehood, how operation of Truth; all things on earth are, 104.

Fate, Seven Administrators in Seven Circles of Heaven are, 5; and Harmony establish, and cause of generation and destruction, 10, 108; all subject to, 79; of the Evil to suffer and to obey Justice, 79, 80, 108; those having Mind, not subject to, 79, 80, 132; dominated over by Mind, 80; bodily things subject to, 108; cause of disposition of Stars, *ibid.*; subserves Providence and Necessity, 109; a Power of Providence, none can avoid it, *ibid.*; rules over all things, 116; regulates union of Soul and Body, 123; Fate and choice, 131; has no power over Reason, having God for Guide, 132.

Father of all things, The God, Life, and Light, 6-15; created typical Man in His Image, *ibid.*; of Universe, constituted of Life and Light, 11; an Epithet of God, 23; has no Name, 41; Ingenerate and Eternal, 48; and *see* "God," *post.*

Fire, pure, or heat, 2; instrument in Creation, 2, 62; issues from moist Nature, *ibid.*; and Spirit, *ibid.*; God of, issued forth by Word of The God, 4; agency of, in Creation, 2, 6, 122; divided things light and heavy, 25; gives maturity to Men, 9; shines on all, 94; earth sustains not, 62; punishment of wicked, 12.

Fortune, what, 115.

Generate, Generation, are things apparent, 36; of quantities and qualities and moveable, 65; Essence of Life and change in Time, 68; must be by other and that one preceding and ingenerate, 96; Two in Creation only, Maker and that generate, 97; these are inseparable, *ibid.*; must be generator and generate; one by Union, 98; changeable and not true, 102; how far may be, *ibid.*; corruption necessary for, 103; are phantasies, *ibid. See* Entities.

Gluttony, unsurpassable evil, 44.

God, The ("O Θεός), Father, Life, and Light, created typical Man in His own form, 8, 11-16; will of, 10, 30; what He is, 21; in Holy Word said increase and multiply, 16; intelligible in Himself, 18; to us, *ibid.*, 48, 105; is superessential, nonapparent, 18, 36; self-existent,

21, 22, 55, 56; alone good, 22, 42, 94, 99; by His nature, 20, 23; One and Only, 30, 32, 34, 37, 71, 72, etc.; glory of, 24; gives all things, receives nothing, 23, 56, 76, 94; maker of all things, *ibid.*, 30; Father of all things, and of man, 37, 40; without envy, Father of Body, Soul, own kindred Father of Man, 97; Reason and Mind, 82; by Word constituted Entities, *ibid.;* Beginning and Cause of the Entities, Life, Light, and Spirit, 21; Mind, Nature, Matter, Wisdom, 27; Holy, of Whom all Nature Image, 37, 40; above all Power and Excellence, *ibid.;* always making manifest though non-apparent, 36; non-generate, *ibid.*, 48; the Good in God, 42-99; nothing else good, 22, 23; cannot exist without doing, 74; contemplation of, guide to Heaven, 35; not visible, touchable, separable, unlike body, 31, 97; may be made apparent, 36; appears throughout world, 37; this His Virtue, 76; to be contemplated and prayed to by Understanding, 37; visible and to be contemplated in his works in Heaven and Earth, 37, 75, 85; orders course of sun and stars, 38; fabricated circles of Heaven, and whole world, sea, and earth, *ibid.;* not spoken or heard, 58; superior to all, 66; dedicated Earth to Himself, 31; Maker and Lord of all, in particular of Man, 38, 39, 40; His Essence to be pregnant of, and make all things, and Natures, 40, 94; all things full of, 70; is self-working, 72; nothing made without Him, 40; world and all things in Him, 70, 74, 85; nothing in world not Him, 72, 73; nothing apart from Him, 70; is the Entities and Non-Entities, 41, 55, 56; has no Name, all Names being all things, 42; His Name very great, 137; is intelligent Mind energizing, *ibid.*, 69; all things generate and ungenerate, none generate without Him, *ibid.;* nothing superior to or compeer with Him, 43, 70; not to be seen with eyes, 44; willing to be seen, visible to Mind and heart of the good, 46, 76; manifest throughout all things, 76; Fountain and Founder of all things and natures, 68, 94; is the Beautiful and Good, Happiness and Wisdom, 44, 56, 68, 73; these integral, inseparable properties of Him, 44, 45; sows the seeds of, and Virtue, Temperance, and Piety, 52; Creator of Universe like Himself, 48, 53, 69, 106; beginning, comprehension, and constitution of all things, 50; Prince of order, Guide of worlds, 70; not insensible, mindless, or inert, 54, 70; if inert, no longer God, 72; all things energizing energize through Him, 84, 85; energy of His Will, 55, 56; is the making Power, 94; is all things not yet in being, *ibid.;* made all forms of one Idea, 74; how to understand, 75, 76; ignorance of, sum of evil, 76; will be met and known by the good, *ibid.;* holds converse with Man, 84; parts of, 85; is Energy and Power, *ibid.;* has neither magnitude, place, quality, figure, nor time, although Generator, 86, 92; simple, incomposite, His Glory One, this, as it were, His Body, 98; is both Maker and Father, and why, 97, 80; makes nothing evil, but all things, 76, 92, 99; is not Maker only, but conserver, *ibid.;* has one Passion, the Good, *ibid.;* compared to agriculturist, 99; sows immortality, change on Earth, life and motion in Universe; cannot be understood, impossible to express in speech, 105; may be apprehended mentally, *ibid.;* is Truth Itself, 103, 105; is eternal, 106; is Immutable Good, 115. *See* also Spirit, Trinity, Word.

Gods in plural, 22, 24, 28; in constellations and stars, 27; or Angels, 24; distribute seminal nature in Creation as ordained, 26; circling course of, 28, 29; Man comparable with, or superior to, and why, 67; shall not descend to earth, 67; moved with World, 85; intellectual and sensible, 125.

Good, The, beholden by those with Mind, 32; excellence of, 34; God is only, 42, 43; cannot be in this world, and why, 44, 57; in the ingenerate only, 43; dissimilar to all else, 44, 57; cannot co-exist with Passion, 43; generated by worldly course becomes evil qualities, 53; cannot be purified from evil here, 43; proper to, to become known, 57; moves with God in the Universe, in permanence, 85; spectacle of, sanctifies, 57; is intellectual splendour and immortality, 57; sometimes induces sleep of body, *ibid.;* seen in Divine silence and repose of senses, 58; beauty of, deifies Soul in body, transforms into image of God, *ibid.*

Grass and green herbs created, 26.

Grief and joy, energies of Sense, and rational, and how, 121; are Ideas of Passions, and evil, *ibid.*

Harmony of creation, what, 7; of the Seven, 9; established minglings and generations, 10; of the body, 104, 117, 127; action of, 122, 123; of the four materials of the World, 122; how it acts in birth and with Spirit, 123; is immutable, *ibid.;* differences in, of, in three forms of figure, form, and image, *ibid.*, and 126, 127; its relation to Stars, 127; dissolution of [*see* Body and Death].

Hate of body necessary, 33.

Head contains Soul, 60; what is united to immortal, and what distance from mortal, *ibid.*

Heaven and Earth, double, unchangeable, incorruptible, and the reverse, 69; Eternity of, *ibid.;* Heaven unchangeable, without blame, receptive of incorruptibles, and has nought common with earth, 115; general description of qualities, 114, 115; mutual relations with earth, *ibid.;* contrast with earth, *ibid.;* Heaven first of Elements, Earth last, 115; Heaven, Seven Circles of, 26.

Hermes, as guide, preaches to men repentance and wisdom, 14; invites them to thank God, 15; his prayer of, to God, 16; is Holiness of God, *ibid.;* passes into Life and Light, 16.

Hymn to God the Father, 15; subjects of, 42; how and when to be sung, 93; of the Regeneration, 93-95; secret, *ibid.*

Ignorance of God, greatest evil. corrupts Soul, 46; is complete evil, 76.

Idea, Ideas, the Father full of, 49; their qualities in sphere, *ibid.;* God has one, 74; incorporeal, what, 74; some shewn in bodies, *ibid.;* what they are, 75.

Identity, Essence of Eternity, 68; Bodies of Universe have, 82-3.

Image of God will guide to things above, 35; contemplation of, *ibid.*

Imagination, Phantasy, 36; of things generate only, *ibid.*

Immortality, Immortal, man is, has not mortality, 10; is present in mortal bodies, 115; whoso sins greatly, deprived of, 11; man of mind light and life, has, 11, 12; in all things, matter, life, spirit, soul, 84; animals have, especially Man, *ibid.*

INDEX. 163

Impiety, how punished after death, 63, 64.

Incorporeal, the, moves World, 19; is the place in which the Universe is moved, 21; what it is, 21 [*see* Soul, Spirit]; Good, Truth, and Light, rays of, *ibid.*; intangible, conservative of Entities, *ibid.*; non-apparent to body, 34; most comprehensive and powerful, 75; always movers, 81; always energizes, *ibid.*; moved by Mind, *ibid.*; subjects of Passion, *ibid.*; cannot be comprehended by sense, 105; three species, qualities, properties, and that received by us, 107; First Essence is, *ibid.*; properties and qualities of bodies, *ibid.*

Increase and multiply, God's command, 10.

Inert, God is not, 72, 73; equivalent to non-existence, *ibid.*

Ingenerate, God is, unimaginable, and non-apparent, 37; yet appears in all things, *ibid.*

Injustice, absence of, justifies, 90.

Intellect (Νόημα) is Reason of Soul, 129.

Intellectual things, and intelligible Gods, 125.

Intelligence (Νόησις), of First God, Man of Mind has, 50; of Creator, 107; according to Essence, property of Soul, 117.

Intelligent only understand God, and believe in Him, 55.

Intelligible Essence, what, 107; not under Necessity, 108.

Intelligible (νοητός), God not so to Himself, but to us by sense, 18; each an Essence, 82.

Irrationals, creation of, without Reason, 6, 26; renewal of, 29; Energies of, how operating by Nature only, 118.

Justice and Endurance, 90; ordained over men, avenger of evil, 106; subjects them to fate, *ibid.*; is Divine and cannot err, *ibid.*; how generated, 127; by thinking Reason, 128.

Knowledge (Γνῶσις), received by Baptism with Cup, 32; enables to obtain The Good, 34; with Piety is the way to God, 45; is Shining Light, 46; of God is Piety, 52; makes evils good, *ibid.*; is Virtue of Soul and made Divine, 59; how it differs from Sense, *ibid.*; alone saving for Man, 51; by it Soul becomes good, *ibid.*; banishes Ignorance, 90.

Language, how differing from Voice, belongs to Man only, is enunciative Reason, 81, 82.

Law, Avenger and Convicter of evil, 78.

Life, is union of luminous Word out of Mind, 3; with the Soul, 73; World, place and creator of, 53; and always in it, 83; and Immortality, God is, 70-73, 85; of God, what, 74; Life one, therefore God One, *ibid.*; will of Father is plentitude of, 83; Motion, energy of, *ibid.*; in irrationals, 77; intelligent, afforded by Soul, 126.

Light, and Voice of, out of Chaos, 2; issues forth to Chaos, 24; Holy Word descends from it on Nature, 3; in numberless Powers, *ibid.*; God the Father is, 11; God, cause of, 22.

Light things separated upward, heavy downward, 23.

Love of Body, cause of Death and darkness, 10, 11; of self, hating Body, obtains Mind and Science, 33.

Magnitude and increase through Spirit, 123.

Maker (Ποιητής) of all things, God Father of all things, is but One, 37-39, 56; not that only, but is all things, 56; cannot be two or more, and why, 71; can and must be but One, 97, 98; im-

INDEX.

pious to deny this, *ibid.;* precedes, that generate follows, *ibid.;* Making is body of God; not making not God, 98; not maker of evil, *ibid.*

Man, Image of Father God, 6, 39, 40; beheld in Water by Creator of World, 8, 50; His own form, *ibid.;* twofold, mortal and immortal, 8-13; harmonious servant, masculine, feminine, *ibid.;* generate by God the Father, from Life and Light unto Soul and Mind, 9, 11; generations of, how sown, 28; created for what purposes, Contemplation of God, &c., 29-31; excels other animals, and how, in speech and mind, 31, 67, 84; ornament of Divine Body, *ibid.;* Beauty of, Divine Image, 39, 40; how fabricated by Creator, 39; cannot be without Him, 40; cannot be destroyed, being work of God, 48; Divine Animal, 67; having Mind, has sympathy with World, Intelligence of First God, 13, 50; divided into Body and Soul, 51; belongs to World, is its offspring, 61; saved by knowledge of God, *ibid.;* at death leaves garments and takes fiery tunic, 62;

Man, God-fearing, has Knowledge, 52; has sense and understanding in union, 56; wicked, has understanding from demons, 53; evil, as mortal and moveable, 60, 114; immutably so, 50-114, 115; and as animal, 116; First of things mortal, 60; of Mind is above gods, and why, 67, 77; on earth a mortal God, ascends to Heaven; with World administers all things, *ibid.;* having Mind and Reason, immortal, *ibid.;* passes into Life again, 81-84; susceptible of, and joint in Essence with God, 84; with God holds converse, and so he knows future things, *ibid.;* of Mind hymning the Father with the Powers, 14, 94; attaining Knowledge, becomes in God, 95: how different from other animals, 85; cannot be true, and why, 100, 101, as man, 102; constituted of many things and changeable; a Phantasy, 102; a succession of phantasies, 103-4; generation of, 114, 115.

Many, The, The Entities not to be discoursed of to, 115; understand not Philosophy, 116; thereby disposed to evil, will refer evil to Fate, *ibid.*

Matter or Material, eternal, 49; originally without order, 2; Material World, beautiful, not good; Matter, how dealt with by God, 48, 49; from Matter differs, 53; qualities generated from, *ibid.;* Matter is from four things, Earth, Air, Fire, Water, *ibid.;* made immortal by Eternity, 69, 84; order of, regulated by Providence, 81; is One, 83; full of Life from God, 85; not energized by Him is mere mass, *ibid.;* Energy of Materiality, *ibid.;* generated by God, 111; receptacle of Generation and Ideas, *ibid.;* is variable, dissoluble, and eternal, 111, 114; how moved and warmed at Creation, 122.

Metempsychosis, 23, 63; of Soul not into wild beasts, 63.

Mind (Νοῦς), speaks as Poemandres, 1, 15; of the Almighty Supreme, *ibid.;* Masculine, Feminine, 4; offspring of Word, Creator, God of Fire and Spirit, *ibid.;* is Life and Light, 6; is present with Holy and Good, 12; shuts out works of body, *ibid.;* and Reason incorporeal, 21, 59; is from God, 2, 32; is recognition of God and science of Divine things, *ibid.;* Mind, Word, creative, 5, 6; of all things, 62; afar off from wicked, 12; not imparted to all men, and why, 31; how to be obtained, 33; received by Baptism into Cup, 31; Discourses with the Harmonies, God is not, but cause of, 22, 95;

INDEX.

Science of, what is, 32; those having, hasten from Earth to One and Only, *ibid.;* has Intelligence of First God, 50; those who have, become in God and are immortal, 84, 95; spoken forth by understanding in dreams, 51; has Soul for envelope, and why, 62; swiftness of; has Fire for body, 62; on Earth has not Fire, and so knows not Divine things, 63; is Essence of God, and united to Him as Light to Sun, 77; Men with, behold God, is God, 77; a good physician to Soul, 78; those who have, are not subject to Fate, and escape Vice, 79; is Soul of The God, 80, 82; principal of all things, and dominates all things with Fate and Law, *ibid.;* in brutes, works with natural appetites; but is not passion, 80, 81; is impassible, 114; with Reason, will guide to God, 82; Mind in Soul, Reason in Mind, Mind in God, 82, 114; can alone understand Regeneration, 89.

Monas, Unit, or Beginning, 34, 35; comprises and engenders every number comprised of none, 35.

Mortal, that which is distant from the Head, 60; relation of, to immortal, 115.

Motion (Κίνησις), conditions of, 16; in somewhat, *ibid.;* motor stronger than thing moved, that in which moved contrary to thing moved, 17; is capacious Energy, 18; in the incorporeal and ingenerate, not in the stable, 18, 19; in place, *ibid.;* of Planets, contrary to other Stars, 17-19; of errant and unerrant spheres explained, *ibid.;* not in a void, 20; of material, is generation, 60; of World, orderly, spherical, not up and down, 60, 71; Soul originates, 128; of Soul and Body; of corruptible bodies, *ibid.*

Name of God, 36; has no Name, being superior to a Name, and why, 41; has all names, *ibid.;* dignity of, 137.

Nature, Elements of, constituted by will of God, 4; image of God Creator, 8; enamoured of Him, *ibid.;* receives beloved form, *ibid.;* mingled with, man brought forth Seven Men, 9; from Air and Water, *ibid.;* Periodical Circle of, 28; renovated by Divine Power and Necessity, 29; constituted in The Divine, *ibid.;* what it is, 55; of The Good and The God, the same, *ibid.;* rays of World energize through the Elements, 66; of the One; administers Universe through Mind of One, *ibid.;* is the Mind of, and energizes Irrationals, 77, 118; properties of, and relations with Body, 116-117; corporeal merely, abandoned by God; of Universe moves all things, 122; of Universe permeates and surrounds it, *ibid.;* produces things generate, *ibid.;* is sensible Essence, having in itself all sensible things, 125; assimilates Harmony of body with Stars, 127.

Necessity, 107-8; intelligible Essence not under, but irrationals subject to, *ibid.;* keeps together the World, 108; a Power of Providence, 109; subservient to Providence, 115, 108.

Number (*see* Harmony); comprised in the Monad, 35; belongs to all composite bodies, 83; unities generate, and augment, *ibid.;* of Body, what, 104, 123.

Ogdoad, what, 13, 93.

One and Only, Beginning is from, 61; abides, unmoved, administers all things, *ibid. et seq.*

One Maker only, one Soul, one Life, one Matter, 80-98.

One are all things, especially Intelligibles, 80.

One, God's glory, 98; Generate and Ingenerate, One by union, *ibid.*

Opinion (Δόξα), of Sensible things, 125; and Sense are of Thought, 131; with Thought, has communion with Reason through Sciences, *ibid.*

Order (τάξις) of Creation cannot be conserved apart from Maker, 38; nor without Place, Measure, and Maker, 39; may be defective somewhat, yet under a Master, *ibid.*; by One Maker only, 71; of Heavenly bodies, One and indissoluble, 49; in earthly animals defective, *ibid.*; of World, 85.

Passions of Body, 32; of World, 74.
Passion, belongs to things generate, 32, 43; cannot co-exist with The Good, *ibid.*; all things in Body have, 81; what Passions are, *ibid.*; energize; all things moveable and immoveable have *ibid.*; energize with Senses, 121.

Phantasy, what, 102-3-4; Men are, *ibid.*

Philosophy, cannot be pious without, 112; unacceptable to the many, 116.

Pious, Piety (Εὐσέβεια), beauty of, 14; become in God, *ibid.*; shewn by choice of the Incorporeal, 33; and Knowledge way to God, 45; those who have, hated and despised by the many, *ibid.*; strife of, is havng known God, 63; what pious is, and should do; will philosophize, 112; pious know Truth, thank Creator as Good Father, will love Good God; will live and be happy, must war with self and body, *ibid.*; only way to goodness, *ibid.*

Place, properties of, 116, 117; motion must be in, 17.

Planets, Seven, 18, 134; how moved, *ibid.*

Pleasures of body bad, 10, 11, 32; those given up to, cannot admire Good, 32.

Poemandres, meaning of word, 1, 93.

Powers hymning the Father, 13; with purified Man, 14; of God, 14; above Eighth Nature, *ibid.*; purify men, 90; intellectual, 91; sing to God, 93.

Providence (Πρόνοια), of God effects minglings and generations, 10; and Nature are Instruments of the World, and order of The Matter, 82; each, Essence of Intelligibles, *ibid.*; and Necessity over Divine Order, 106; governs whole World with Reason, 108-9; World first has, then expanded in Heaven, 108; Fate subject to, 109; no place destitute of, 109; self-sufficient Reason of God, *ibid.*; is Order, 115; World generated, and all things governed by, 115.

Punishment of wicked, 64, 65.

Qualities of World enclosed by Father Creator in sphere, 49; made good and evil by energizing in the World, 53.

Reason (Λόγος) and Mind in Man immortal, 81; enunciative, *ibid.*; Reason in Mind, Mind in God, 82-114; how differing from Instinct, 118, 119; relations of, with thinking Essence, 128, 131; is Intellect of Soul, 129; not in the Irrationals, *ibid.*; contemplates Beauty of Essence, 130; knows things honourable, *ibid.*; of Essence, in being Wise, *ibid.*; having Essence, self-determinate, 131.

Renewal of, flesh and seeds, how, 29.

Regeneration, Regenerate, cannot be saved without, 87; mode of, 88; who is Generator of, *ibid.*; not understood by Senses, and does not belong to Four Elements, 89; Mind alone understands, *ibid.*; accomplished by being rid of twelve Vices, through Powers of God, 90, 91; what it consists in, 92; the

INDEX. 167

Regenerate immortal; born of God and Son of The One, *ibid.*; hymn of, how and when to be sung, 93; not to be disclosed to all, 96.

Sacrifices, rational (λογικὰς), 16, 94, 95; to God, Father of all things, 95; through The Word, *ibid.*; acceptable thus, *ibid.*

Science (Ἐπιστήμη), (*see* "Arts"); is gift of God and incorporeal, 59; using Mind as organ and end of knowledge, *ibid.*

Sciences and Arts, energies of the rational, 117; brutes have not 118.

Seeds and green herbs created, 26.

Sense (Αἴσθησις), deprivation of, death, 50; and understanding connected influence Man, 51; is material, *ibid.*; cannot be apart from, *ibid.*; comes upon World from God, 54; in all Entities, 59; how differing from Knowledge, *ibid.*; of Body to be laid aside to understand, 89; to be relinquished for Regeneration, 91; cannot comprehend incorporeal and invisible, 105; difference of, from Energies, 120; differ from each other, and how, 121; are effects of Energies, 120-121; and connected with Passions, *ibid.*; are Corporeal and Mortal, bodily, good and evil only, *ibid.*; not in Immortal bodies, *ibid.*

Sense of Soul, what, 122.

Sensible Gods, as the Sun, images of Intelligences, 125.

Seven administrators, 5.

Seven Circles of Heaven, *ibid.*, 26.

Seven Men produced by Nature, 9.

Silence, pregnant with good, 15; and Repose Divine, 58; contemplates The Good, *ibid.*; Intellectual Wisdom in it, 87; of Virtue, 76.

Sinners, great, deprived of immortality, and why, 11.

Sleep, effects of, on body, 57, 124; fore-provided by the Creator for the preservation of the animal, *ibid.*

Speech, Enunciative Reason, 81; puts Man above animals, imparted by God to all, 31; sister of Mind and Understanding, 51.

Son of Father of all things, the Typical Man, 6, 7; Father delivered over to Him all creatures, *ibid.*

Son of God, One Man by will of God, 88.

Soul (Ψυχὴ) is immortal, and its energy, 47, 58; moves World, 19; cannot be moved by body, *ibid.*; how even in body transformed and deified, 58; Souls are divisible and different sorts of, *ibid.*; are parts of Soul of the Universe, *ibid.*, 61; of good man passes into Choir of unerring Gods, *ibid.*; how deified and transformed, 58; some happy and unerring, these the perfect Glory of Soul, *ibid.*; vice of, ignorance of Good, 59; virtue of, Knowledge, *ibid.*; this makes men Divine, *ibid.*; entangled with Passions is evil, and ruled by body, *ibid.*

Soul and spirit, how they operate, 60; is not the blood, *ibid.*; of Youth, how developed, 62; contracted into Spirit at death, *ibid.*; is punished according to desert, *ibid.*; departing from body, what it becomes, *ibid.*, and 65.

Soul, envelope of Mind, Spirit of Soul, Soul in Body, Mind in Soul, 62, 82; Soul of pious, how rewarded, *ibid.*, and 65, 66; Impious is punished in its proper Essence, *ibid.*, and how, 64, 65; does not degrade into a beast, 63, 65; community of Souls, what, 65; superior take care of inferior, 66; having Mind of The One blessed, *ibid.*; apart from Mind, powerless and irrational, 66, 67; inert, has not Mind, *ibid.*; Soul of Universe full of Mind and of God, 69; all things full of, and moved by, 71; one Soul only, 72; great activity and power of, 75; always with Mind, *ibid.;* shut up in body, how debased and depraved, 76, 77; Irrationals have not, *ibid.;* disease of, is Atheism, 78; not having obtained Mind as pilot overcome by appetites and evil, *ibid.;* is above Fate, 80; having elevated itself to Good cannot fall away, 112; vehemently loves its forefather, *ibid.;* in body, must war with body and conquer, 113; is an Entity, *ibid.;* Sensible is mortal, Rational immortal, *ibid.;* moves every being, 114; is energy of motion, 124; is incorporeal, Eternal, rational, thinking, Intelligent Essence, having Reason as Intellect, 116, 126, 127; concerned with Harmony Form and Figure, *ibid.;* having finality in itself, and Life according to Fate, 127; has communion with body in Time, Place, Nature, 116, 126; energies of, how working through bodies, 119; works through bodies, but not always in body, *ibid.;* associated with bodies through Harmony, 123; has no love for body, but creeps into with the Spirit through Fate, 123; gives body intellectual motion, *ibid.;* affords intelligent life, 127; may be in Body moveable, 130; and self-moveable and moving others, 116, 126; is from Incorporeal Essence, 128; motion of, in body, *ibid.;* ideas of, 129; Divine part of, has energy of Self, without Vehemence or Desire, *ibid.;* separate from body, remains Self in intelligible World, *ibid.;* rules over Reason, *ibid.,* 130; has two motions, essential self-determinate, and bodily of Necessity, *ibid.,* 131; is Understanding and Thought, 131; to be exercised here to behold The God, the Beautiful, and the Good, 137.

Soulless cannot move soulless, 20.

Spectacle of Good sanctifying, 57; intellectual splendour of, sometimes induces sleep of body, *ibid.*

Sphere. *See* World.

Spheres, errant, moved by inerrant, 7-18; contrariwise, by the stable, 19; Arctic moved round some point but not restrained by Stability, 19.

Spirit (Πνεῦμα), God, cause of, and employed in Creation, 2, 25, 62, 122-3; the Mind of Fire, *ibid.;* in God, 94; The God sent forth by Word; another Mind Creator, God of Fire and Spirit, 4; Divine, wrapped round all Constellations, moving them, 27; encompassing Spirit, 123; of Man, how operating, 60; returns into Soul at death, 61; is envelope of Soul, *ibid.;* judicial of appearances, 130; has Senses as organs, *ibid.;* Opinion belongs to, *ibid.*

Stars, and Fate, 5, 106, 109; appear in Signs and Constellations with Gods in them, 27; circular course of, *ibid.;* order of determined by number and place, 37; unequal in courses, *ibid.;* sensible, God's images of Intelligences, 125; influence of, on Earth, 27, 135; none can avoid force of, 109; said to generate sub-ministers, 135; some perishable, 136; are appendices of nature, *ibid.;* how differing from Constellations, 137.

Subsistence. *See* Existence.

Sun, greatest of Gods in Heaven, 37; after First and One Creator, 103; intrusted with Creation, *ibid.;* is Truth, *ibid.;* Hermes salutes it, *ibid.;* Image of Creator, God, 125; creates animals, &c., *ibid.*

Sun and World, Father of things according to the goodwill of God, 56.

Tanæ, 135.

INDEX.

Temperance, knowledge of, is joy and great virtue, 90.

Thanks to God at Evening, 15. *See* Hymn.

Thought (Ἔννοια Διανόια), 1, 131, etc.; Opinion and Sense belong to, 131; Understanding interwoven with, *ibid.*

Thoughts (Νοήματα) good from God, evil from demons, 51.

Time, made by and in the World; its Essence Change; generation accomplished in, 68; Times are three, past, present, and future, 110; are but one and cannot be disjoined, *ibid.*; of bodies, 114; properties of, 117.

Trinity, enunciated, 94, 95. *See* God and Son.

Truth, belief in, how attained, 55; what is truly such only, 89, 96; banishes deceit and brings Life and Light, 91; in Eternal bodies only, not in Man, 100, 101; on earth none but imitations only, 101; may be understood by Man of goodwill, *ibid.*; Who the First Truth, and why, 103; eternal and perfect, 105.

Understanding (Νόησις Νόημα), or Intellect differs from Mind, 50, 51; an essential of Man, *ibid.*, 51; united with Sense is Reason, *ibid.*; generate, by Mind, influences Man, *ibid.*; Speech cannot be without, 51; can exist without Sense, *ibid.*; with Sense comes from God, 53, 54; but if with wickedness demoniacal, *ibid.*; necessary to belief in Truth, 55; self going, 131; with Thought, are Soul, *ibid.*; recognizes Man as immortal.

Unit (Μονάς) or Cup, 34; hath in itself the Decade, and all numbers, 92.

Universe (Τὸ Πᾶν) moved in the incorporeal, 21; created by God and is eternal, 48; composed of Material, and World, 50; motions of, compared to those of a head, 60; full of Soul, and of God vivifying it, 69; Eternity keeps it together, God energizes it, *ibid.*; God is, nothing in it not Him, 86, 94; motions of, by nature, 122.

Uranus and Kronos forefathers had vision of The God, 57.

Vehemence in Soul (Θυμός) is material, 127; ratio of, with Desire and Reason, 128; energies of, far from the Divine, 129; belong to irrationals, *ibid.*

Vices, how man purified from, at death, 13; of Soul is ignorance, 59; cured by Mind, 79; twelve principal, 90; to be eliminated by ten Virtues, 92.

Vices and Virtues, how connected with Zodiacal signs, *ibid.*

Virgin of the World noticed, 130.

Voice, animals have; how differing from language, 82.

Void, none in Nature, no Entity void, 20.

Water, in beginning, intermingled with earth, and pure fire from, 2; separated from earth, how, 6; Deity contemplated form of Man in, 8; cupiscent in creation, 9, with Spirit in Chaos, 24; is on earth to resist fire, 62; created for Man, 94.

Wicked, how punished, 12; by fire, and subject to Justice and Fate, 106.

Wickedness, reign of, is earth, 52.

Will of God, loosed bounds, and made Males and Females; made the World, 10, 30; created the Entities, Man, and all things, 30, 31, 40; World, organ of, 53; is His Essence, 55; His energy, *ibid.*; without it nothing can be generate, 56; sows Wisdom and Good, 87; through Son of God regenerates, 88.

Wisdom of God, what is, 69; in silence, 87; intellectual, what, sown by will of God, *ibid.*

Word (Λόγος), the Spiritual, 2; luminous, out of Mind, Son of God,

3; is union of Mind, Father God, and the Word; is Life; are not distinct, *ibid.;* The God by Word begat Mind, Creator God of Fire and Spirit, 4; of God to pure creation of all Nature of same Essence with Creative Mind, 5, 94; of Supreme Authority received from Mind, 15; made the World, 30; the Mind Shepherdeth, 94; praise to God through, 95.

World (Κόςμος), formed of Elements after an Archetype, 4; Illimitable, 3, 4; by Word of Creator, *ibid.*, 30; out of Elements by Will of God, *ibid.*, 31; greater than any Body is moved, 17; in that greater than itself, 18; in the incorporeal ingenerate God, *ibid.;* by things within either Soul, or Spirit incorporeal, 19; whole of, Divine in nature, 29; order of, how effected, 39; not good except in making, 43; plenitude of evil, why, 44, 57; but not itself wicked, 52; cannot perish as created by God, Eternal and Immortal Animal, 48, 49, 50, 69; formed spherelike, *ibid.;* is Second God from the God, and in the God Son of the God, 48, 54, 61, 69; Man is from, 50; has pure sense and understanding from God, 53, 54; is organ of Will of God, makes and unmakes all things, 53; engenders all things alone, *ibid.;* called Κόςμος fittingly, and why, 54; material God, and First of possibles, Second of Entities, 59; deficient sometime, and ever generated, ever in being, 60; First Animal, but not good, *ibid.;* subject of God, and hath the Man, 61, 66; Man subject to it, *ibid.;* made by Eternity material, *ibid.;* Energies of, restitution and destruction, 68; Time is in, *ibid.;* will never perish, nor things in it, 69; is moved in Eternity, 68, 69; its Essence Order, *ibid.;* beauty and vigour of, 70; Passions of, 74; full of all forms, *ibid.;* great God image of greater, united to Him, conserving His order and will, 83; is Image of Universe, and Plenitude of Life, *ibid.;* has always Life, and nothing dead in it, nor can be, *ibid.;* collective is unchangeable incorruptible, but parts of changeable, 84; parts of, are Four, 85; Intelligible, 95; generated by Providence and Necessity, 116.

Worlds, Seven, God, Prince of, full of light, 70.

Worms and flies appendices of Nature, 136.

Worship of God, what it is, 136.

Zodiac, how corresponding with Virtues and Vices, 92, 133.

Zodiac, what, 134; circle of, energized by the Constellation of Bear, 135-6; twelve Constellations in, 137.

Zones, Eight, of Harmony, 13; Man of Mind leaves vices in them successively, *ibid.;* eighth, receives Mind, having proper energy, *ibid.*

www.ingramcontent.com/pod-product-compliance
Lightning Source LLC
Chambersburg PA
CBHW022008160426
43197CB00007B/330